Broken Brotherhood

BROKEN BROTHERHOOD

THE RISE
AND FALL OF THE
NATIONAL AFRO-AMERICAN
COUNCIL

Benjamin R. Justesen

Southern Illinois University Press
Carbondale

Printed in the United States of America

11 10 09 08 4 3 2 1

Library of Congress Cataloging-in-Publication Data
Justesen, Benjamin R., 1949–
Broken brotherhood : the rise and fall of the National Afro-American Council / Benjamin R. Justesen.
p. cm.
Includes bibliographical references and index.
ISBN-13: 978-0-8093-2843-7 (alk. paper)
ISBN-10: 0-8093-2843-7 (alk. paper)
1. National Afro-American Council—History. 2. African Americans—Civil rights—History. 3. Civil rights movements—United States—History. 4. African Americans—History—1877–1964. 5. United States—Race relations. 6. Racism—United States—History. I. Title.

E185.61.J88 2008
323.1196073—dc22 2007028609

Printed on recycled paper. ♻
The paper used in this publication meets the minimum requirements of American National Standard for Information Sciences—Permanence of Paper for Printed Library Materials, ANSI Z39.48-1992. ∞

For Beth and Wayne

Contents

Preface

I first became interested in the National Afro-American Council in the late 1990s, while writing a biography of North Carolina congressman George Henry White, an unsuccessful early aspirant to the group's presidency. As with other aspects of White's life, I found clues to the Council's origins and activities but little documented evidence of its activities or prominence. Most historians who discussed the Council had dismissed it as primarily, if not exclusively, a vehicle of Booker T. Washington and the Tuskegee Machine and all but ignored the Council as otherwise irrelevant to the period. Like other groups of the period, the Council at first seemed a victim of the developing ideological chasm within the ranks of African American leaders.

Years later, when I returned to this subject, my initial research efforts were rewarded with a surprising number of detailed newspaper accounts of the Council's annual meetings, both in African American weekly newspapers—where I had expected to find the accounts—and in a large number of mainstream daily newspapers, where I had not expected to find either extensive or neutral coverage of the meetings. In every city where it met over its decade of existence, the Council received long, generally (and uncharacteristically) objective accounts from the white newspapers—accounts far more balanced, in fact, than from the black newspapers, which were often split between expressions of devoted membership and derisive scorn, depending on the partisan loyalty of the editor.

Because no official records could be located for the Council after the first three years, these newspaper accounts quickly became the only viable option for reconstructing the later history of this long-dead organization. Limited correspondence between Council leaders and others was available and proved to be a rich secondary source for opinion, if not factual detail; but the absence of collected private papers for several of the principals made the search arduous. Memoirs by such key players as Alexander Walters, Mary Church Terrell, Ida Wells-Barnett, and John Green revealed their surprisingly selective memory for detail. Many of the most active members barely mentioned the Council at all, while others, like William E. B. Du Bois, bitterly disenchanted by Tuskegee machinations, all but glossed over their own membership in obvious favor of competing and successor organizations. What was it about the Council that made it so elusive, I wondered?

As I worked, it became clearer to me that the Council had been an inspired but flawed attempt to unify an increasingly fractionalized population, in the face of extraordinary internal pressure and external obstacles on almost every side. That it was even attempted, given the setting in which it emerged, seemed most remarkable to me; that it managed to survive for ten years, beset by internal bickering and sabotage, was little short of a miracle. Many of its members moved on to help found, after 1909, the enduring National Association for the Advancement of Colored People (NAACP). But without the instructive trial-and-error precedent of the Council and its flaws, I concluded that the NAACP could never have succeeded; that most historians overlooked the Council or dismissed it entirely, then, seemed the height of absurdity.

Even though its existence was comparatively brief—barely a decade—the Council was the only truly national civil rights organization during the late 1890s and early 1900s, certainly the only nationwide grouping, with representatives from every state and most territories. And for all its structural weaknesses, the Council was easily the most resilient of a number of smaller, mostly regional, civil rights organizations with which it coexisted or overlapped, some of whose members it even attempted to bring together in one forum: the Constitution League, the New England Suffrage League, the National Suffrage League, the National Racial Protective Association, even the vaunted Niagara Movement, which seemed destined, if only for a moment, to co-opt the Council entirely. None could match the geographic reach of the Council, or the enduring loyalty of its core membership, especially in the conservative South, where most African Americans still resided. None held annual meetings in major cities, attended by delegates from across the nation. Certainly none sent their leaders to the White House for regular consultations.

The Council emerged during a period of almost nonstop organization by African Americans at all social levels for varying purposes. Whether the Council spurred or simply capitalized on the growth of such organizations cannot be determined, but it clearly benefitted from the social ferment. Some of these new groups, particularly the National Association of Colored Women's Clubs, and to a lesser extent, the National Association of Afro-American Women, reflected apolitical yearnings by still-disfranchised groups and served as social feeder groups for the Council; many of its active members became officers or bureau chairs in the Council. The largely male National Afro-American Press Association, whose leaders were all members of the Council, and who met annually in the early years, in the same city and the same week as the Council, was clearly more interested in political issues, often helping to set the public and private agendas for the ostensibly nonpartisan Council by adopting resolutions on important political issues of the day. The Second Baptist Lyceum of Washington, D.C., whose elite membership made it one of the nation's most glittering audiences for learned discussion of political and social issues, sent a delegation regularly.

Other groups, like Booker T. Washington's National Negro Business League, founded in 1900, or Du Bois's Niagara Movement, founded in 1905, represented far more concerted attempts to upstage or displace the Council as a political player on the national stage by neutralizing the charisma of Walters or the acerbic rhetoric of Tim Fortune. Some, as in the case of the National Racial Protective Association, seemed to be subtly encouraged by envious outsiders as preferred alternatives to the Council—less activist, perhaps more easily controlled than the group envisioned by maverick Alexander Walters, whose motives were privately distrusted by many, particularly W. Calvin Chase or Chase's sometime nemesis Booker T. Washington and his disciples.

Other organizations came and went, sending delegates to Council meetings but causing barely a ripple on the greater national ocean of African American activism—the J. C. Price League of Salisbury, North Carolina; the National Industrial Association of Chicago; the Law Enforcement League of Minnesota; and the Citizens' Protective League of Quincy, Illinois, which sent delegates to Chicago's meeting in 1899, for instance. Since almost any organization willing to pay its dues ("Religious and secular organizations which have for their aim and work the mental and moral elevation of the race") could send an accredited delegate to the national convention, many did so, including local Republican (and Democratic) clubs, statewide organizations, and a few obscure groups with unusual names, now long forgotten, like the Afro-American Junta and the Ugly Men's Club of Indianapolis, or Bishop H. M. Turner's Scientific and Ethnological Academy of Atlanta. Many local churches sent delegates, reflecting the religious background of the Council's earliest leadership, and Afro-American schools and universities were similarly encouraged to participate; the Avery College Trade Schools of Philadelphia, Tuskegee Institute, and Atlanta University did so, for instance, in 1899.

Just what the Council's members had in common, beyond a desire to effect change, is often unclear. In retrospect, little real consensus is apparent among the factions that came together annually to debate the issues, and the records of its meetings show that they were anything but serene. The tension at many of these meetings stemmed from a behind-the-scenes battle raging between partisans of both national parties, submerged only with the greatest difficulty at public Council sessions. Most of the Council's members, as might be expected, were

Republicans—as, indeed, were the vast majority of America's black voters at the time—and almost all of its elected officers were Republicans, either nominally or actively so. Walters, long suspected by many as being a closet Democrat, would finally emerge as an anti-Taft supporter of William Jennings Bryan in 1908; and Fortune, as a matter of historical record, had once publicly deserted the G.O.P. to support Grover Cleveland and, beginning in 1898, unleashed blistering rhetorical attacks on William McKinley for courting southern Democrats.

Indeed, why the Council succeeded for as long as it did, with so few real resources and against such great odds, is a puzzle. But like many other historians, I found that I loved the process of assembling a puzzle for which many parts have been lost and others replaced by newer parts that didn't quite fit. Reconstructing the brief life of the National Afro-American Council became a stubborn quest for me. As I surveyed the material I did find, I became increasingly convinced that the story could be best told by compiling the stories of the annual meetings—the Council's single most significant, repetitive activity, from all accounts—against a backdrop of the complex interactions between its four founding members.

Two of them—Booker T. Washington and T. Thomas Fortune, whose complicated relationship has been well dissected by others—had already received considerable attention from historians over the years. George Henry White had been the subject of my own extended research. Only Alexander Walters, who presided over the Council for all but three years of its stormy existence, remained an enigma; his posthumous memoirs focused only on the Council's first year, despite his presence in the organization for long afterward.

Rather than filter their words through extensive paraphrasing, I decided to let these men and their contemporaries tell the story in their own words, with as little interpretation—or interference—as possible. I have tried, in most cases, to add perspective and context, but without choosing sides. That the four titans often talked past each other—and their respective audiences—is obvious, and their separate agendas gradually emerge well enough, without prodding, on their own.

Acknowledgments

Completing this book would not have been possible without the encouragement and support of Cherie Lohr-Murphy, Susan Amussen, Peggy Heller, and John Churchville at the Union Institute and University, Cincinnati; Professor Edna Greene Medford of Howard University; and Robert Chadwell Williams, professor emeritus at Davidson College. My affectionate thanks to all of you for your time and energy and your careful guidance

To the librarians and staff members at the Library of Congress, particularly the Periodicals Reading Room and Manuscript Collection; the North Carolina Collection at Wilson Library, University of North Carolina at Chapel Hill; Perkins Library at Duke University; the University of New Orleans Library; the Moorland-Spingarn Research Center at Howard University; the North Carolina Division of Archives and History; the Ohio State Archives; and the National Archives: my deepest appreciation for your patience and assistance with every request, large and small.

To Dr. H. G. Jones and the members of the North Caroliniana Society of Chapel Hill, who encouraged me with grants for related local projects in 2003 and 2005, my sincere thanks for continuing to believe in the worth of my historical research in African American history.

To my wife, Margaret, who has patiently borne the burdens and watched over me, once again, my love and gratitude for helping nurture this latest project.

And finally, to my sister, Beth, and brother, Wayne, siblings extraordinaire, who never stopped believing that I would one day complete the task, I dedicate this book.

Abbreviations

BTW-C	The Booker T. Washington Collection, Library of Congress
BTW-P	The Booker T. Washington Papers, 14 vols., edited by Louis R. Harlan and Raymond W. Smock (Urbana: University of Illinois Press, 1973–1989)
CT	*The Chicago Tribune*
CG	*The Gazette,* Cleveland, Ohio
DANB	*Dictionary of American Negro Biography,* edited by Rayford W. Logan and Michael R. Winston (New York: W. W. Norton, 1982)
INJO	*Indianapolis Journal*
INSE	*Indianapolis Sentinel*
LOC	Library of Congress, Washington, D.C.
LCJ	*Louisville Courier-Journal*
NYA	*The New York Age*
NYT	*The New York Times*
SPPP	*The Saint Paul Pioneer Press*
WB	*The Bee,* Washington, D.C.
WCA	*The Colored American,* Washington, D.C.
WES	*The Evening Star,* Washington, D.C.
WP	*The Washington* (D.C.) *Post*

Broken Brotherhood

Introduction

The Four Titans

Their backgrounds were remarkably similar: four African American men born in southern slaveholding states in the decade before the Civil War, each privately educated by determined parents, each achieving manhood during the period of Reconstruction and realizing professional distinction in the decades after. Yet their career choices, personalities, and philosophies made them at times the oddest of bedfellows, their relationships marked by an uneasy blend of personal friendship and political differences. Their paths would cross many times during their lifetimes, but their personal crusades, while markedly different in many ways, would intersect in one remarkable common setting, where each sought to advance the interests of their troubled race. And while their only joint venture has long since been forgotten, their dream of a better, fairer nation has survived and prospered, their greatest single legacy to generations yet to come.

The National Afro-American Council became their most memorable common project—perhaps, indeed, the only organization to which all four actively belonged. For a time, these four near-mythic titans of America's black community—Timothy Thomas Fortune, Alexander Walters, Booker Taliaferro Washington, and George Henry White—would come together for the common good, struggling to uplift the less fortunate and help raise the nation's consciousness, drawing in some of the most talented of their colleagues along the way. Together these four men shaped an imperfect brotherhood that held near-unchallenged moral sway over millions of the downtrodden for almost a decade. And while the Council would founder in the end, for a moment in history, Washington, Walters, White, and Fortune would stand together, at its head, proudly proclaiming their belief in the American dream and justice for all.[1]

George White was the oldest, born in 1852 in North Carolina, and the only one raised as a free child by free parents. The others were born and raised as slaves, Fortune in Florida and Washington in Virginia, both born in 1856, and Walters in Kentucky, born in 1858. Walters, the youngest, was the son of mixed-race parents and claimed to be a distant relative of Abraham Lincoln; Fortune and White had black, white, and Indian ancestry, while Washington's father was unmistakably white. Fortune and Washington gained total freedom only after the Emancipation Proclamation, while Walters, in border-state Kentucky, would be freed after the War by the Thirteenth Amendment to the Constitution. Whatever his legal status, White lived as a free child before the war. And despite prevailing restrictions against their race, all four were educated from an early age, either in private settings or in postwar public schools.[2]

White attended privately funded subscription schools before the Civil War and continued his education in both freedmen's schools and a private normal school before entering Howard University at age twenty-one, where he probably met Fortune, seventeen, a first-year student in Howard's preparatory school, in late 1874. White left Howard in 1877 to read law privately.

Fortune, who apparently spent one year in preparatory school and another year in the Howard law department, had left academia permanently by then. A decade would pass before either met Washington or Walters. In 1874, the eighteen-year-old Washington was beginning his own academic career, some miles to the south in Hampton, Virginia, while Walters, the youngest of the four at sixteen, was still completing high school studies in his native Bardstown, Kentucky.

When Fortune and Washington began corresponding in 1887, Fortune was a rising journalist in New York, and Washington was grooming his new industrial training school in Tuskegee, Alabama. They may have met in the early 1880s, when Washington made his first fund-raising trip North on behalf of the struggling school.[3] George White had since become a successful lawyer and legislator, winning a term in the North Carolina senate in 1884. Walters, now a minister, was quickly rising through the ranks of the African Methodist Episcopal (AME) Zion hierarchy and was elected that same year as first assistant secretary for the denomination's General Conference.

By 1889, White would be the nation's only black elected prosecutor, headed on a path toward Congress. He had kept in touch with Fortune, now one of the nation's best-known black journalists, as editor of the *New York Age*, and preparing to found a nationwide organization to protect the civil rights of his race. Washington, not yet the influential power broker he would become by the turn of the century, was making a strong name for himself and his educational philosophy in Tuskegee, Alabama.

White and Fortune next encountered each other, publicly, in Saint Louis in 1896, when White served as a delegate to the Republican national convention that nominated William McKinley, and Fortune covered the convention for the *Age*. White and Washington finally met, in all likelihood, in the spring of 1898, when the first-term congressman from North Carolina's "Black Second" district addressed Tuskegee commencement exercises. While together in Tuskegee, the two men may well have discussed the recent wave of lynchings of black citizens, including the murder of black South Carolina postmaster Frazier Baker. And they may well have discussed the latest call by Walters to resurrect Fortune's defunct Afro-American League. Walters's call, quickly endorsed by more than 150 of the nation's leading black professionals, would soon be published in Fortune's *Age*, certain to be read with interest in both Tuskegee and Washington, D.C. By the end of that year, Fortune, White, and Walters would meet in a crowded church in the nation's capital where the new National Afro-American Council held its first annual meeting. Only Washington, unable to attend, was physically missing from the Council's "brain trust," yet the bonds that linked the men to each other were already well formed.

Fortune, Walters, Washington, and White certainly shared a strong commitment to advancing the interests of their race. Their political philosophies were more distinguishable, although three of them displayed adherence, more or less, to the Republican Party, if varying degrees of loyalty to the leadership of President William McKinley.

As the nation's only African American congressman in the late 1890s, White publicly supported McKinley at every opportunity, indicative of both his personal affection for and professional allegiance to the former Ohio governor. Washington, who declined to seek office and maintained a discreet public silence on partisan politics, was nonetheless among the president's second tier of black advisors and corresponded dutifully with McKinley.[4] Fortune, who had left the Republican Party briefly to campaign for incumbent Democrat Grover Cleveland in 1888, returned to its fold, disgruntled and skeptical, after Benjamin Harrison's election and showed little enthusiasm for McKinley's 1896 candidacy.

Walters was the most enigmatic of the four, a minister, never a politician, yet still a shrewd observer of his secular surroundings. If his political allegiance remained unclear at the time, Walters did not publicly break with the Republican Party until 1908, when he endorsed Democrat William Jennings Bryan over Republican William Howard Taft. Yet his autobiography indicates he had begun to despair of Republicans at least as early as 1897.[5] Suspected by some observers of being a closet Democrat while chairman of the Council, he maintained neutrality at Council meetings—a wise move, in view of its domination by Republicans who publicly derided any partisan moves by a small minority of black Democrats.

But political persuasions aside, the four men shared a philosophical commitment to racial justice. All sincerely opposed lynching. All but Washington publicly condemned disfranchisement of black southern voters as patently unfair and unconstitutional, and even Washington secretly financed court tests of discriminatory electoral laws in Alabama and Louisiana. As far as their own public words could define them, the four men's personal philosophies were roughly compatible, if far from identical. Washington's commitment to "bootstrap" success based on hard work and practical education by black Americans, along with a public willingness to accept segregation and second-class political status, obviously represented the most conservative view. Yet even Fortune, the most radical, was perfectly able and willing to work closely with Washington, leaving himself open to ridicule by many as Washington's puppet.

White, whose public stance became increasingly outspoken after the Wilmington racial massacre, had generally taken a conservative social view in his earlier years, one more similar to Washington's. When they differed over the kind of education all black children ought to receive, for instance, it was in degree more than in ideology, as White explained to an appreciative commencement audience at Hampton in 1899. He had come away from Tuskegee in 1898 with a new appreciation of the Washington philosophy, having witnessed its success in practice. "Now I am a firm supporter of the industrial idea," he said. "The higher education is indispensable to a limited number, but the skilled hand of the mechanic is equally indispensable to our people."[6]

And if the self-educated lawyer believed that blacks still needed their own professional role models—lawyers, doctors, theologians—he knew equally well that both resources and prospects for liberal education were limited by circumstance. White's main qualm seemed to be that too strong an emphasis on vocational education might discourage talented young black men and women from seeking education as future leaders. For his part, Walters repeatedly hammered away at explicit themes invoking hard work, education, family, thrift, and moral behavior by black Americans as a necessary way to resolve long-term difficulties. For all his condemnation of unfair treatment of black Americans by whites, he regularly reminded his listeners of the need to "raise the standard of morality among us," of "our imperative duty . . . to eliminate as far as possible all the immoralities of our race. We should create a healthy public sentiment among us on this line."[7]

Walters thus echoed the Washington line, if from a purely religious perspective. As a bishop, he tended to deliver annual addresses that sounded more like sermons than political speeches, although in matters of civic justice and political equality, Walters could be as outspoken as anyone. But he was far less quick than White to praise Republicans—and noticeably slower than most "respectable" Republicans to condemn Democrats. On the subject of the new segregation, including the "Jim Crow" laws beginning to crowd American state legal codes, only Washington seemed publicly willing to accept the new lines drawn by increasingly rabid southern lawmakers. Despite grumblings from the infant left wing of America's black political spectrum, Washington's "Atlanta Compromise" of 1895 had generated only muted criticisms from black activists by 1898.

Like Washington, White was a prudent, gradualist conservative, although his views on social equality were often wildly misstated in the white press. White never publicly opposed the new segregation, however distasteful personally. So long as black citizens were treated equally and fairly—as was nearer the rule in North Carolina than elsewhere in the South at the time—the congressman was resigned to the inevitable, after the Supreme Court's 1896 ruling in *Plessy v. Ferguson*. Not so Fortune, whose fiery rhetoric on the subjects of racial justice and equality for black citizens often bordered on incitement to defensive violence by mistreated blacks. If Fortune spared his mentor, Washington, he spared few others.

Walters's religious scruples forbade him from endorsing any real or coded call to arms, yet he was disturbed enough by the upswing in violence to insist that blacks must "organize for self-protection." Indeed, his call in March 1898 for the formation of what would become the Council followed the brutal murder of postmaster Frazier Baker and expressed his belief that the perpetrators would escape punishment.[8] Yet it took something far more alarming than one postmaster's death to galvanize black sentiment. The flash point came in November 1898, with the Wilmington racial massacre, in which at least seven black citizens were killed in a virtual coup d'état by armed whites against elected Republicans in the state's largest city. By year's end, Republicans who tacitly allowed or even favored second-class status for blacks came under withering fire from journalists like Fortune, amid increasing reports of lynching and racial violence elsewhere.

If Fortune spared Washington from direct criticism, more and more black leaders began to find the educator from Tuskegee an easier target. Washington shrewdly shrugged off the criticism. Meanwhile, White had become the target of opportunity in his own home state, his words now widely misquoted by the state's largest newspaper and the man himself labeled, however falsely, as a confirmed race-mixer daring any white man to deny him social equality. Both were caricature at best, if so frequently employed as to seem unassailable in the public mind. It was the dawn of the era of white supremacy politics in North Carolina, and of an open battle between Josephus Daniels, fiery Democratic demagogue, and White, the nation's last African American congressman. Daniels's rhetoric would help inflame the state, nurturing the Wilmington violence and toppling the state's Republican-Populist fusionists from leadership. Eventually, once-progressive North Carolina would join the tide of southern states disfranchising black voters and drive White into self-imposed exile. Yet in mid-1898, the state's situation was still fluid, and black voters still active.

Many of the nation's politically influential black leaders—particularly those with strong connections to Republican national leadership—still hailed from North Carolina. That many of the new National Afro-American Council's leaders also came from North Carolina was hardly surprising. For nearly thirty years, the state had supplied national appointees to federal positions, as well as four of the nation's twenty black congressmen seated since 1870. The current circle included former congressman Henry P. Cheatham, now recorder of deeds for the District of Columbia, and religious leader Owen L. W. Smith, U.S. minister to Liberia, as well as John C. Dancy, U.S. collector of customs for Wilmington. Among the southern states, only Virginia had more signers of Bishop Walters's call than North Carolina. If Alabama boasted the nation's best-known black educator, it boasted few other influential black names in national circles—and no one from Alabama was listed as calling to revive the old Afro-American League.[9]

In Alabama's comparative quiet, the political battle unfolding in North Carolina was a secondary issue to Booker T. Washington. The Tuskegee educator saw no reason to alienate such potential contributors or supporters as Daniels, who tended to praise less aggressive black leaders, like Cheatham, as proper role models for their race. As always, Washington had his own agenda, one more concerned with maintaining white support for educational ventures and nurturing quiet backroom dealings with national Republican leaders than with helping White win another term in Congress.

Still, Washington could only have been alarmed at the withering attacks on White during the campaign. And although Daniels's efforts failed to unseat White, who narrowly won reelection in a Democratic landslide, the situation there boded poorly for the future of race relations across the South, home to almost 90 percent of the nation's black citizens. Mindful of their precarious situation, many southern black leaders remained wary of the new Council. Its initial geographic makeup tilted most heavily toward the northeast, both in early membership and in views on those issues of greatest importance, at least to Walters and Fortune—lynching, disfranchisement, and other dangers to Afro-American welfare and safety. Southerners were generally more moderate and less inflammatory on the issues than their northern brothers. Only gradually would southerners assume a larger role in the Council, gingerly pushing

Walters aside, momentarily, and driving Fortune away entirely—but that shift lay years ahead.

For the moment, in 1898, the emerging Council was yet represented by no single leader or face. Together, Fortune, Walters, Washington, and White best characterized the infant Council in its earliest stage of development. Walters, the smooth, enigmatic, and ambitious bishop, was the elected head, determined to create a functioning organization from scratch. Fortune, brilliant and erratic, was the new Council's heart, rash and often reckless, less patient with detail. Washington, the shrewd and circuitous manipulator, waited calmly offstage, the as-yet unseen hands of the future Council, content for now to work through his protégé, Fortune. White—the earnest eyes and idealistic, naive, and unofficial voice of reason—also waited for his own chance to lead, but at a distance, seemingly unaware of others' hidden agendas.

They were close acquaintances and clearly seemed to respect each other. Whether this constituted mutual trust, however, was not yet apparent—and whether they could hope to form one body, one smoothly functioning unit, to lead their race in a time of crisis, was yet to be determined.

1

Resurrecting the League

Rochester, 1898

Once a hotbed of abolitionism, Rochester had sent many of its sons to battle against the hated institution of slavery during the Civil War. New York's third-largest city was thus a fitting site for a monument to Frederick Douglass, great and lamented leader of his race, who had lived there for twenty-five years and was buried in Mount Hope Cemetery. In 1898, Rochester's black population remained comparatively small—just six hundred of its roughly two hundred thousand citizens, or fewer than half a percent—in a state where most inhabitants of African descent still lived hundreds of miles away in the metropolis of New York City, but feelings for Douglass still ran strong and favorable among the city's population.[1]

Mayor George Warner had equally warm regards for his few black constituents. "We have in this city a large number of colored inhabitants, whom we esteem as worthy citizens," Warner told the opening session of the Afro-American Conference on September 15. "Our city was friendly to the colored race in days when that friendship was criminal, and she is friendly still." It could easily have been a Warner campaign speech, but this was no local campaign kickoff. Instead, it was an unprecedented push for a truly nationwide civil rights movement, and Warner's remarks were encouraging and optimistic, even flattering, to the initiators. "There are thousands of your race all over the Union who grace every profession and calling," he said, "and I am sure that a body of men more capable of dealing with questions of public importance it would be difficult to find.[2]

"Should anyone assert today that the colored people are not capable of becoming good citizens and enjoying the liberties a short time ago presented to them, you may answer by referring him to the words uttered in Fitzhugh Hall yesterday," Warner added. The statue dedicated a day earlier was still unfinished, not yet unveiled, but the memory of Douglass suffused his audience in the Common Council chambers. Son Charles had posed for his father's statue, slated to stand in front of the New York Central railroad station. "Not the least good done by that great man for his race was his demonstration of the ability to prosper under good laws," said Warner.[3]

Among his listeners were Bishop Alexander Walters and journalist Tim Fortune, prime architects of the conference. Both had hoped to build on the legacy of the late abolitionist by convening a conference of the mayor's "good citizens." The Walters appeal, published in Fortune's newspaper in mid-March, had been for a "meeting of the leaders of the race at an early date . . . to suggest a remedy [for] the present condition of affairs," including the recent murder of one black postmaster and the attempted murder of another. More than one hundred Afro-American men had endorsed the call, nearly a third of them from New York alone.[4]

Fortune's unsuccessful Afro-American League had pursued similar goals in 1890, and the New York journalist had selected the date and place of the meeting to capitalize on the drawing power of the Douglass name. "My excuse for calling the conference at Rochester is to take advantage of the race sentiment which will be invoked by the unveiling" of the monument, he wrote in August. Clearly the need existed for a nationwide organization "to stem the tide of wrong and injustice of which the race is made victims."[5]

Yet if he was unwilling now to lead the resurrection of the league, Fortune willingly deferred to Walters and other "responsible men and women in all parts of the country" to take action in any feasible way. After a decade of acquaintance, he trusted Walters's instincts as much as his own. In 1888, Walters had become the pastor of the city's Mother Zion Church, bringing him well within the circulation area of the *Age*, successor to the *Freeman*. A year later, Walters had endorsed Fortune's new Afro-American League venture, thereby inaugurating an alliance between the two that would last for years.

Most of those in the Rochester audience in 1898 lived in the city or elsewhere in the state. No more than thirty hailed from outside New York, wrote Minnesota journalist John Quincy Adams, a signer of Walters's call. Other endorsers had not made plans to attend the unveiling, giving them little time to arrange travel to Rochester when the call was published, just three weeks in advance; these included Booker T. Washington, Congressman George White, U.S. Treasury register Judson W. Lyons, and brothers Archibald and Francis Grimké.[6]

Their presence might have bolstered the conference's image, although a number of those who did come were already distinguished, regionally and nationally, including New Jersey prelate Walters, Chicago journalist Ida Wells-Barnett, former U.S. minister to Liberia John H. Smythe, and U.S. customs official John C. Dancy. Journalist and former city council member Chris Perry of Philadelphia, whose weekly *Philadelphia Tribune* served the largest urban population of blacks in the Northeast, followed Warner to the stage, praising Rochester for its generosity in hosting the conference and declaring that "no other city was better fitted for this conference."[7]

Almost all of those within Perry's earshot were also black, two notable exceptions being revered suffragette and former presidential candidate Susan B. Anthony and the widow Douglass. Tim Fortune was certainly mindful of the presence of both, taking pains to refer, indirectly, to Helen Douglass's race. In his remarks, he pointedly called for uniform laws of marriage and divorce throughout the Union; long after emancipation, as he reminded his listeners, twenty-four states still prohibited miscegenation. Fortune also referred to an issue stemming from the recent war with Spain. He was apprehensive over the treatment of foreign peoples of color—notably Cubans, Filipinos, and Puerto Ricans—now under U.S. rule, and he feared how "Southern sentiment" in race relations might affect the new territories. "If this country proposes to rule the mixed populations of the newly acquired possessions as it has the colored people of the south, there will be revolution upon revolution in all of them," he said.[8]

This was typical Fortune hyperbole, flashy and apocalyptic, but his major point was more oblique. He had agreed to convene this meeting because 150 members of the race had asked him to do so, but he was not yet convinced that "the colored race is . . . educated up to the point of sustaining a large organization. Two or three men have to bear the weight of the whole thing."[9] Few who knew Fortune were surprised by his equivocation, however sour a note it sounded. John Adams, assessing the meeting a week later, tended to agree with him. "Judging by the small attendance, it seems that Mr. Fortune's words are true," Adams wrote in the *Appeal*. "It is possible to make the organization a great power in righting the wrongs of the race, but there must be more enthusiasm than was shown at Rochester," he added.

Given his own poor track record, Fortune displayed little real enthusiasm for the venture. His Afro-American League, organized eight years earlier, "has pretty well died," he said. "I do not believe the old league can be revived. But I thought it would be well for us to meet together and talk the situation over."[10]

Fortune could talk, and write, a good game. He was certainly brilliant and always controversial, and his writings were widely read by educated blacks. Yet the Florida native and self-made journalist seemed to lack the gift of follow-through and could rarely inspire others to follow his causes for very long. More like a shooting star than a guiding light, he often lapsed into shrill attacks at just the wrong moment, rather than building consensus or brokering compromises. His idealistic network of local Afro-American Leagues, which he helped create in 1887 and sought to take national in 1890, had fizzled out after just three years.

Still, Fortune's strident outbursts against racial injustice made good copy, and his speeches were usually colorful and inspiring. But his militance and erratic personality, especially under the influence of alcohol, tended to make him less reliable for managing group projects. Even his own league had passed him over as national president in 1890, preferring Livingstone College president Joseph C. Price, and relegating Fortune to secretary. That 1890 Chicago convention had drawn an impressive number of delegates—more than one hundred, from twenty-three states—and if conventioneers preferred Price as president, their hearts were with Fortune, who listed six principal grievances the league should rectify: suppression of voting rights in the South, lynching and mob violence, inequitable distribution of school funds by race, the South's penitentiary system, discrimination against black railroad passengers, and denial of public accommodations to black citizens.[11]

Fortune also persuaded Chicago delegates to adopt his preferred constitution, which created a strictly nonpartisan body whose officers could not hold elected public office—a purist position designed to shield the league from accusations of Republican puppetry. Then Price miscalculated badly by attempting to consolidate the league with a second national group he also chaired, the Citizens' Equal Rights Association. That move backfired, driving away important leaders who might have reinforced the league's appeal among the rank and file.[12] Hardly any active Republicans bothered to join the league, and contributions remained low.

By the time a second convention was held in Knoxville a year later, the league was foundering. Those few delegates who attended had to pay their own way to Tennessee. In desperation, the delegates replaced Price with Fortune, then hastily amended the constitution to allow the league to take political actions as necessary. After member W. H. Heard was compelled to leave a Pullman car in Jim Crow–era Tennessee, Fortune, according to his biographer, pinned hopes for future success on a risky antidiscrimination test case. (The legal effort proved too expensive and was dropped after an unspecified out-of-court settlement.) By 1893, the entire experiment was in shambles, and the league defunct, Fortune said in August of that year, because of "lack of funds, lack of mass support, and lack of support from race leaders." His attempt had been premature, and he was thoroughly discouraged and disillusioned.[13]

Price's death shortly thereafter sealed the fate of a once-bright idea, and five years passed before a young clergyman persuaded Fortune to renew the quest. In 1889, Alexander Walters had enthusiastically endorsed the call for a national league, when still serving New York City's Mother Zion Church, and reportedly served as the president of the city's first league chapter, while Fortune chaired the state league. After his subsequent elevation to the church bishopric freed him from more restrictive parish duties, Walters quickly assumed an even more commanding position on social issues. Alarmed by the increasingly repressive racial atmosphere of the 1890s, he and Calvin Chase, among others, prodded Fortune, beginning in 1896, to resurrect the dormant league. Walters's 1898 appeal for action quickly recruited many new supporters, including influential clergymen.[14]

The urbane, cosmopolitan Walters was two years younger than Fortune. Both were good public speakers, both intellectually gifted, both passionate supporters of civil justice for their race, yet Walters's calm demeanor and mature grasp of both organizational and policy issues made him appear far older than the headstrong editor, and far more reassuring to other leaders. The two were like fire and ice, in almost perfect balance, so long as they maintained a discreet distance. Walters's steely approach could easily have dampened Fortune's excitable prose; Fortune's hotheadedness might have weakened his new mentor's reputation for icy resolve. Yet working in careful tandem, they could inspire more followers than either could hope to do alone.

Before his alliance with the pacifist cleric could bear fruit, however, Fortune would be compelled to tone down his violent metaphors. As early as 1887, Fortune had recklessly envisioned the possible use of "weapons of violence" if "peaceful methods of agitation, through the ballot and the courts," did not achieve the desired ends. Under heavy fire from friends and critics, he soon retreated from this position but still occasionally resorted to fanciful exaggerations that he was routinely forced to retract. No one seemed able to restrain the irrepressible, unruly Fortune, although Walters appeared at least willing to try and would certainly have his hands full now. At times, Fortune seemed a force of nature, battling the will—and the patience—of the man of God, both in writing and behind the speaker's rostrum. Just three months after Rochester, in an impromptu Washington speech, Fortune would publicly express a desire for "stabbing" President McKinley because he was not fighting energetically for racial justice. His words proved an easy weapon against him in the hands of his detractors.[15]

Even Fortune's friends, gamely trying to control the damage by insisting his remarks were metaphorical, would be taken aback. Almost always his own worst enemy, the journalist sometimes seemed lucky to have any defenders at all.

In Rochester, Fortune's initial ambivalence did not stop his fellow conferees from electing him temporary president of the new group, pending presentation of a full slate of permanent officers for the first year. But his term would be short-lived, lasting only a little past the first day's luncheon recess. Fortune's uncertain mood deteriorated noticeably after a verbal afternoon clash with conservative lawyer and former diplomat John H. Smythe, who insisted on joining the committee. Now president of the Negro Reformatory Association, Smythe had served as U.S. minister to Liberia under presidents Hayes, Garfield, and Arthur and was arguably the most famous Afro-American in Rochester. But his views favoring separate marriage laws and racially segregated schools did not sit well with northern activists.[16]

Fortune quickly ruled that Smythe's "different" views on such subjects made him ineligible for membership. But Smythe had allies in the crowd and successfully appealed to the conference for a reversal of Fortune's ban. Fortune vacated the chair in a flash of anger, saying he "would not preside at a meeting where people who held such views were allowed to take part." Cooler heads intervened, convincing the conferees not to alienate Fortune—or, worse, insult Helen Douglass—by endorsing segregation and antimiscegenation laws. Fortune, enticed back to the chair, requested a formal re-vote and let the conference reconsider its stand, declaring this time that Smythe was not a member. Fortune was vindicated, and the former diplomat left the meeting.[17]

Yet Fortune's victory did little to improve his temper or his personal views on leadership. Bishop Walters next delivered the nominating committee report, recommending Fortune as the permanent president of the new National Afro-American Council. But the nominee declined, citing a lack of confidence in the race and the new group's prospects. In response to one black newspaper's accusation of "petulance" for refusing to lead the new Council formed to his specifications, Fortune would cite poor health and overwork as other reasons. Ida B. Wells-Barnett, famous for her sharp tongue and sharper pen, needled Fortune into suggesting another leader who could display "utmost confidence" in the movement. Thus the presidency passed, almost seamlessly, to Walters, whose enthusiasm was more visible, while Mrs. Wells-Barnett became the first secretary. Other officers included John Dancy of North Carolina as vice president, John Thompson of Rochester as treasurer, and a seven-member executive committee that Fortune had to be begged to chair.[18]

A committee on address next presented a brief declaration of principles for the new organization, covering four major civil rights issues—lynching, the convict lease system, the separate-car law, and the need for black representation on the nation's labor commission—and two less urgent but still timely issues: the desire for an official Afro-American exhibit at the upcoming Paris Exposition, and the question of Cuban immigration. Fortune could easily have written the report himself, although Ida Wells-Barnett probably did.[19]

"The lynching evil is still with us, the most grievous ill to which our race is subjected," the committee report began, citing ten thousand victims of mob violence over the past two decades and 167 victims in 1897, as well as the infamous murder of Frazier Baker in South Carolina. "We recommend that the executive committee be empowered to carry on the agitation against lynch law throughout the length and breadth of the land, and Postmaster Baker's case in particular," the report continued.[20] In other recommendations, the committee on address called for a report on the convict leasing system to be given at the next meeting; urged Afro-Americans to reduce train travel to an absolute minimum in protest of separate-car laws; and urged a committee to report to Congress on the issue of a race-pride exhibit in Paris. None of the issues were electrifying, but all were important to black leaders.

Fortune's short battle with Smythe and the wording of the declaration had accomplished two ends—one clear, one more subtle. The Council meeting had clearly established Fortune's position as the agenda setter for its mission, but perhaps more importantly, it had underscored his temperamental unsuitability for its actual leadership. While in the chair, Fortune seemed tense, distracted; with someone else at the helm, Fortune could afford to relax and speak his mind, unburdened by basic details of organizing or running the group. As executive committee chair, he could preside over meetings and let others do the work.

The Council adjourned on September 16, giving its executive committee the power to draft bylaws and a constitution, as well as set the next meeting date. The Rochester meeting had made preliminary structural decisions—creating four officers and the executive committee, and providing for a "national council [to] consist of five representatives from each State, two of whom should be women." A state council needed at least ten members. Annual fees were set at a minimum of $5, Walters recalled in his memoirs.[21] But there was still a great deal to accomplish before the Council could function efficiently. News of the Council's existence needed to be spread across the nation, and new members recruited in every state. Before another meeting was held, careful planning was of critical importance. Groundwork for state and local councils needed to be laid, and a structure of operational committees drawn up.

Establishing the Council was a calculated risk, for without sufficient interest among Afro-Americans, the new group might yet follow the example of the old league and fail for lack of membership and money. Opposition from conservative leaders like Smythe might still block Council effectiveness. Booker T. Washington's opinion needed to be assessed, and the "Wizard" himself carefully cultivated. Much of the management burden lay squarely on the shoulders of Alexander Walters, barely forty and the "youngest bishop in either branch of the great African Methodist Church."[22] His organizational skills, still untested outside the church environment, made the charismatic new leader something of a question mark. Already a busy man, his ability to handle his new responsibilities—and his unpredictable executive committee chair—could well determine whether the Council flourished or disappeared. Keeping the Council in the news would require massaging the egos of a broad range of newspaper editors.

Walters would gain unexpected help, as brutal fate soon intervened, guaranteeing a high level of interest in the new Council's potential. By the time the group met again, an uprising by armed whites in Wilmington, North Carolina, against the city's Republican-controlled government and its black officials, both elected and appointed, galvanized public sentiment among the nation's Afro-Americans, dominating newspaper front pages of both races for weeks in November. Tragic as it was, the Wilmington massacre would present a glorious opportunity to the new Council, but it also presented a set of harsh political challenges to a nonpartisan group, which now had to attract a core group of electrified members and change forever the focus of the Council's work and mission.

2

The Black Judases

Washington, D.C., 1898

Rochester had provided an unexpected opportunity for Alexander Walters to demonstrate his leadership skills on a broader stage. No national organization comparable to the new Council had ever survived for long; most had collapsed within months or years, victims of internal difficulties, both administrative and financial, or external pressures. If the Council were to endure, its foundation would need to be secure, its goals precise, and its leadership unified. Recruitment of new members was the key. It was a tall order for the untested bishop, whose only experience so far had been within the walls of a highly structured religious denomination.

Yet as Walters returned to his Jersey City home, his optimism far outweighed historical precedents. Before leaving Rochester, he and other leaders had discussed ways to stimulate participation in the organization, including sites for future meetings. For all its hospitality and symbolic appeal, Rochester was never likely to generate much of a crowd; its isolation and the expense of getting there, particularly during winter, were strong disadvantages. To maximize future attendance, the Council needed a centrally located site, one with a larger Afro-American base.

Weather and time were other factors. Waiting too long to meet again might dampen the enthusiasm awakened in Rochester. As winter drew near, a southerly site would be far more appealing. Six weeks after leaving Rochester, Walters decided to invite interested delegates to the nation's capital the week after Christmas, citing availability of reduced holiday train fares. A natural choice by almost every criterion, Washington was easily accessible by train from all directions and featured both tourist sites and a reasonably affluent population of black citizens, numbering nearly ninety thousand, the nation's largest. Advance publicity would be provided by two black weekly newspapers, Calvin Chase's *Bee* and the newer *Colored American*, edited by Edward Elder Cooper, and almost certainly by two white daily newspapers, the *Evening Star* and the *Washington Post*.[1]

Yet drawbacks remained. Washington was still largely a southern city, and an increasingly segregated one. Congress, while technically in session, would recess during the Christmas holidays, making possible calls on sympathetic Republican congressmen unlikely. Washington's winters were far milder than those farther north, but heavy snows were not uncommon in late December, making weather a concern for visitors from the South. But such considerations were secondary, and on November 1, Walters issued an open letter to interested parties to convene in Washington on December 29, "to consummate the work so auspiciously begun at Rochester, giving ample time between the issuing of the call and the date of the meeting for all needed." A nationwide spate of lynchings and widespread racial discrimination made such a meeting imperative, if Afro-Americans were to "organize and perpetuate an organization for self-protection."[2]

Such an organization was almost unanimously favored by editorial sentiment among Afro-American journalists, Walters declared. Among them was Ed Cooper, head of the District of Columbia's new branch of the Council, which was handling arrangements for the meeting. "The Afro-American press," Walters wrote, "is almost a unit in its demand for a national organization which has for its objects a fair representation in the government;" resisting mob and lynch law and demanding the arrest and punishment of mob participants; resisting "tyrannical usages of railroads, steamboats," and other forms of transport; and action on a litany of issues involving discrimination against members of the race.[3]

The bishop hoped to attract a broad cross-section of sensible leaders to the meeting, but only those who could afford the dues. The meeting was open to those "willing to contribute $5.00 annually towards carrying out of the purposes of the Council," a small but not insignificant sum. Among those certain to attend the Washington meeting were three members of the black elite: high-ranking office-holders Henry P. Cheatham and Judson W. Lyons, both appointed by President McKinley, and the nation's only black congressman, George Henry White (North Carolina Republican), a McKinley favorite about to win a second term.[4]

The president had enjoyed heavy support among black Republicans in 1896 and had appointed a record number of black men to federal office during his first year. Midway through his term, however, he faced dwindling enthusiasm among black supporters disappointed by his recent lack of ardor for using black soldiers during the war with Spain. Some black leaders had lately begun to chafe under McKinley's inattentiveness to critical issues affecting Afro-Americans. Fortune, who proclaimed himself a loyal Republican, expressed doubts with a growing shrillness; his pronouncements, in fact, would soon begin to puzzle observers and alarm some of his friends.

In the first week of November 1898, neither Walters nor anyone in Washington could have foreseen the deadly drama about to unfold four hundred miles to the south. Even the shrill, racist tone of North Carolina's recent legislative campaign—and the furious rhetoric directed against George White, seeking reelection from the adjacent "Black Second" district—seemed purely political, a passing fancy. White supremacy, however trendy as a campaign tactic in the hands of Democrats, seemed out of place in traditionally peaceful North Carolina—at least to those on the outside.

On the ground in Wilmington, however, racial tensions and political infighting approached a dangerous climax. The state's largest city, predominantly black, had long been a bastion of Republican sentiment, effectively neutralized by the Democrats' statewide hegemony since Reconstruction. Until the mid-1890s, Wilmington-area Democrats had controlled most local offices, and Republicans had settled for electing half of the county's state legislators. In 1894, the Democrats lost control of the state's general assembly to Republican-Populist "fusion." Two years later, the state elected a Republican governor—its first since Reconstruction—and the emboldened legislature quickly amended Wilmington's city charter, allowing the governor to appoint half of a ten-member city council and ensure Republican domination. Democrats battled the changes in vain; the state supreme court resolved the results of the March 1897 municipal election in favor of the Republicans, including at least two black city council members.

Without a Democratic-controlled legislature, local Democrats had no hope of winning back the city council. So to win back the legislature, Democrats across the state embarked on a well-planned but unusual course in 1898, fighting so-called "Negro domination" of the state in favor of explicit "white supremacy." Democratic newspapers, including Wilmington's own *Morning Star* and *Messenger* and the state's largest daily, the Raleigh *News and Observer*, mounted a shrill offensive against fusionists, whose precarious alliance was already disintegrating. George White, the nation's only black congressman, became the much-reviled symbol for "Negro domination" in the white supremacists' campaign; his rhetoric at the state party convention in July was widely mischaracterized by leading white newspapers as favoring social equality for blacks.[5]

In August 1898, an editorial in Wilmington's black-owned newspaper, the *Daily Record*, inflamed local whites by exploring the subject of interracial sex, which Alex Manly suggested was both widespread and often consensual, even between white women and black men. Manly's editorial was regularly reprinted and widely denounced throughout the South as the November 8 election approached and racial tensions mounted. It could not have appeared at a worse moment. Desperate to avoid violence, the state's Republican leadership withdrew its local slate of candidates in New Hanover County. The election itself was generally peaceful, although black turnout was quite low, particularly in Wilmington, with rampant fraud widely suspected and many black voters intimidated by roving bands of "red shirt" bullies. Across the state, Democrats won an overwhelming majority of both houses of the general assembly, and with it, certainty of regaining control of a restructured Wilmington city council. (One of the state's few Republican victors was White, who narrowly won reelection to Congress.) But postelection euphoria quickly turned into open hostility after belligerent whites gathered the next day to demand the departure of Manly and other black leaders, along with many Republican officeholders. When black leaders failed to respond by an arbitrary deadline, an angry armed mob stormed black neighborhoods on November 10, burning down Manly's newspaper plant, shooting at least seven black men to death, and driving hundreds of city residents into nearby woods for safety. A white former sheriff was nearly lynched before being rescued and banished, along with dozens of white Republicans. The Republican mayor and city council members were publicly forced to resign, replaced immediately by Democrats, and all but ridden out of town on a rail.[6]

Local leaders played down the number of shooting deaths, estimates of which ranged from seven to more than thirty black citizens and one white man. But one thing was immediately clear: The city of twenty-five thousand had been "redeemed" in the nation's first, and only, armed coup d'état. Even the Republican governor, nearly lynched himself on his way back from voting on election day, seemed terrified. Meanwhile, national newspapers trumpeted the violence in front-page headlines. In the nation's capital, the mood seemed alarmed and confused. The president's cabinet discussed the violence but made no recommendations; the president certainly had the authority to intervene, if requested to by the state's governor, or if the violence continued unabated, but only the attorney general, who was then absent, could confirm this. Exiles met in Washington with Department of Justice officials, but to little avail.

Farther north, Alex Manly—rumored erroneously to have been rescued from Wilmington by Congressman White—soon turned up, unharmed, in New Jersey, where his speeches drew enthusiastic black crowds. A mass meeting in New York, convened a week later by Fortune, drew a mixed-race crowd of six thousand to the Cooper Union, where one speaker said the U.S. government should "send for Dewey," military hero of the battle of Manila. Fortune, for once, was remarkably restrained, saying "We are here to start the fight for right and justice. We come with no vindictiveness in our hearts, no dynamite in our sleeves, and no Winchesters in our closets. . . . We represent a State to-night that is appealing for the rights of its citizens in a sister State."[7]

As days turned into weeks and nothing happened, North Carolina's beleaguered black citizens slowly realized that the federal government was not going to intervene to restore the elected local government or punish anyone for the violence. Frightened, despairing, and suddenly impotent politically, Governor Russell was unwilling even to ask for McKinley's help; Russell's black followers were defenseless against attack and almost leaderless. Their only hope lay in Congressman White, who carried the case to friendly audiences in Massachusetts and Canada on a December speaking tour, and blamed the atmosphere of violence in his home state on provocative speeches by South Carolina's outspoken U.S. senators, John L. McLaurin and "Pitchfork Ben" Tillman. Wilmington's "men and women [were] shot down like dogs by a bloodthirsty mob under the pretense of law," he told Boston listeners, and their appeals for justice were being ignored. White sought to keep the issue alive and on the president's mind, but he was unable to persuade McKinley to acknowledge it, even tacitly, during a brief train stop in North Carolina on a scheduled trip South.[8]

Drawing up the program for the Afro-American Council's first real meeting required much time during the weeks after the announcement. It was to be carefully choreographed, beginning with Walters's annual address and ending thirty-six hours later with the Council's "Address to the Country" and tributes to seven heroes of the race. In between, the schedule allowed for fifteen presentations on various subjects of interest to those expected to attend, followed by panel discussions featuring a carefully selected cross-section of impressive names. But how much of the program was delegated to members of the Committee on Programme, headed by lawyer-sociologist Jesse Lawson, is not clear. Lawson was also first vice president of the local chapter of the Council, charged with handling meeting arrangements. Walters, preoccupied with other tasks, may simply have approved much of the work done by Lawson's committee.[9]

According to the printed program, topics included both timely ones, such as lynching and political rights, and more traditional long-range subjects, such as achievements and progress of the race. Presenters and panelists were to include politicians, journalists, religious leaders, and educators. Among the more notable scheduled speakers—and their hot-button subjects—were Booker T. Washington ("Industrial Education"), Congressman White ("Protection of American Citizens"), and firebrand journalist Ida Wells-Barnett ("Mob Violence and Anarchy,

North and South"). Veteran Georgia political leader William A. Pledger drew a fairly controversial topic: "Our Place in the Politics of the Country."

Paul Laurence Dunbar, arguably the nation's best-known African American writer, was also recruited, perhaps for his drawing power alone. (Dunbar's subject was appropriate but dull: "The Negro in the Department of Letters.") But whether by design or choice, several well-known orators drew lesser assignments. Fortune was assigned "Our Economic Status." Former congressman George W. Murray received the topic "Our Progress in Business," while the subject given former Gov. Pinckney B. S. Pinchback was timely enough, in view of the war with Spain, if unlikely to provoke headlines: "The Negro in the Wars of the Nation." Second-tier subjects and presenters included "The Church as a Factor in Solving the Race Problem in America" (the Reverend Elias C. Morris of Arkansas), "Power of Organization" (Bishop Abraham Grant of Pennsylvania), "The Influence of the Press"(Edward E. Cooper), "The Champions of Human Liberty" (Magnus L. Robinson), "Representation on the Bench" (R. S. Smith), "Higher Education" (Professor Kelly Miller of Howard University), and "Work among Our Women" (Mrs. Jesse Lawson).[10]

Panelists included a glittering array of well-known African Americans, from former congressmen John R. Lynch of Mississippi and Henry P. Cheatham of North Carolina, and recent candidate James C. Napier of Tennessee, to local leaders George William Cook and John W. Cook. On the list were U.S. postage stamp agent John P. Green; Daniel Murray, assistant librarian of Congress; many local ministers; and local attorney Robert H. Terrell. Terrell, second vice president of the local Council, was a rising star in District circles; the Harvard graduate and former local schoolteacher was a law partner with former congressman Lynch. Others on the agenda included federal customs collector Dancy and Ohio Bishop Benjamin W. Arnett, considered a top confidant to McKinley, along with distinguished state political leader James Lewis of Louisiana, attorney Edward E. Brown of Massachusetts, bishops James W. Hood of North Carolina and Lucius H. Holsey of Georgia, and New Jersey educator James Monroe Gregory.[11]

It was a busy schedule, with little room for flexibility, and the agenda made no provision for either question-and-answer sessions or for a business meeting. Given the tendency of many speakers to speak longer than their assigned times—speeches lasting an hour or two were not uncommon at other African American venues—there was little room for unexpected developments or spirited debates by the panels, much less the audiences. Indeed, the unwieldy number of agenda items—fifteen sessions, two speeches, and assorted shorter presentations—was a dizzying prospect for a two-day public meeting, requiring split-second timing and a firm hand at the helm. Even with Fortune effectively muzzled—and no one could predict how long that might last—Walters could not choreograph or control the performances offered by other speakers, some of whom he barely knew. And while the prelate was certainly capable of forceful behavior, almost all of his professional experience lay within religious meetings, with familiar faces, accepted rules, and fairly predictable outcomes.

The minor flap over John Smythe's insistence on joining the Council in Rochester, a mini-revolt that had very nearly driven Fortune away from the meeting, remained an omen of possible trouble ahead. When one of the scheduled speakers for Thursday night's session—George White, a theatrical orator but coolheaded, sensible, and a safe bet for his topic, "Protection of American Citizens"—needed to be replaced a week before the Council met, planners selected panelist John Green, a lawyer and former Ohio state senator, appointed by McKinley as U.S. postage stamp agent. If Green's political credentials were impeccable, his familiarity with the very sensitive topic was less clear; perhaps White agreed to supply his friend and replacement with notes.

Walters's opinion, if any, on the choice is not known. Lawson's December 23 letter inviting Green gives no clue as to the reason for White's withdrawal—presumably a scheduling conflict—or who might have suggested Green as a last-minute alternative, only that all speakers on the subject would be limited to fifteen minutes speaking time.[12] His selection would very nearly derail the infant Council on its first evening of deliberation. For all Green's legal prowess and political connections, he would prove to have little independent knowledge of the topic or of its political sensitivity among his listeners, or of the folly of pretending to know more than he did; indeed, his role as the Council's virtual "court jester" would continue for years.

But that was yet to come. As the Council meeting drew nearer, Walters appeared to concentrate on issues of far greater importance: galvanizing the faithful and attempting to convert skeptics like Calvin Chase, editor of Washington's oldest existing African American newspaper, the *Bee*. So far, Chase was a Council holdout, although he would attend as a delegate from his own organization, the National Racial Protective Association. He agreed to publish Walters's letter "Low Rates for Delegates" in his last edition before the meeting, but only alongside a much longer, more pessimistic column by Walters, entitled "What Must We Do To Be Saved?"

In that column, Walters admitted that McKinley appeared to have "abandoned us to our fate" but cautioned those attending the Council against rash actions or judgments. "Let Afro-American men and women . . . gather . . . not as an angry mob, but as sober, loyal and thoughtful citizens, and consult together as to what is the best to do at this crisis." Only such deliberate action might yet sway the president to change his mind, Walters reasoned. During this same week, Fortune's incendiary speech before Chase's organization made headlines in Washington. Chase's newspaper clearly preferred Tim Fortune's outspoken rhetoric to Walters's caution, a preference subtly demonstrated by the two columns the *Bee* devoted to reprinting the *Evening Star* account of the December 19 meeting, adjacent to Walters's letter.[13]

Fortune's torrid attack on President McKinley had been reported widely in the Washington press, prompting the *Star* to condemn him editorially. And while Chase defended Fortune and the speech, other black journalists were alarmed. Even if taken out of context, the Fortune statements were "rash and ill judged utterances" that were "unfortunate" and "dangerous," said John E. Bruce.[14]

The Wilmington massacre and McKinley's silence remained burning issues for Fortune. McKinley was only now returning from his controversial tour of the South, where he had visited Tuskegee and met with black leaders in Savannah but had yet to denounce, or even acknowledge, the Wilmington violence. Worse, he had placed flowers on the graves of Confederate leaders, nearly an act of treason in Fortune's overheated view. Personally, as Fortune had already confided in Washington, "I despise the man."[15]

If McKinley's actions in the South and silence on violence had discouraged Walters, they infuriated Fortune, who publicly accused the president of going back on his word. "I came down here to fight the President. He has gone back on us," the journalist had all but screamed at the Racial Protective Association meeting. "I want the man whom I fought for to fight for me, and if he don't I feel like stabbing him."[16] Whatever Fortune meant by that phrase—and it is almost certain he did not advocate political assassination as a tool, or intend any physical harm to McKinley—it was a poor choice of words, and a public relations gaffe of the highest order. (His equally ambiguous wish, for the "death" of the U.S. Supreme Court, did nothing to lessen the impact outside black circles.)

In the same speech, Fortune said that too few whites had died in the violence at Wilmington; for every black citizen killed in there, he said, a white man should have been killed as well. Afterwards, he insisted, almost pathetically, that he had been misquoted, and meant only to say he would "stab" the president "at the ballot box" yet stubbornly repeated his statement about Wilmington.[17]

Fortune's attempts to explain his rhetoric—by accusing the *Star* of "twisting" his words—fell on deaf ears, as did Chase's rather flimsy defense: that the *Star* had reported Fortune's words fairly enough, if selectively, but misinterpreted his meaning, and in any event, nothing he had said deserved censure. Free speech, after all, was guaranteed to all. But freedom of speech was one thing, common sense another. Fortune, long the provocateur, had suddenly begun to sound more foolish, if not deranged, and many white newspapers said as much. The journalist was an enemy of his own people and should be repressed, wrote one Washington newspaper after the McKinley debacle, ridiculing the "usual whimper of the man who allows his tongue to run away with his head."[18]

Meanwhile, black newspapers clucked and chided Fortune, not for his words so much as for providing the opportunity for public scorn to be expressed. (Even if Fortune had been inebriated—common enough, as others whispered—it was no excuse for such an outburst.) Chase's suspected role in all this appears to have been something of an open secret. If few liked the arrogant, ruthless Washington socialite and lawyer, known for his singularly independent opinions and biting sarcasm, incurring his wrath by tangling with him publicly was a risk advisable only to the supremely self-assured. New York journalist J. M. Holland claimed privately—to Booker T. Washington, as well as to the president's private secretary—that Chase had set Fortune up to discredit him, first by plying Fortune with drink, then brainwashing him into making key inflammatory statements.[19]

If Chase was playing such a duplicitous game, he was fooling perhaps only Fortune—certainly neither Mrs. Holland, nor the respected editor of the *Evening Star*, Crosby Stuart Noyes, whom she quoted as somewhat sympathetic to Fortune but scornful of Chase. For his part, Booker Washington kept his own counsel. He sent Fortune Mrs. Holland's letter. What else he may have said, privately, was almost certainly stern but sympathetic; he was, after all, Fortune's patron. Fortune's reply, hardly penitent in tone, ridiculed Mrs. Holland and accused the newspapers of deliberate misrepresentations "to back up the President's Southern position."[20]

Washington had little to gain by making public statements about the Wilmington violence and could ill afford to endanger his budding relationship with McKinley, after coaxing him to appear at Tuskegee. Yet Washington's public reticence about Wilmington was hardly for lack of private concern. Just two months before the massacre, Washington and his wife had paid a well-received visit to Wilmington, where he addressed more than a thousand listeners, peacefully, at a local church.[21] The November violence was a frightening aberration from the atmosphere he remembered, and a distressing reminder of deteriorating local relations between the races.

Washington was doubtless aware of George White's unsuccessful attempt to persuade McKinley to call attention to the Wilmington violence, symbolically, by visiting another black college campus in Greensboro on his way to Atlanta and Tuskegee. Washington was also scheduled to address the Council—on his favorite subject, industrial education—along with Fortune and Walters, but the Fortune incident, so fresh in the minds of Washington journalists, threatened to overshadow any favorable publicity he could give the theme. No record is available of the text of the Tuskegee leader's letter withdrawing from his appearance, which was read during the Council's opening session. It was one of a number of deviations from the original program announced over the next two days, including the absence of John B. Wight, the District of Columbia commissioner slated to welcome the delegates.[22]

The Council meeting seemed to be taking on an independent existence, resisting Walters's best efforts to choreograph it, almost as if it were a stubborn human being. The mood among African American leaders in general seemed a shade darker than usual, far less optimistic than even a few weeks earlier. Like a tremor days before an earthquake, Fortune's shrill attack on the president reflected subtle new tensions, deep within the ranks of African Americans, over what path the race ought to take in resolving the larger issue of race relations. Nowhere, perhaps, was the dilemma more thoughtfully expressed than by an unsigned author—probably a black Democrat—in the *AME Church Review* that fall. "The Negro in Politics" warned that blacks were "fading from view in national politics," even in the North, in part because some "old" [read, Republican] leaders of the race were now "engaged in fighting each other" for purely personal advantage. The only remedy, in the author's opinion, was for all black voters to be able to "experiment" with a far more independent course than before: in short, "to affiliate with any political party without being ostracized."[23] It was a utopian solution and, while unlikely to succeed, eerily predicted the eventual exodus of black voters into the Democratic Party in the 1930s.

The Council was determined to avoid partisan internal battles; Article XI of its constitution enshrined its "nonpartisan" nature. But to succeed as a truly united organization, the Council needed to accommodate all viewpoints, without rancor or bitter infighting. Walters understood this, as few others did, and envisioned a calm, statesmanlike air to the sessions. Yet his optimism was tempered by more realistic precedents, at other gatherings, of spirited discussions and frequent unruly outbursts. After all, loud public disagreements over policy among African American leaders were nothing new, if rarely a sign of serious internal hostility, and only desultorily noted by the mainstream press.

Always the pragmatist, Walters had tried to set the stage for a sober, productive discussion of important issues by including a wide range of influential and respected speakers. But the Fortune fiasco was not a good sign for the Council, while withdrawals by Washington and White threatened the careful balance of speakers. What had so recently seemed like a glorious opportunity to fashion a sensible, united front on important issues seemed to be in danger of slipping away.

Bishop Walters arrived in Washington quietly just after Christmas, to preside over the December 28 meeting of the executive committee at Galbraith AME Zion Church, of his own denomination. The committee, formed in Rochester, had since been enlarged "to cover all the States and Territories," but its new bulk did not deter it from quickly disposing of organizational work left over from September. One major action was to appoint Ida Wells-Barnett as financial secretary and national organizer, at an annual salary of $500. (Her selection as financial secretary was criticized in the black press, and by August 1899, she had been replaced.) The committee also approved changes in the first day's agenda, differing somewhat from the printed program: shortening the morning session by ending with Walters's address and delaying addresses by Bishop Grant and former representative Murray until the evening. The segment "Protection of American Citizens," by John Green, was postponed, not even appearing in the first day's agenda provided to local newspapers.[24]

The Council meeting was slated to open the next day in the far larger Metropolitan Baptist Church on R Street, Northwest, in an auditorium seating one thousand people, just a dozen blocks from the White House, an impressive setting. But blocks away, another gathering of African American intellectuals, the American Negro Academy, was winding down its own two-day meeting, featuring scholarly papers and discussions on past and present issues of interest to the race. With just twenty-eight U.S. members, the academy's collective voice nonetheless carried an air of solid respectability, including local residents such as Professor C. C. Cook of Howard University, attorney Robert Terrell, and the Reverend Francis Grimké, pastor of the city's largest black church, as well as Professor W. E. B. Du Bois of Atlanta University and Georgia college president R. R. Wright.[25]

Some of them, Du Bois and Terrell included, were becoming active in Council activities, although Terrell's enthusiasm would subside after his appointment as principal of the local high school. One of those in attendance who would not enjoy Council membership, however, was John Smythe of Richmond, former U.S. minister to Liberia, whose conservative views on race matters had already disqualified him in Rochester but who presumably found at least one presentation at the academy more to his liking. That scholarly paper—highlight of the meeting, said the *Post*—was titled "The Entrance of England and Japan Upon Their Progressive Stage," a seemingly innocuous topic. Professor Cook, however, discussed the applicability of those historical precedents to the more recent question of the "equilibrium between the white and colored peoples in America." For many historical reasons, Cook argued, African Americans were ill-suited to press forward in pursuing civil and social equality with whites and, in his opinion, should not attempt to maintain a place in national or state politics.[26]

Cook's paper drew a polite and attentive reception, even if "the audience evidently was not in sympathy with some of the views advanced." And the title to his article? "Not Born to Conquer," subtitled "Inherent Weakness of Race."

Revenue was not the issue upon which Bishop Walters expected to focus during the Council's first hour, shortly after noon on December 29, yet it assumed a large presence, momentarily, at least, after the reading of the call to action. The call had been drawn up in Rochester and was now being repeated for the benefit of new members. The Rochester group had also voted to impose a dues requirement of $5 per delegate—an "annual tax," according to the constitution. The amount was not insubstantial, for some the fruit of a week's work.

Calvin Chase would have spent that much on one evening's wine, perhaps, yet the well-off socialite still rose to complain loudly about the amount. "There was nothing in [Walters's] call," said Chase, "concerning an annual fee of $5, and he moved that the item be stricken out. The president declared the speaker out of order, but Chase insisted upon being heard. While he was appealing from the decision . . . a motion was made that a committee on credentials be appointed." The motion prevailed, the committee was appointed, and Chase took his seat "amid great applause."[27] So much for a choreographed beginning.

Grumbling about the payment of dues raised a delicate issue for the new Council, now four months old and still operating on a shoestring budget. The Rochester meeting had been conducted "at no expense to the organization and [with] no money collected," according to treasurer John W. Thompson. The Washington meeting brought the Council's first recorded expenses, a total of $127.70 for rental of the church, printing costs, and traveling expenses for financial secretary Wells-Barnett, according to Thompson's cumulative report in 1902.[28]

In Washington, Wells-Barnett paid those bills and turned over another $150.30 to the treasurer, or the equivalent of thirty payments of annual membership dues.[29] If the Council were to build up reserve funds for the next annual session, or pay any salaries—such as the $500 annual salary discussed for Wells-Barnett as financial secretary (the only paid position listed so far)—it needed to generate far more revenue. In the meantime, traveling expenses for Walters, Fortune, and Wells-Barnett, plus printing costs for the Council constitution and other minor expenses, would consume almost all of the money collected in Washington. By late July 1899, the official treasury held less than $10.[30]

The bishop's thoughtful annual address soon captured the rapt attention of his listeners, as he implored them to make their voices heard on the subject of "complete political, civil and social rights" for all members of the race, or risk being "unworthy of the name of freemen." Action—prudent action—was imperative, he declared. Silence had gained nothing so far for African Americans, particularly the vast majority who still lived in the South.

Walters had surprisingly few charitable words for white leaders, even for President McKinley. "Shall we remain silent when the President of the United States, who could not have been elected without our votes, is utterly silent in his last message to Congress concerning the outrages in North and South Carolina . . . ?" he asked. "Silent while the officials of the States of North and South Carolina admit they are powerless to protect our rights? Silent, while Mississippi, Louisiana, and South Carolina, by statutory enactments, have practically disfranchised their negro populations, and other States are preparing to do the same? Shall we not speak out when innocent men and women of our race are burned at the stake, hung to the limbs of trees, and shot down like dogs?"[31]

Yet speaking out alone would do little to burnish their race's reputation among dominant whites, Walters continued. It was one thing to demand that the South "do unto the negro as they would have the negro do unto them," but entirely another for blacks to "scorn manual labor" in the process, as so many young people now did. Encouraging industry among African Americans was essential, as was the need to elevate "the standard of morality among us . . . [and] eliminate as far as possible all the immoralities of our race." Refusing to support "immoral ministers, teachers, politicians and all other leaders" was just a start.

The bishop's "stentorian" voice rang through the cavernous church auditorium as the first session closed, his "commanding personality" and "princely bearing" firmly establishing him in his listeners' view as "the ideal chieftain to head our columns in this crisis now confronting us." There could be "no real peace in America until this [race] problem is solved," he warned—and even if it took another hundred years to attain real equality, Afro-Americans would continue to bear much of the burden for their own destiny. Much depended on how members of the majority race reacted to the example set by black leaders. Walters admitted he could not understand how any among his race—or who claimed to be a friend to the Negro—could "advise us to be quiet and let the white man have his way." Surely the time had come instead for the colored men to act—and to act with firmness, calmness, and after due deliberation.[32]

His well-chosen words would still be ringing in delegates' ears when the Council reconvened at 7:30 P.M., before an estimated crowd of one thousand. For a while, at least, the evening's agenda followed Alexander Walters's careful plan. Letters of regret from Booker T. Washington and others were read aloud, before the first speaker, former representative George W. Murray, addressed the Council. The farmer and schoolteacher had served one full term and part of a second in the U.S. House before his final defeat in 1896 and was now involved in the real estate business in Sumter County, South Carolina. He declared that Afro-Americans were entitled to "as large a share of business as was represented by their population," and that the real problem in business was an internal one. Black citizens should support their fellows in entering upon and conducting various business enterprises, he said.[33]

Murray's words aroused nods among fellow businessmen but little passion among the rest. That task fell to the next speaker, John Green, who strongly defended the president, saying "no man in the white House had been more zealous of the rights of the negro" than McKinley, both before and after his election to the presidency. It was only logical, then, that the president's recent silence on the issue of racial violence must be due to "the advice of some of the prominent men of the colored race."

Green was opening a political Pandora's box, albeit with his foot, and "the groans, which had been coming every little while from certain quarters of the audience, grew loud and general." The meeting quickly degenerated into a furious Babel of shouts. Fortune finally managed to seize the floor and demanded to know the names of these "black Judases." Even the next speaker—the usually dependable Bishop Abraham Grant—defied Walters's introduction, preferring, he said, to speak only after Green responded to Fortune's request. A motion to that effect was quickly carried, and Green was hustled off the stage by Grant and other members of the Committee on Address.[34]

Under interrogation, Green admitted to inquisitors that he "did not get his information from the President, but from a close personal friend of the President, and that he did not ask his informant the names of the black men who gave such advice." Green's admission, relayed moments later by Fortune to the convention at large, drew wide laughter and applause. The incident had passed, yet a subtle fault line had already emerged among the delegates.[35]

The three remaining speakers drew warmer receptions for their remarks. Bishop Grant advised that "the thing for the negroes to do, if they want to help rule this country, is to help own it. The question is not what the white man is going to do with us, but what we are going to do with ourselves." Next, Ida Wells-Barnett put down her secretary's pen to discuss recent incidents of lynching and mob violence, characteristically jeering at Booker T. Washington's "great mistake in imagining that the black people could gain their rights merely by making themselves factors in industrial life." Politically speaking, black voters should help block the nation's current experiment with colonialism "until this nation can govern at home," she concluded. "Let the negro place himself with the party that is opposed to expansion."[36]

Former congressman Cheatham, now the D.C. recorder of deeds, took strong issue with Wells-Barnett, offering a rare conservative viewpoint on both racial violence and the most prudent response to the racial dilemma. His remarks, at first greeted with audible hisses and groans, gradually gained the respectful attention of his listeners, finally ending amid "considerable applause." As he saw it, "hot-heads" in the North were "were making it impossible for the negro of North Carolina to live peaceably in his home," by inciting even worse friction between the races in the South. Afro-Americans should instead "show to the world that we want peace instead of strife; reason instead of passion; protection and friendship instead of confusion and harshness," proving that the black voter was "worthy of all franchises and privileges which a government has bestowed upon him, and that no wrongs which have fallen upon him will destroy his patriotism or weaken his confidence in our glorious government."[37]

The recent violence in Wilmington was deplorable, yet Cheatham saw no paradox in McKinley's silence. Instead, he was convinced that by visiting the South—"as the President of the whole country, not the North nor the South, or the East or the West, not the blacks nor the whites, but the President of the United States and the friend of all"—McKinley had in fact already made the most appropriate response to the situation. "I believe his appeals to the Southern people to lose sight of all past prejudices, and that all sections of the United States unite in one grand union of brotherhood, will go a long ways toward bringing about a more substantial recognition of the rights of the black man in the South as a citizen," Cheatham said.

Grateful for the calming tenor of Cheatham's appeal, Walters gaveled down objectors just after 10:00 P.M. and ordered the evening session adjourned, before leading the audience, in "good old camp-meeting style," in a spirited rendition of the doxology—"Praise God from Whom All Blessings Flow"—and pronouncing a benediction "over the tumultuous and excited audience."[38] The long first day was over, and the bishop needed his rest.

Coverage of the previous day's meetings no doubt dominated discussions over delegates' breakfast tables on Friday. But a smaller story about an unrelated White House visit by a handful of black Pennsylvania leaders doubtless raised a few eyebrows. Pennsylvania congressman John Dalzell, a popular six-term Republican, had led a small but determined delegation of Pittsburgh citizens into an audience with President McKinley, where the group had appealed for just enforcement of the laws and the enactment of legislation to prevent injustice to black Americans. Their memorial petition referred to the recent wave of lynchings of colored men without cause—other than their color—and condemned prevailing racial conditions in the South. Those named were the Reverend G. W. Kincaid, Dr. W. D. Clinton, J. W. Holmes, the Reverend J. E. Howard, the Reverend W. S. Bentley, and H. F. Cumbach.[39]

None of them was known to be active in the Council. But their visit, duly noted in morning editions of the *Washington Post* and the *New York Times*, suddenly seemed an important precedent—and a reminder of how much work the Council still needed to do to achieve legitimacy and influence. (The *Post* story, appearing only after its much longer account of the Council session, did not mention the Council at all. The much shorter *Times* article devoted two paragraphs to the Council meeting and a third to the Dalzell delegation.)[40]

George White leaped into action, and barely twenty-four hours later, a larger Council delegation would also be received, however briefly, by the president on New Year's Eve. In the meantime, however, the Council grappled with a more daunting task: an open rebellion over the text of the address to be carried to the nation's leader. The "intense feeling" described by journalists at the earlier session seemed to have subsided when Walters gaveled Friday morning's session to order. But what began as "complete tranquillity" disappeared soon after the bishop led his new flock in singing "Nearer, My God to Thee," and a troublesome new issue emerged. Who should approve the draft report prepared by the Committee on Address—the executive committee, as Walters clearly preferred, or the convention itself?[41]

For the next two hours, "disorder reigned . . . the chairman calling vainly for quiet and order, before a yea and nay vote was taken," wrote the *Star.* "Everyone on the floor endeavored to be heard at one and the same time." Bishop Walters's ruling—that the executive committee would receive the draft, and report in turn to the convention that evening—was loudly appealed, prompting a chaotic floor vote in which tellers appointed to count the votes could not agree. The Walters ruling was eventually sustained, but the carefully prepared morning agenda "went to smash," including scheduled addresses by six speakers, some pushed into the evening session. Among the casualties: prominent poet Paul Laurence Dunbar, whose face "grew longer and longer" as he waited. "Finally he could stand it no longer and throwing his overcoat over his arm he strode down the aisle and out of the door," never to return.[42]

Perhaps not surprisingly, coverage of the events by the two major white newspapers, the *Star* and the *Post*, was largely negative. The *Post* dismissed "professional Negroes, such as Walters, Grimké, Fortune, &c" as opportunists who had no firsthand knowledge of the situation in the South and were "agitating from a safe distance and for purely selfish purposes," reserving its editorial praise for Cheatham and Pledger, "who know what they are talking about, and have nothing to gain by falsehood and incendiary counsel."[43]

Headlines using words like "pandemonium" and "disorderly" did little to soften the "vein of ridicule, mingled with contempt" and "notoriously unfair reports" perceived and later criticized by the *Colored American*. "Our three dailies . . . most shamefully discredited a conference in which 10,000,000 of black people looked for inspiration and hope," Edward Cooper wrote. "The meeting was characterized as a tumultuous mob. . . . Creditable deeds were minimized, and the few unpleasant incidents maliciously magnified." Even as one of those whose speeches were delayed or dropped in the confusion, Cooper believed the convention was still "the best the race has ever held" and "was as orderly and dignified as any gathering of enthusiastic men could possibly be."[44]

The executive committee, however, saw other villains. One resolution adopted during the Friday recess blamed a small group of unnamed troublemakers for exposing the Council to public scorn Thursday night. "Certain persons, not members of our council, but whose attendance we could not well prevent, [gave] expression to their prejudices and irrational emotions in a manner that was mistaken by some as an expression on the part of this council," read the resolution. The Council supported the McKinley administration's efforts to "guard and to promote the welfare of all the people, regardless of class race, or section," and anyone who said otherwise was simply wrong.[45]

The purposes of the Council were positive, if vaguely expressed: to "dispassionately consider the conditions under which the Afro-American is working out his progress as an American citizen," to "devise means of ameliorating such incidental circumstances as operate unfavorably," and to "utilize such opportunities as promise greater good."[46]

Friday afternoon's recess did little to improve the situation among the delegates, some of whom, not acquainted with the niceties of parliamentary procedure, spent much time trying in vain to be recognized during the evening session, which was "attended by much confusion," wrote the *Post*. Nor did the recess improve the general outlook of the one speaker whose remarks were covered, the Reverend Marsell of Philadelphia, who scolded McKinley for trying to "conciliate the old Confederate" and blasted the "damnable heresy" expressed by one southern black leader: that the Negro had been "given the ballot too soon."[47]

Walters grew visibly exasperated with the disrupters, said the *Star*, declaring at one point, in a "huge voice, which fairly shook this big building: 'You are all out of order. Take your seats.'"[48] But the disruptions were well orchestrated, and Walters grew hoarse trying to outwit them, as he sought to introduce the next item of regular business, the Council's address to the nation, which was unenthusiastically adopted without debate. The Council did take two notable actions, endorsing a House bill establishing a home for aged and infirm Afro-Americans, and proposing creation of a daily Washington newspaper as a policy organ for the Council. Before adjourning, the Council ordered the printing of an engrossed copy of its "address to the public," as drafted by the committee, to be presented the next day to the president. A "rather mild affair" after the heated debate of the morning, the address was "a disappointment," in the opinion of the *Star*.[49]

"We are not opposed to legitimate restriction of the suffrage, but we insist that restrictions shall apply alike to citizens of all races," the address said in part, while vigorously opposing the separate-car law as "unjust and oppressive." But its most controversial demand—that Congress act to reduce the representation of those southern states that had disfranchised black voters—was unlikely to find resonance in the White House, particularly after the Council expressed its regrets, albeit mildly phrased, over a related issue: "that the President saw fit to treat with silence this vital matter [mob violence and lynch law] in his recent message to Congress."[50]

The group charged to deliver the address to McKinley was far larger than Dalzell's contingent, or the Iowa delegation they found waiting in the White House on Saturday to deliver its own petition. Indeed, the Council's delegation included perhaps the single greatest number of Afro-American men—more than twenty—in the White House at any one time to date. And while two lists of those visiting differ slightly, it was surely the most distinguished group of black leaders to date, including one sitting congressman (White), two former congressmen (Cheatham and Murray), a former governor (Pinchback), three bishops (Walters, Clinton, and Arnett), a U.S. collector of customs (Dancy), and the U.S. Treasury register (Judson Lyons), among others.[51]

Walters presented the president with a copy of the Council's address, which did contain an olive branch, asking him "to use his good offices in presenting to Congress the subject of the recent lynchings of colored men in the Carolinas . . . [and] to exert his influence in all proper ways to improve the conditions of the colored race." After a fifteen-minute audience, the group withdrew, "greatly pleased with their interview." The Iowans next presented their memorial on race troubles "signed by the colored people of that State" and reported an equally cordial reception.[52]

Precisely how many composed the Council's delegation, and how they were selected, is not clear, although the two published lists of attendees are similar. As one of its last official actions, the Council had authorized a fifteen-member committee, chaired by Walters. In all, twenty-two names appear on both lists, plus another five on one or the other, but not both. The names did not, as one newspaper reported, encompass the Council's "executive committee," which actually included more than seventy members—or even its newly elected slate of officers—but comprised a mixture of both, with a few extras.[53]

One Council member listed, but who almost certainly did not attend, was executive committee chairman Tim Fortune, who had so recently criticized—threatened—McKinley. Angered by his inclusion in one published list, he even wrote a sharply worded letter to the *Washington Post*, vehemently denying that he had crossed the executive mansion threshold.[54]

Days later, the *Colored American* commended the Council for its "moderate" speeches and "perfect composure" while in the White House, pointedly ignoring Fortune's anguish over being suspected of participating. And although no commitment was obtained from the chief executive, the newspaper reasoned that the Council had done its best, and McKinley would do "the right thing" eventually, given enough time to consider the matter. "No public utterance may be expected until the President feels that it is expedient to speak," said the *Colored American*. "Give the President a chance to think—and a rest."[55]

As for John Green, the president's defender, the reviews were mixed, and mostly negative. Still, one Ohio friend cheered him on by ridiculing "that aggregation of mal-contents, as well as the cowardly silence of the President's friends (?) . . . Oh that you had told that T. T. Mis-Fortune to go and ask the President if he desired," wrote former state legislator Jere Brown, who congratulated Green for his courage. Brown condemned the Council meeting as "the most disgraceful affair that has ever occurred in our history" and urged Green to have nothing more to do with the likes of Walters, Fortune, Wells-Barnett, or Harry Smith. "You are the only redeeming quantity that participated," he wrote in late January.[56]

In the meantime, plans were underway for a different kind of pressure, in the form of a Washington-based daily newspaper, to spell out Council policies and further organizational goals. The newspaper was the brainchild of *Atlanta Age* editor William A. Pledger, a veteran of Georgia Republican politics who had browbeaten the Council leadership into contributing $2,000 for the project and delegates into providing another $500.[57]

The first issue was projected to appear in September 1899, just after the Council meeting in Chicago. Pledger was given the task of soliciting stock for the enterprise, which was estimated to need $50,000 for equipment and other expenses. For assistance, he named a committee of more than two dozen members, including a variety of religious leaders, political leaders, educators, and journalists—and one major figure who had not yet addressed the Council, Booker T. Washington. Pledger's dream was glorious, but hardly practical, at least not without sustained financing and a solid business plan, including national advertisers. Most U.S. black newspapers at the time were weeklies with shoestring budgets, staff members who generally were employed elsewhere at full-time jobs, and which were dependent on annual subscriptions or hidden support from power brokers. Moreover, it was still not clear that a black-oriented daily newspaper could consistently attract enough readers to survive without a significant continuing subsidy. If the newspaper was probably no immediate threat to established weekly newspapers, like Washington's own *Bee* and *Colored American*, or even Fortune's *Age* in New York, the proposal raised troubling issues: How many black readers cared enough about politics to buy two (or more) black-oriented newspapers? Was the nation's black community ready for a truly national newspaper?

Such issues would be of interest primarily to working journalists on Pledger's committee, including Fortune, Chase, Cooper, Wells-Barnett, and three other notable names: John Mitchell Jr., editor of the Richmond *Planet*; Chris Perry, editor of the *Philadelphia Tribune*; and Washington's Richard Thompson. And while the newspaper's capitalization goal was no small sum for the fledgling Council, at least some of that was already being sought from unnamed "prominent white men," according to Pledger. Cooper found the newspaper "an experiment well worth trying," but if the goal could not be met, he believed whatever money was raised might be better spent shoring up the position of "the country's best Afro-American weekly . . . to make it an invincible agency for race elevation."[58]

The project never materialized. By the time the Council met next in Chicago in August 1899, the idea of a house newspaper had been scrapped, despite energetic plugs by notable Washingtonians, including Robert Terrell. Ironically, a daily newspaper devoted to coverage of news and issues of interest to Afro-Americans did begin publication in Washington in 1899, but it would be the privately operated *Record*, produced by the refugee Manly brothers of Wilmington, North Carolina, and reportedly financed by an $800 loan from Alexander Manly's patron, George White. White's ties to Manly were close and would remain so for several years, until Manly moved to Philadelphia, after serving as White's private secretary. Some said White had actually helped spirit Manly away from the violence in Wilmington under cover of darkness, an unlikely scenario, at best. Three weeks later, White was on a northern speaking tour, including stops in Boston and Nova Scotia, where he mentioned the Wilmington situation but made no reference to his personal knowledge of the riots or Manly's escape.[59]

White's election to his second term in Congress had been by a narrow margin, his once-powerful political base all but neutralized, yet he forged ahead. Once again, he would be the only black serving in the House, when the 56th Congress convened in December 1899. In the months ahead, he would be preoccupied with pressing matters, including chairing the Council of Colored Citizens of North Carolina, a new group seeking to stabilize race relations in his increasingly polarized state; his new membership on the House District of Columbia Committee, as the first black ever; his plans to introduce a bill making lynching a federal offense; and his wife's rapidly declining health.

But the congressman nevertheless made as much room as he could in his schedule for Council activities, serving as a member of the executive committee of the D.C. chapter—the nation's first, proudly sporting "Afro-American Council No. 1" on its letterhead—and agreeing to join a special national subcommittee on operations, intended to oversee the Council's operation between annual sessions. In May, he emerged as the most visible local Council booster, addressing a large audience at the Second Baptist Church and offering "the official expression of the Council" to enthusiastic listeners. "Possibly at no time in the history of our freedom has the effort been made to mould public sentiment against us and our progress so strongly as is now being done," White said.[60]

"The forces have been set in motion and we must have sufficient manhood and courage to overcome all resistance. A race of people with the patience, forbearance, physical development and Christian manhood and womanhood which has characterized us during the past 285 years will not bow down at the bidding of any man or set of men, and it would be well that all the bloody host of lynchers and assassins all over this country should learn this now." National action was needed, he said, to "lance . . . this festering sore which tends to sap out the life blood, before the putrefying cancer destroys our body politic." Organizing black citizens, part of the Council's primary mission, was an important part of the process, he added, contending "that it would do for the black man all that it has done for the white man." White also cited "the wise and sober plea of Booker T. Washington to the people of the land—to rise above themselves, above race, above party; above everything that hampers the sympathetic and friendly relation of the element here thrown together by a decree of God."

In closing, White called on "all, old and young, male and female, [to] join hands and hearts in the prosecution of this work until there are no race problems to solve, no lynchers to condemn, no rapists to be hanged, no barriers to be removed, yes, press on until there is no North, no South, no East, no West, but one indissoluble union, all striving to make more glorious our common country." Other speakers repeated the themes on behalf of the Council, including Cheatham, Green, Lyons, Pinchback, Manly, and Thompson. But the star was clearly the nation's only black congressman, whose theatrical gestures and eloquence held his audience spellbound for an hour and drew "bursts of applause [at] every telling sentence and declaration."[61]

Whether their urgent joint appeal would fill the membership roster—and coffers—of the new Council with life enrollments, at $50 a throw, remained to be seen.

3

All Eyes on McKinley

Chicago, 1899

In some ways, the initial relationship between the Council and President McKinley resembled a failed courtship, marked by unrealistic expectations on both sides and more by abiding affection than by real passion. If so, the Council's delicate romance with McKinley, over by the spring of 1899, had been unsatisfyingly brief for both. The president's personal commitment to racial equity in appointments and his sense of racial justice remained real, yet his ability to act on them had been pushed aside by his cautious nature and the rude political realities of 1898 and 1899. The Council, unable to achieve its immediate goal of an outright public commitment, peevishly pondered how to lure McKinley back as winter became spring and plans were drawn up for its midwestern meeting in August.

For months, Bishop Walters had hoped the president would end his silence and make some visible move to quell the growing frustration felt by many black leaders over the Wilmington massacre, but so far nothing had happened. Then new events in the South exerted new pressure on the White House. Federal indictments, announced in early April against thirteen white South Carolina men for Postmaster Baker's murder, were a bright spot, but the actual trial, held just days later, was a bitter disappointment to black observers. Three men were acquitted, after the government offered no evidence against them, and charges were dismissed against two more. The all-white jury deadlocked on a verdict for the remaining eight defendants, forcing a mistrial.[1]

News from neighboring Georgia was equally disheartening. A half dozen black citizens charged with arson were slaughtered by a white mob in Palmetto in mid-March, followed by the brutal burning and mutilation in April of a black man falsely charged with rape but later publicly exonerated, whose name, Sam Hose, would become a rallying cry for years to come. According to several black newspapers, a black minister who dared to defend Hose was also lynched.[2] The lynch mob seemed to know no bounds, as George White later told the House of Representatives. Across the United States, a total of 166 persons—all but ten of them black—were lynched during the sixteen-month period ending in April 1899, White said. This included Sam Hose, who had killed his employer only in self-defense, according to disinterested white witnesses, and had never touched his employer's wife, but was himself murdered before he could be tried.[3]

The Council's executive committee met in Washington in April, according to the *New York Age*, although correspondent Robert Terrell gave no details, simply praising the "real, forceful" leadership of Walters and H. T. Johnson ("two strong men of whom the every day world did not know much" prior to the December gathering). Terrell, who soon relinquished his vice presidency of the local council to his wife, became inactive after his appointment as principal of Washington's Afro-American high school that same spring.[4]

By early May, when religious leaders gathered at New York City's Zion Church for the Afro-American Conference—not related to the Council—the mood among black leaders had grown increasingly despondent, even cynical. Indignation permeated the speeches of those addressing the conference, wrote the *New York Times*. Not surprisingly, the speaker given greatest coverage was the irrepressible Tim Fortune, apparently granted leave by Walters for the occasion and introduced, without a trace of irony, as "too conservative." Sober but never somber, Fortune rose to the occasion, attacking McKinley as "a man of jelly, who would turn us all loose to the mob and not say a word. He may not mean to do so, but he is vacillating, uncertain, and . . . a man of putty and jelly, influenced by others. What we want in a President is a man with a bar of steel down his back—like Thomas B. Reed," outgoing speaker of the Republican-controlled House.[5]

Walters had set the stage for Fortune's tirade, warning his listeners that "We have now reached a condition where we must surrender to the white man or fight, and I now declare that we will fight for the manhood and the negro's right." In case anyone misunderstood him, Walters added, "We are numerically weak, but we have God on our side, we have justice on our side, and I say let us fight it out to the finish." Fortune took his cue well, blaming the upsurge in southern violence against blacks on McKinley, the "one man in Washington who has done more to breed disquiet and create these outrageous acts than any one else [and] permitted the people who committed these outrages to think they had the liberty to do so." Walters and fellow bishops had already set June 4 as a day of prayer by black Americans, and Fortune now instructed black Americans to give fifty cents each to a fund "to hire Pinkertons to send South and bring the leaders of the mob to trial."[6]

The mob's one positive accomplishment, added the Reverend H. G. Miller, was the new harmony between colored religious denominations. "True Christian lives" lived by Afro-Americans were the best antidote for outrages, Miller said. But he was in the minority, even among clergymen. Two months later, Fortune's newspaper would openly oppose the renomination of William McKinley for president, primarily because of his poor record on lynchings. McKinley had failed to halt "the reign of mob law which has terrorized the southern states ever since he has been in presidential office," the *New York Age* declared. The gauntlet had now been thrown down, though not everyone was impressed; Fortune's nemesis, Calvin Chase, snidely insisted that Fortune's anger stemmed not from principle, but from failure to receive a federal appointment.[7]

Three months later, the national Council would unveil its own, decidedly less pacifist remedy to the lynch mob: a federal statute imposing the death penalty on anyone convicted of "lynching, burning, cutting, maiming, or by taking the life by an unlawful means of any person" accused without due process of law."[8]

The nation's second-largest city boasted a large, increasingly influential black population in 1899, with more than thirty thousand black Chicago residents listed in the 1900 census. They amounted to less than 2 percent of the city's total but were beginning to make their mark in city circles, most recently with the appointment of Ferdinand L. Barnett as assistant state's attorney for Cook County. Two black weekly newspapers served Chicago: the militant *Conservator*, edited by Barnett's wife, Ida Wells-Barnett, and the more moderate *Appeal*, published by brothers Cyrus and John Adams.[9]

More than three hundred delegates and attendees, mostly clergymen and educators, were listed as assembling in Chicago on August 17 for the Council's second annual convention, held at Bethel AME Church.[10] Among those present, according to the *Chicago Tribune*, was the elusive Booker T. Washington, whose last-minute withdrawal from the Washington session had disappointed so many delegates in December. At least fourteen local councils and three state councils (Illinois, Indiana, and New York) sent official delegates, with the remainder representing legally constituted member groups, ranging from the ordinary—schools, churches, newspapers, and civic organizations—to the unusual, such as the Black Man's Burden Association of Philadelphia, and two Indianapolis groups: the Ugly Man's Club and the Afro-American Junta.[11]

But few other figures of real national prominence turned up for the meetings, so disturbed were they by rumors that the Council was preparing to launch an open attack on President McKinley. Missing were Fortune, reportedly too ill to travel; Bishop Arnett, McKinley's most influential black advisor; and three high-ranking McKinley appointees—Lyons, Green, and Cheatham—who had conferred with the president on this very subject weeks before. Washington and his wife, Margaret, were both in Chicago, and both were publicly expected to attend, although only Mrs. Washington was slated to speak, on the final day. Washington himself did not appear at a formal Council session—Fortune, mindful of mounting criticism, had warned him to stay away entirely—but he did address delegates at an unofficial dinner August 18.[12] By the end of the convention, it was Mrs. Washington's abrupt withdrawal from the schedule—in a polite note she sent the Council—that raised the hackles of the Reverend Reverdy C. Ransom, whose "caustic comment" on the convention floor seemed to startle other Council leaders and observers such as the *Tribune*. The youthful pastor of Bethel Church was an outspoken social activist and a rising star, eventually due to become an AME bishop.

Ransom declared himself offended by the wording of Mrs. Washington's note asking to be excused, first demanding that her name be erased from the official program, then proceeding to attack her husband for staying away. His rhetoric briefly matched the unusual combination outside of average late-summer heat—86 degrees—and high humidity on Chicago's streets that week, which killed one citizen and prostrated several more. Walters quickly took the floor to defend Washington's nonattendance, claiming that the Wizard "could not afford to be . . . connected with the discussions of an organization which might be radical in its utterances." To do so might destroy his "usefulness in connection with many classes," presumably southern whites. The Council agreed with Walters, and Washington's friends forced through a resolution formally endorsing the Tuskegee educator. But as Walters had predicted, the "radical utterances" that had caused Washington to distance himself soon precipitated a crisis among those active "in the cause of uplifting the colored race," including northern white philanthropists, said the *Tribune*.[13]

Chastened by the uproar over his remarks, Ransom soon claimed—in letters to the *Chicago Inter-Ocean* and to Booker T. Washington—that he had been misquoted. He had never used the terms "traitor, or a trimmer, or a coward" (perhaps someone in the audience had), and he had been "unwise" to have mentioned the educator at all, he told the *Inter-Ocean*. His curiously phrased apology to Washington blamed Tuskegee supporters for "much of the misrepresentation." Ransom had certainly meant no disrespect to a man whose career he regarded "as one of the most fruitful and remarkable of any man of our race."[14]

W. E. B. Du Bois, who wrote about the convention weeks later for the *Independent*, ignored the Ransom furor, while admitting that many factions were evident in Chicago. "The convention was composed largely of professional men and schoolteachers, with a few clerks in public service, merchants, farmers and workingmen," Du Bois wrote. But except for a few "conspicuous figures"—Walters, Bishop Turner, Wells-Barnett—"they were men of average ability, rather talkative and excitable," and not nearly so cultured as their female counterparts at the separate NACW gathering.[15]

Walters opened the conference with his customary eloquence, yet his tone differed markedly from that of December. His annual address was noticeably pessimistic on several key issues, particularly the likelihood that most white Americans would stop discriminating against their black neighbors—or that racial violence in the South would soon subside. The goals of the Council remained to guarantee life, liberty, and the pursuit of happiness to all Americans, regardless of race, and to remove "the barriers erected by prejudice" against Afro-Americans, said Walters. "In a word, we desire the opportunity to struggle, unfettered, for the things which some of the white people of this country think are 'unattainable' by negroes, but which they are careful to keep out of their reach." And while black citizens sincerely wished to cooperate with southern authorities investigating "heinous crimes . . . said to have been committed by negroes," they were often justifiably skeptical of official ability to protect those apprehended and assure them a fair trial. "No self-respecting negro will turn over to an angry mob a man of his race to be mutilated and burned," Walters declared.[16]

The public issue of American expansion abroad continued to be a sensitive subject for the race, in light of their own experience. Walters claimed to believe in the economic benefits of expansion but questioned the nation's commitment to extending democratic rights outside the continent. "I do not think that America is prepared to carry on the work of expansion at this time, especially if it be among the dark races of the earth. The white man of America is impregnated with color-phobia; he has been taught for centuries that the black man, no matter where he dwells, has no rights which the white man is bound to respect; hence he is unprepared to grant to dark-skinned peoples the most favorable opportunities for development. No matter how intelligent or cultured a man may be, if his skin is dark that is a sufficient reason at any time why his rights should be ignored." As leader of the entire nation, the president bore a heavy responsibility in protecting black America, Walters concluded. McKinley must "use his influence by word and deed to secure to all American citizens . . . a fair and impartial trial by jury" as well as to "grant to Afro-American soldiers who deserve it promotion to be commissioned officers in the regular army."[17]

The evening session featured more optimistic addresses by Du Bois and Mound Bayou, Mississippi, mayor Isaiah Montgomery, drawing a crowd so large that "two women fainted and had to be carried from the church." Du Bois, from Atlanta University, delivered a lecture entitled "The Business Enterprises of the South and How to Foster Them," while entrepreneur Montgomery discussed the success of black enterprise in his all-black town of Mound Bayou. Du Bois was introduced by the presiding officer and "confessed pessimist of the Council," Georgia bishop Henry McNeal Turner, who later rose to expound upon his controversial plan for mass emigration of American blacks to Liberia. Du Bois took direct issue with Turner, concluding that difficulties faced by Afro-Americans "are not insurmountable," and that progress was being made, particularly on the business front in the South, and insisting that fleeing to Liberia would be "cowardly."[18]

Turner's controversial plan involved transporting up to seven million men, women, and children to Liberia for a mere $15 apiece, as he then explained in the evening's final address. He planned to ask Congress for $105 million to accomplish this goal. In the South, Turner said, "there is no hope for the race . . . the white race always has been and will be the dominant race. The white race either rules or exterminates." The "only salvation for other races is to get out of its way or be crushed," yet such a plan could not be compulsory.[19]

Turner's pessimism, if not his solution, was shared by other leaders, including Washington, who were "more despondent at present than they have ever been before." An upcoming New York conference of representatives from societies overseeing private educational efforts among southern blacks proposed to take up the view that disfranchisement of black voters was probably a positive act in the long term, since it "would remove one of the prime causes of the trouble in the South," the *Tribune* wrote. Bishop Walters acknowledged the imminence of the conference but disagreed with its thrust, arguing that "the Israelites were given forty years in the desert to prepare for Canaan, and the colored people have not had so long as that yet."[20]

If Israelites had been allotted forty years, the Council's female members had been given barely forty weeks to prepare for their new roles. Yet they were already assuming active roles at the annual conventions. While only four of nearly one hundred official delegates named publicly were women, the Council was committed to equality of participation by gender and was designating one seat in three from each state on the executive committee to a woman. So far, twenty-five women filled executive committee slots.[21]

Few of them were national figures. Gertrude Mossell of Pennsylvania, Josephine St. Pierre Ruffin of Massachusetts, Lillian Taylor Fox of Indiana, and Julia Layton of Washington, D.C., were more widely known outside their home states than most of the others, although none was an official delegate in 1899. That distinction fell to just four women: Wells-Barnett, from Chicago; Mayme Weir, representing the Law Enforcement League of Minnesota; Mrs. R. Jerome Jeffrey, of Rochester; and Elizabeth Carter, whose affiliation was not listed.

As yet, only a handful of the Council's major officers were women. Two of those named to posts in Chicago were Elizabeth Carter, recording secretary, and Julia Layton, corresponding secretary. The Council's original secretary and best-known female member, Wells-Barnett, was named to head the antilynching bureau, one of nine bureaus, but relinquished her other post—that of financial secretary—to journalist John Bruce. But even if their numbers and positions were still limited, the Council's female members were quickly establishing a distinct public identity, separate from that of their male counterparts, and were already generating publicity in their own right. Much of their Chicago image came as a result of the separate convention of the National Association of Colored Women (NACW), formed in 1897 and headed by Mary Church Terrell of Washington, D.C. The NACW convention had begun a day earlier, featuring a lively debate over the constitutionality of Mrs. Terrell's continued service as president, one which Ida Wells-Barnett happily joined after claiming to have been snubbed by convention planners.[22]

Citing a one-term limitation for the presidency, Massachusetts delegate Carter and others from New England had apparently threatened to bolt the convention if Mrs. Terrell were reelected. By Thursday, however, the storm had blown over, Terrell was reelected, and Miss Carter "was in a mollified frame of mind" by the time the convention closed with a farewell banquet, attended by guest speaker Margaret Murray Washington, the Wizard's wife. After a group visit to Jane Addams's Hull House, the women's club delegates adopted a number of resolutions, one opposing discriminatory separate-coach laws being enacted across the South and another favoring the establishment of kindergartens and schools of domestic science for young black students. Delegates also deplored the recent death of activist Colonel Robert Ingersoll, who had bequeathed $1,000 to the John Brown monument fund.[23]

Walters encouraged the NACW delegates to attend Council sessions, even inviting its leaders to come to the platform and address the full convention. Accepting the offer were Mrs. Terrell, Miss Carter, and Mrs. Jeffrey—each a current or future officer of the Council—and five other women.[24]

The text of Margaret Washington's remarks at the NACW banquet did not appear in newspaper accounts, nor did those of Mollie Terrell or local leader Fannie Barrier Williams. Two nights later, remarks by Mrs. Washington and Mrs.

Terrell at the Council's closing banquet would figure more prominently, at least in *Tribune* coverage. Mrs. Terrell's sincere admonition to her listeners to help "obliterate" objectionable traits displayed by the race—such as stealing chickens and gossiping—"caused a commotion," the newspaper wrote. "We are continually doing small things that are heaped up to our detriment," the cosmopolitan world traveler warned, perhaps with tongue slightly in cheek. "The Irish, the Germans, and the Jews do not cause censure of their respective races in any manner."[25]

Responding to a separate toast on the subject of "Character Building," Mrs. Washington expressed her own satisfaction with the Council's adopted resolutions—all but the part referring to her husband—but at least one unnamed delegate reassured her that "the sentiment of the resolutions was not directed at Mr. Washington." (That delegate was Walters, according to Wells-Barnett's memoir.)[26]

The statement was true enough. While discernibly critical of McKinley, not one of the resolutions adopted on the convention's final day even hinted of a break in official ranks with the Tuskegee leader. But the precedent had been set for future attacks on other leaders by the very tone of the resolution directed at the president. "We are heartily grieved that the president of the United States and those in authority have not from time to time used their high station to voice the best conscience of the nation in regard to mob violence and the fair treatment of justly deserving men," read the shrillest of the texts. "It is not right that American citizens should be despoiled of life and liberty while the nation looks silently on, or that soldiers who, with conspicuous bravery, offer their lives for the country should have their promotion result in practical dismissal from the army."[27]

A substitute resolution drafted by Chicago's Théophile Allain—chairman of the Afro-American Cook County Republican Club—would have softened that language, giving McKinley more latitude in action and assigning no personal culpability to his inaction. But the Allain text, offered as a minority report, was voted down by the full convention, after provoking "violent debates and much personal feeling." In an August letter to friend Booker Washington, the Louisiana Creole blamed the failure of his resolution in Chicago on the absence of office-holders "who should have been there and who were afraid to face the music," namely Lyons, Cheatham, Green, and Arnett.[28] (Allain himself fared no better in his quest to replace Walters as Council president.)

The lynching issue provoked the Council's most pointed resolution, calling for the enactment of federal legislation to punish lynchers. The only proper response to the "grave crisis" facing the nation over treatment of Afro-Americans was positive action by the government, specifically through "such national and constitutional legislation as shall at least secure as great protection from mob violence to Americans as is today afforded citizens of foreign countries resident here." Lynching "is an offense against civilization which demands punishment, and we believe that it lies in the power of congress to enact such repressive legislation as shall prevent justice in America from becoming a by-word and a mockery."[29]

To thwart labor union discrimination against black workers, the Council next proposed appointing a committee "to wait upon the labor leaders and the National Industrial commission" and promote cooperation between the races. A reaction to McKinley's failure so far to appoint a black to the National Labor Commission, the resolution was the shrewd ploy of Reverend Ransom, who had insulted Mrs. Washington and tried, but failed, to goad the Council into breaking with her husband's accommodationist strategy (and his focus on industrial training), even though Ransom had once suggested Washington as a candidate for the labor post.[30]

"We have but two particular grievances against President McKinley personally," the Chicago minister claimed. "We do not mean to become allied with either party, but what we want is equitable consideration. If one party can't give it to us, perhaps the other can. . . . We made it plain to Mr. McKinley that we would rather have one of the Labor Commissioners than all the political offices he could give us."[31] The versatile Ransom chose his battles carefully and did not intervene on the delicate issue of disfranchisement, which many observers had expected to draw far more attention at the convention. Perhaps for this reason, that subject's resolution produced a far less direct assault.

The South's growing tendency toward depriving black voters of the franchise was "dangerous and un-American and bound to bear bitter fruit in the future," but the Council's hope seemed oddly vague: "that the good sense of the nation and the wisdom of its officers of justice will prevent the further progress of this final plan." Even so, it was the Council's "unalterable resolution to strive by all power and manly means to vindicate our privileges and fulfill our duties right here in the land of our birth." The Council's strong criticism of McKinley generated the biggest national headlines after the convention, but Ransom's personal criticisms of Washington followed the educator to his own next stop, in Saratoga, New York, where Fortune, described in the minutes as "dangerously ill," was recovering from his recent surgery for an unspecified ailment.[32]

Contacted there by journalists, Washington deftly deflected the barbs. "When I left Chicago it was with the very happiest understanding with all the leading spirits of the council, from President Walters down," he told reporters. "We agreed as to the good that could be accomplished along the lines which I regard as for the best interests of my race. Some of my race think I ought to participate in political activity and discussion. Personally, I have not entertained this view, and I shall not so do." He clearly dismissed Ransom as representing a small minority among blacks. "Whatever a few critics may say in public and in private as to my work and to my course," Washington said, "I have the satisfaction of knowing I am sustained by the knowledge that I enjoy the confidence, the sympathy, and the respect of the most thoughtful and forceful members of the Afro-American race."[33]

New officers were elected on the final day, with Walters easily reelected president (despite a challenge from Allain and former Illinois legislator John C. Buckner) and also for the first time, elected as executive committee chairman. Joining him on the ballot were nine vice presidents, most of them clergymen, fewer than half of them present; only bishops George Clinton of North Carolina and Lucius Holsey of Texas, Chris Perry, and George White were in Chicago. Absent were Fortune, the Reverend Elias C. Morris of Arkansas, and bishops Arnett, Grant, and Cicero Harris.[34]

Delegates once again selected John Thompson as treasurer, naming C. H. Thompson of New York as sergeant-at-arms, Fred McGhee assistant recording secretary, and Ransom chaplain. New financial secretary John Bruce and others faced the continuing task of recruiting new members and raising funds. More than $300 had been raised since December, including Chicago dues payments, but disbursements there consumed much of that.[35]

Bureau chairmen named by the Council included a number of well-known figures, such as Ida Wells-Barnett (antilynching) and former governor Pinchback (literary). Bishop Henry Turner, apostle of Liberian resettlement, was named to head the emigration bureau. Among up-and-coming individuals selected were Professor W. E. B. Du Bois (business bureau) and librarian Daniel Murray of Washington, D.C. (legislative bureau).[36]

Du Bois, participating actively in his first convention, was visibly perturbed by the open attacks on Washington. He told reporters he would be "very sorry if it went out into the world that this convention had said anything detrimental to one of the greatest men of our race." Ransom's words "were ill-timed and foolish" and did not represent the convention's true spirit. Not yet the bitter opponent of Tuskegee accommodationism that he would become, the enigmatic Du Bois was still defending Washington. It was a role the Wizard's secretary relished reporting: "Du Bois and others sustain you well in the Chicago *Record*," wrote Emmett Scott days later.[37]

White's role at the convention was mostly backstage, perhaps because he was there only to defuse anti-McKinley sentiments. In any event, his few public remarks in Chicago drew minor mention in the local press, which ignored his congressional status and misidentified him on at least two occasions—once as a physician, then as a bishop. It was a curious departure from his usual assertiveness on critical issues of the day.[38]

Nowhere, perhaps, was the absence of White's rhetorical flourishes—or the barbed imagery of Tim Fortune—more noticeable than in the drafting of the Council's annual address to the nation, which lacked the fire and distinctive flair of its shorter, snappier predecessor. After the excitement of Ransom's attack on the Washingtons and the furor over the resolution critical of McKinley, the address was a flat and rather dull postscript, clearly authored by committee. Mostly lawyers and ministers, the drafters displayed geographical balance but little sense of rhythm or cadence. From Georgia's doleful Bishop Turner to Minnesota's iconoclastic Democrat, Fred McGhee, and Boston's dry attorney Edward E. Brown, the committee labored to construct a laundry list of debating points, and a handful of sincere, anticlimactic demands.[39]

Its labored introduction traced Afro-American accomplishments and their faithful service to the nation since emancipation, after which the address established the Bible's "golden rule" as the guiding principle for black citizens. "Having now complied with every condition which our civilization imposes upon him, he asks that that civilization guarantee to him immunity from outrage and wrong in the exercise of his rights as an American citizen and in the enjoyment of his freedom as a member of society."[40]

If white Americans claimed superiority over blacks, where was the proof of that superiority? Surely not in America's past "consideration for the weak and the humble," or the "insults and outrages heaped upon the Afro-American people of this country by the whites of a certain section." Afro-Americans claimed no "perfection in any department of life," condemned "every act of violence committed by any Afro-American against anybody whomsoever," and pledged "to do all in our power, as citizens and electors in the United States, to bring before the bar of justice every perpetrator of wrong and outrage."

But the race problem persisted, and Afro-Americans fervently believed that lynching stemmed from unjustified white hatred. "The white people made the problem and they must solve it. Afro-Americans do no lynching. To stop lynching the lynchers must be brought to terms, and they are all white." To prevent further drift into anarchy, the United States must seek to punish the "national sin" of lynching before it was punished by "national calamities." International complications spawned by lynchings of "five Italians in the state of Louisiana" demanded the arrest and punishment of the perpetrators, but murders of American citizens deserved no less, unless somehow the southern "part [was] greater than the whole" of the nation, a mathematical impossibility.

Expressing the Council's "abiding confidence in the ability of the government to act in every instance," the address sought a half dozen major actions, from providing "an equal chance with the whites" for Afro-American soldiers to the appointment of an industrial commission "to inquire into the condition of the Afro-Americans in the United States," and proportional appointment as census takers and supervisors in 1900. The Council proposed appointing at least one black as a commissioner to the Paris exposition; a $20,000 payment to the family of Postmaster Baker, as well as justice for his assassins; and passage of a federal antilynching law.

The address closed with an appeal to all Afro-Americans "to cultivate a friendly feeling among the races in America; that patriotism be taught in each local Afro-American council and that good citizenship shall be the watchword in every home and around every fireside where Afro-Americans are assembled."[41]

With its adjournment, the Council began planning its next meeting, to be held in Indianapolis in August 1900. This would fall after the quadrennial political nominating conventions, but just before the presidential election. Lobbying from both political parties would intensify as the next conclave drew near.

Less than a year after its founding, the Council had indeed exploded onto the national news scene, but mostly through its successful criticism of McKinley (provoking mixed reactions from white newspapers), and its thwarted criticism of Booker T. Washington. Quick to scold the Council for the tone of its most controversial resolution, the *Chicago Tribune* called the Council "unfair in its indirect censure of the President," although other resolutions, such as that on labor discrimination, were deemed "within bounds" and offered "good advice."[42]

Black editors tended to downplay the Council's most controversial resolution, couching descriptions of the meeting in more dignified terms. "Representative men and women from all over the state were present, and worked earnestly for the good of the race," wrote the *Appeal*. The *Colored American*, more defensive than others, summarized the meeting as "a success from every viewpoint. It was a disappointment only to those who expected it to take a radical position in regard to the cowardice of the administration on the Negro question. . . . Nobody insulted the President or any of his friends—if he had any there." Du Bois found the "effect of the debating and conference was good, and behind all froth and intemperate or irrelevant talk there was distinct evidence of sensible restraint and careful well-reasoned leadership."[43]

When the executive committee convened in December at Washington's Conservatory of Music to reassess their efforts and plans for Indianapolis, the mood was one of confidence and renewed purpose. It had now been a year since the Council paid its careful respects to President McKinley, hoping to nudge the White House into open support for its goals, and no presidential assistance had yet materialized. It had been four months since the Council had begun to ratchet up its pressure on McKinley.

Fortune, pleased by the group's action in Chicago, continued to believe the Council was headed in the right direction, except, perhaps, for tolerating Ransom's attacks on Washington. While he disagreed with certain of its policies, he seemed confident that the new Council would succeed where his old league had not. He had agreed to serve on the executive committee—if only as a member from New York, no longer as chairman—and to chair the committee's interim panel on resolutions and soon sought Washington's advice on their content.[44]

Members considered several resolutions, including one Fortune particularly opposed: the endorsement of Indiana representative Edgar Crumpacker's proposal to reduce the representation in Congress of southern states disfranchising black voters. Fortune, one of the few black leaders to oppose Crumpacker's amendment to the decennial reapportionment bill, "insisted it was a false step."[45] Other opponents warned that such action would be counterproductive, effectively legitimizing southern efforts to evade the Constitution's so-called "Reconstruction amendments."

In other action, the committee voted to create a special subcommittee, nominally representing eight states and the District of Columbia, to act on behalf of the Council "between sessions . . . with general legislative power." Conveniently, six of its members lived in Washington, and the rest within a reasonable distance. Out-of-state members included Edward E. Brown of Massachusetts, John Bruce of New York, and H. T. Johnson of Pennsylvania. Local members included chairman Jesse Lawson (New Jersey), Daniel Murray (D.C.), Pinchback (Louisiana), Lyons (Georgia), Richard Thompson (Indiana), and George White (North Carolina).[46]

White was already burdened with increasing legislative duties; in December he was named to the House Committee on the District of Columbia, along with continuing work on the Agriculture Committee. But working separately with fellow subexecutive members Brown and Murray, White soon took up the Council's challenge on another issue, lynching. In early 1900, White introduced his long-sought bill to make lynching a federal offense. On the next to last day of 1899, after the executive committee's adjournment, White had taken a break to host a late luncheon at a local restaurant for a dozen colleagues; only Alex Manly, his private secretary, was not a Council official. Journalist John Bruce recounted the meal in great detail for the *Colored American*, offering a rare public glimpse into the private social world of influential African Americans.[47]

After dining on such delicacies as boiled turkey, chicken gumbo, and lake trout, washed down with North Carolina scuppernong wine, the group retired to cigars and an expansive discussion of both the Crumpacker amendment—strongly favored by Pinchback—and the Council's overall work, including "the best means of enlarging its scope and work." Walters, just back from a private meeting with McKinley, was "enthusiastic and optimistic, and gracefully acknowledged compliments on the successful sessions of the executive committee."

Booker T. Washington was not present, but quickly learned of much of the committee's actions from Fortune, and might well have smiled on the camaraderie. Washington was on good terms with most of those present, if not in agreement with all their policy decisions, and was a potential ally with strong political connections, as well as a superb fund-raiser. Forewarned, he would react favorably to the Council's first substantive request for assistance, in the form of a February 1900 letter from Richard Thompson, which relayed the Council's desire to pursue a court test of Louisiana election law.[48]

"Knowing how deeply interested you are in this matter," Thompson wrote, "I feel no diffidence in laying the facts before you, and giving you perhaps a long-awaited opportunity to place your sympathies in a direct and tangible form." He enclosed the legal bureau's finance committee circular, "appealing to the country for aid in the work of testing the validity of the Louisiana election laws and to correct other evils . . . in the way of the negro's progress."

Washington had been placed upon a list of potential donors designated for "special letters," and whatever amount Washington wished to contribute—up to a per-member quota of $100, Thompson hinted—would be credited to Thompson. It was an interesting exercise in what amounted to a budding role as an undercover operative for the veteran journalist, now becoming a trusted confidant of the Wizard. Just how much Washington eventually contributed to the project is not known—perhaps $250 or more—but he raised significantly more by soliciting influential white donors.[49] Yet requesting Washington's assistance remained a double-edged sword, since the Wizard rarely involved himself in activities he could not either control completely or, at a minimum, strongly influence.

The Louisiana test case would become the Council's largest single undertaking over the next three years. Even though not yet a Council member, Washington would soon become the project's most ardent—and most secret—supporter. A month after receiving Thompson's letter, he met privately in Washington, D.C., with White, Lawson, and Fortune to begin drawing up plans for proposed legal action.[50]

Washington's involvement would also provoke the first real test of the Council's collective will and independence. As the group moved, slowly but inexorably, away from its Chicago dalliance with anti-Washington radicalism, its search for stability would have unexpected consequences, including an early search for new leadership.

4

Playing at Presidential Politics

Indianapolis, 1900

Given the Council's recent history, it was almost inevitable that its nonpartisan pledge would be sorely tested during a presidential election year. As leaders prepared for the late summer session in Indianapolis—scheduled after national nominating conventions, and just ten weeks before the general election—the Council could not expect to avoid the spotlight, especially if black voters might well provide the margin of victory in certain northeastern or midwestern states, as many believed had happened in 1896. Both parties would be certain to pursue whatever advantage might be gained among black voters, by whatever means.

Yet in the spring of that year, the conventions lay months in the future. Instead of partisan strategies, two unrelated events formed an intriguing backdrop for Council plans for the summer: Bishop Walters's appeal for black Americans to commemorate the centennial of abolitionist martyr John Brown's birth (May 9) and simultaneous rumors about Walters's retirement as Council president. The Brown centennial should be marked in churches and elsewhere by "public services in honor of the grand old hero," Walters declared in black newspapers that spring. Collections should go to treasurer John Thompson, "for the use of the council in prosecuting a case which it has before the supreme court of the United States," being handled "by our only congressman, Hon. George H. White, and ex-Senator Edmunds."[1]

If characterizing the court test as "before the supreme court" was premature—it would not be filed in Louisiana courts for another year—the importance of the projected case could not be overstated. George White was closely involved in preparing the case, while former senator Edmunds's involvement was peripheral; the aging Vermont Republican, now in private practice, offered free services in civil rights cases. The Louisiana disfranchisement test, known simply as *State ex rel. Ryanes vs. Gleason*, would dominate the Council's agenda for three years, with a daunting legal price tag of $5,000.[2]

More significant than its cost or its strategic importance, however, was its symbolism. The decision to retain legal counsel and pursue the Louisiana case was Walters's first concrete accomplishment since heading the Council. Yet the achievement was dwarfed by the breaking news, in black newspapers across the country, that it might be his last, perhaps only, real legacy. Rumors had begun circulating that spring of the bishop's plan to step down. (Calvin Chase suggested to Booker T. Washington, somewhat disingenuously, in March, that he, Washington, should replace Walters.) In May, the *Colored American* reported that Walters had announced plans to "retire from the presidency . . . in favor of Congressman George H. White." If Walters's retirement would surely provoke "universal regret," Edward Cooper claimed that "if a successor is to be chosen, no other man would fill the bill as happily as our manly lawmaker, Mr. White."[3]

As the nation's only black congressman, White was arguably the Council's best-known officer—and less likely to provoke dissension than Washington. But was he a consensus choice? Two weeks later, Harry Smith's Cleveland *Gazette* argued that "nothing would so quickly ruin the prospects of that splendid organization as the nomination and election of a politician to the presidency," no matter how well-qualified Walters and others thought White to be. "The president should be a man who is above political influence," and White was "too imbedded in politics for such a position." The three-term Ohio legislator was a maverick Republican, and no particular admirer of White, now completing his second term in Congress. Smith was also a vehement opponent of Booker Washington's politics, and had recently fallen out with the McKinley-Hanna wing of the Ohio party, but represented Ohio on the Council's executive committee, and would soon join White as a vice president. At any rate, Smith's opposition was at best a minor obstacle, if Walters truly wished to anoint White. Months later, White claimed that the bishop had approached him "some time ago" and "asked him to accept the office at a time when he did not want it," complaining that he was losing too much time from clerical duties. White had agreed, reluctantly, but would go to Indianapolis in August fully expecting to be elected.[4]

As one of nine sitting vice presidents, White had built-in rivals for the higher position, including Fortune and five of Walters's fellow bishops. Whoever succeeded Walters, the difficult issue of salary—and the funds to pay for it—would surely arise. Since 1898, Walters's denomination had paid his bishop's annual salary while he devoted weeks on end to Council duties. Complaints that he devoted "too much time to the work of the council and too little to the work of his church," however, had finally forced Walters out, it seemed.[5]

The Council's constitution listed only one paying job—that of financial secretary—but none of the possible contenders would likely agree to take the job without a guaranteed salary. Fortune, perennially broke, was always first in line for reimbursement of his Council travel expenses; the *Age* was barely surviving, and he could not afford to work for free at anything. Walters's fellow bishops faced his same difficult choice, even if their denominations agreed to permit them to devote large amounts of salaried time to running the Council. AME bishop Arnett carried the greatest national political influence, as an unofficial McKinley advisor, but he was also the oldest and frailest.[6]

White was accustomed to a comfortable lifestyle. He had earned a prosperous living as a lawyer before entering Congress and now drew an annual salary of $5,000. Yet he was now facing severe financial difficulties due to his wife's chronic illness and substantial medical expenses, and he did not plan to move his family back to North Carolina if he left Congress when his term expired in March 1901. He had put off a decision on seeking reelection from his predominantly black district until after state voters decided the fate of a constitutional amendment disfranchising illiterates—political code for black voters—on August 1, four weeks before the Council convened. White was publicly optimistic about the vote, yet his home-state political base was steadily eroding. If he chose not to run again, he would need to support himself as a lawyer in Washington or another large city while running the Council part-time, and even then he would require a Council salary.

But could the Council afford even a part-time president whose salary was not subsidized by an outside employer? With no financial reserves, it depended on annual dues and a few donations for almost all its revenue. The Council's fund-raising had not picked up since Chicago, and Pledger's drive to capitalize the proposed newspaper had stalled, while Council expenses continued. A total of $118.75 was spent between September 1899 and January 1900, mostly for printing and travel expenses, against income of just $42. That left less than $50 in Council coffers when the convention opened, or less than half a week of White's Congressional salary.[7]

Before the Council's convention opened, all three national political parties were slated to hold national nominating conventions. The Republicans met in Philadelphia in June, and the Council selected George White to head a delegation before the G.O.P. convention subcommittee on resolutions, bearing the Council's major request: platform planks condemning lynching—similar to one from 1896—and southern disfranchisement of black voters. Eager to attract as many southern black voters as possible in 1896, the Republicans had vigorously opposed lynching.

"We proclaim our unqualified condemnation of the uncivilized and preposterous practice known as lynching, and the killing of human beings suspected or charged with crime without process of law," read the 1896 platform.[8]

As a party delegate to the 1900 convention, White was the obvious choice to present the Council's case, with at least one natural ally on the convention subcommittee: former Mississippi congressman John R. Lynch, now an army paymaster. But Lynch's suggested amendment on disfranchisement was rejected outright, and he fared no better with White's lynching plank. Harry Smith's *Gazette* furiously lashed out at Lynch, who Smith called "wholly responsible for the mutilation and practically the ruination of the Afro-American council committee's resolution."[9]

The final platform stated, simply, that lynching should be condemned, a statement considered a "small and insignificant shadow of the [original] resolution against lynching." Smith's heated exaggeration of Lynch's role—and, by implication, White's inability to deliver—was linked to remarks by Representative Lemuel E. Quigg (a New York Republican), from the full resolutions committee, who claimed that the subcommittee had been "unanimous" in approving both the platform content and all deletions of proposed language. The Republican platform did produce a toothless plank on disfranchisement, condemning "revolutionary . . . devices of State governments, whether by statutory or constitutional enactment, to avoid the purpose of this [Fifteenth] amendment," but the statement on lynching was a pale reflection of its far bolder 1896 predecessor.[10]

White's antilynching bill was now trapped in the House Judiciary Committee, and his national party was not helping matters. Chagrined by the G.O.P.'s failure to support his effort, White returned home to campaign, quietly, against the proposed constitutional amendment. Modeled after an 1898 Louisiana provision, the North Carolina amendment also contained a "grandfather clause," exempting illiterate white voters whose ancestors had voted in 1867, one year before freedmen had regained the vote there. White confidently predicted that North Carolina voters—nearly a quarter of them black—would handily defeat the amendment. But his own antilynching bill and his subsequent public battle with ardent white supremacist Josephus Daniels had badly weakened both his political influence and his powers of prognostication.[11]

National Democrats, hobbled by their dependence on southern votes and candidate William Jennings Bryan's own lukewarm attitudes, said nothing in July on either subject. The People's Party, linked to the Democrats nationally, said nothing about lynching but still managed to repeat their 1896 plank condemning "the wholesale system of disfranchisement by coercion and intimidation advanced in some States, as un-republican and un-democratic."[12]

None of the platforms affected North Carolina's overwhelming vote in favor of the disfranchisement amendment. Even predominantly black counties rolled up large majorities in favor, leading to charges of large-scale fraud. While a court challenge was contemplated, it could not be undertaken until the amendment went into effect (1902) and was eventually scrapped. Stunned by the outcome, White said little for weeks. His first public comments, made to the national press just before departing for Indianapolis, were darkly scornful of his state's party leaders, especially former ally Jeter Pritchard.[13]

White told the *New York Times* that he had decided not to seek reelection to Congress for three reasons: his wife's poor health, wrecked by recent political attacks on him; his belief that even if fairly elected, he could not secure a certificate of election; and his lack of "sufficient means to carry on a political fight that can only prove expensive." But he also felt compelled to leave his home state, which had subjugated the Negro to such a point that "an educated colored man can no longer remain there. . . . I cannot live in North Carolina and be treated as a man." He still needed to work and hoped "to practice law in New York, or . . . some State up this way."

The state's decision to disfranchise black voters had cost North Carolina its only black congressman, along with another "50,000 colored people in the next eight to ten years," he predicted. But the constitutional ploy was "not really political. The political part of it is a mere subterfuge, and is a means for the general degradation of the negro." Independent political action would become commonplace, as result. "I do not believe the black man has much belief in any political party. He must paddle his own canoe. He must think for himself and act for himself. Legislation will not help him." Nor, apparently, would white Republican politicians like Senator Jeter Pritchard, who "are Republicans in order to get the negro vote to maintain them in office, but they do not want the negro to hold office." Pritchard had recently told state Republicans "that if the Democrats meant what they said about preventing negroes from holding office he would join them in passing through the Joint Assembly legislation placing those counties in which the colored people are in the majority under white control," said White.[14]

The two politicians had known each other for nearly two decades, having once served in the same general assembly. During White's first term in Congress, Pritchard had been the South's only Republican in the Senate and had assisted him in appointing a record number of black postmasters, even accompanying White to the White House. Now the white veteran had betrayed his black ally by assuming the mantle of leader in the emerging "lily-white" faction of their fragmented national party, and his treachery was disheartening.[15]

White seemed exhausted and sad as he prepared to travel to Indiana, where even the local white newspapers were predicting his election to the Council presidency. He was unaware that his new nemesis would be joining him in Indiana, as a major convention speaker. That news would trigger an explosive confrontation with Bishop Walters and derail the passing of the torch.[16]

In planning the Indianapolis agenda, Bishop Walters had carefully eyed ways to maximize publicity. The site of the four-day convention would be the senate chamber of the Indiana statehouse, the Council's most public venue yet. The convention would open on August 28, one day after the annual meeting of the National Afro-American Press Association, guaranteeing coverage in virtually all major black newspapers, including the city's own *Freeman* and *Recorder.* Both local white newspapers, the morning *Journal* and the afternoon *Sentinel*, were given detailed advance notice of the Council sessions and its program, and both devoted extensive coverage to it.

Already juggling a busy schedule, Walters was committed to attending a religious conference in Wisconsin just before the Council convention, as he told Washington by letter in mid-August, and could not attend the Boston conference of the new National Negro Business League. Wells-Barnett and others had criticized the timing of Washington's conference as unnecessarily competitive, but Walters assured Washington of his continued trust ("Don't think for a moment that I believe you disloyal to our cause.")[17]

It was no secret that Washington was slated to address the Council, thereby publicly laying to rest any suspicions of his lingering resentment after the Chicago controversy. Yet Walters shrewdly held some of his cards back. As he later explained, he had intended to "secure a fair and impartial discussion" during the convention of a controversial topic, disfranchisement of southern black voters, by inviting "two prominent men of both parties . . . to express their views" on the subject. Yet he did not announce their names until the day of the speeches.[18]

The executive committee had authorized him to invite whoever he wanted. Yet given the angry reactions of at least two members—White and Jesse Lawson—to the announcement, Walters had apparently not informed even the committee of those speakers he selected: Senator Pritchard, a Republican, and former West Virginia governor William A. MacCorkle, a Democrat who never appeared. If Walters hoped to minimize possible protests by telling no one else until the last moment, it seemed part of a broader strategy to retain total control of the convention. In his first unofficial action in Indianapolis—the night before the convention opened—he attended the evening session of the press group, proving "an interested listener" to debate over an official resolution endorsing the

McKinley administration. After being introduced to the audience, he cautioned the editors against actions "touching the indorsement of political parties." Walters even "hinted at plans already near maturity . . . which would throw a stronger light on the situation and enable Afro-Americans to find their friends."[19]

Alex Manly's stirring account of the Wilmington race riot and his life-threatening escape into exile provided less comfort. The nation's leading black editors soon faced a mini-revolt, barely squelching the adoption of a resolution construed by most as supporting the McKinley administration, after certain members protested vigorously against "bringing politics into the association." But the line drawn between official and unofficial endorsements—and between the two organizations, supposedly separate—was blurred considerably by publication of an open letter signed the next day by twenty-three association members, who declared their "unreservedly . . . consistent support of McKinley and Roosevelt in the coming election." If Walters's admonition had helped stave off an official endorsement of McKinley, the journalists seemed worried that official neutrality might somehow be misinterpreted as opposition by political observers.[20]

The letter revealed an almost embarrassingly cozy marriage of the two organizations. Not all the signers were even active journalists, although several had once been, but eleven were already Council executive committee members: Cyrus Adams, Fortune, George Knox, Lillian T. Fox, William Steward, Dancy, Pledger, James Lewis, John Adams, and even George White. The signers represented "more than five-sixths of the membership present," the most surprising being Fortune, now proclaiming allegiance to a leader he had once called "a man of jelly."[21]

As the editors moved on to their next venue, political tensions could only continue to grow. Indeed, the air of the city seemed thick with political intrigue, extending well beyond Walters and the press association. In a national election year, both national parties were jockeying for political advantage among delegates. The *Journal* cited such a report from the *Chicago Post* and took pains to cover every possible angle, such as a "secret meeting of colored men in the cellar under Vaughan's saloon," on the eve of the convention.[22]

Unable to gain access to the meeting, a reporter interviewed bystanders, who characterized those gathered as "Bryan people" afraid of public ridicule for voting Democratic. The underground meeting was part of Mayor Thomas Taggart's "scheme to attempt to swing the Afro-American Council for Mr. Bryan," said an unnamed leader of the Iron League, a local black Republican group. Taggart hoped to dilute the traditionally Republican black vote by tricking blacks into casting "single shots only for president," and thereby invalidating their ballot; ballots so marked were discarded. Meanwhile, national Republicans had apparently launched their version of "dirty peanut politics" by sending two local black operatives—John J. Blackshear and attorney W. E. Henderson—to nearby cities "on a mission to secure republican delegates to pack this convention." The drive, supposedly masterminded by the state's Republican committee chairman, failed when Henderson revealed his true purpose to a "double agent" in Evansville.[23]

If hopes of swinging the Council to Bryan were a long shot, only slightly more likelihood existed for its embrace of McKinley, or so George White said. He was "unalterably opposed to the convention giving its indorsement to either presidential candidate for the reason that our constitution declares we are a nonpartisan organization." Most Council members were Republicans, said White, making a Bryan vote unlikely. "I am a Republican to the core and expect to support McKinley by stumping in several states . . . yet I am opposed to our council indorsing him," he said.[24]

Preoccupied by his own troubles, White was probably unaware of the Republican "line" on Indianapolis, sparked by Ferdinand Barnett's letter to John Green, warning of Democratic intentions to infiltrate the Council and "secure the passage of a resolution unfavorable to President McKinley." Barnett hoped for a "good representation from Washington" in Indianapolis "to thwart the purposes of the Indiana demagogues." Yet his own position was delicate. "You know I would not prostitute [the Council's] plans for political benefit, and you also know that I have seen too much of democratic duplicity and deceit to stand by and allow a lot of schemers . . . to antagonize the President," he told Green. "I write you this matter confidentially because my position in the service of the [Republican] National Committee will be misconstrued" if he were known to be pushing Republicans to "pack" the Council.[25]

Green put the matter directly before McKinley. "What will you have us do in view of the previous?" he asked in a handwritten postscript on Barnett's typewritten letter, noting that "obviously, Mr. Barnett is endeavoring to counteract the bad work of his wife during the past year." Mrs. Wells-Barnett's militant sympathies were well known, and amply enunciated in the pages of her Chicago newspaper. Still, both she—as something of a resident gadfly—and her husband remained active in the Republican campaign at this point. Whether Wells-Barnett knew of her husband's warning from the wings to Green, however, is not at all clear—probably not, although few conservatives (or Tuskegee sympathizers) trusted either Barnett or his wife.[26]

Indianapolis was a bustling midwestern city, home to state government and nearly a quarter-million inhabitants, according to the 1900 census. Its fast-growing black population accounted for 15,931 residents, or just over 9 percent of the city's total, and represented the third-largest black population of any midwestern city, after Chicago and Saint Louis. Largely Democratic in politics, the city boasted a growing black middle class and at least three black weekly newspapers. Two were Republican in viewpoint: the *Freeman*, edited by George L. Knox, and the *Recorder*, edited by William H. Porter and George P. Stewart. The upstart *World* was edited by ardent Democrat Alexander Manning.[27]

Though hardly a hotbed of black Democratic sentiment, Indianapolis did reflect a growing trend toward independence among midwestern black voters, one the *Sentinel* trumpeted optimistically, predicting that "one-half the [Indiana] colored vote will be cast this year for the democratic ticket." The eastern city of Richmond had already formed a large Democratic club, reacting in part to insulting comments about performance of black soldiers in Cuba, made months earlier by vice presidential nominee Theodore Roosevelt.[28]

It was up to high-ranking Republican officials to discourage defections. Indiana's attorney general, William L. Taylor, was flattering in his welcoming remarks to Afro-American Council delegates on August 28. In the absence of the state's governor, Taylor cited the "giant strides" made by black citizens since 1865 and "the distinguishing characteristic of the Afro-American . . . that he is always and everywhere a patriot."[29]

"The progress of the colored race in the last thirty years is the marvel of this age, and would be the marvel of any age," Taylor told the delegates and visitors, who filled the lower floor and the senate galleries. "Think of it: men sitting before me were born and reared as slaves. Yet, within this little span of the years of freedom, you have sprung forward with giant strides. You have occupied seats of honor in the State legislatures, in the House of Representatives and the Congress of the United States," Taylor said. "You are honored here to-day with distinguished representatives of the great departments of the government."

The implication was not lost on his listeners. Since 1865, political success for blacks had almost always come as a result of their loyalty to the Republican party, whose officeholders were amply represented in the audience: White, Green, Lyons, Dancy, and two future U.S. ministers to Liberia, Dr. John Crossland and the Reverend Ernest Lyon. Crossland, a Saint Joseph physician, was a member of the influential Missouri delegation, whose trip to Indianapolis was arranged by that state's Republican national committeeman. Lyon, a prominent Baltimore minister, sat on the advisory committee of the Republican national committee.[30]

Following Taylor onto the platform was Irish-born mayor Thomas Taggart, a Democrat who made a few "gracious remarks" and then called for the federal government and "all citizens, regardless of color" to contribute "in a pecuniary way" toward fulfilling Council goals. It was a cryptic, coded encouragement, perhaps, to the few Democrats within earshot, including McGhee, former diplomat

J. Milton Turner, Tennessee's C. F. Crossthwait, and magazine publisher James W. H. Howard. Taggart, new chairman of the Democratic National Committee, was no stranger to the world of partisan racial politics. He counted on Manning's *World*, reportedly subsidized by Democrats, to remind black readers of the growing political advantages, locally, of switching parties. Manning, who had supported Bryan in 1896 and was nicknamed the "official courier" of the National Democratic Committee, had no apparent difficulty preaching party gospel.[31]

The independents, as represented here by Fortune and Ransom, were the convention's swing vote, arguing that neither political party could be trusted to protect black voters, and that racial prejudice was as strong in the North as in the South. Ransom would even endorse Booker T. Washington's work in education, a year after his Chicago diatribe against the Tuskegee educator. But political groupings, always evident just beneath the surface, were shelved for the moment. After local committee chairman George Knox completed the welcoming addresses, the morning session ended with a series of brief responses by four delegates: White, McGhee, Pledger, and Madison C. B. Mason of Ohio, secretary of the Freedmen's Social and Educational Societies. After lunch, delegates would hear from Walters, as the first major order of business.[32]

Taylor's morning appeal to patriotism among the delegates was underscored by the spirited singing of a stanza of "America," as delegates returned for the two o'clock session. Bishop Walters's voice, "both musical and of great volume," reportedly filled the senate chamber, offering an inspirational lead-in to a far more sober—and politically tinged—message. "It is evident to the thoughtful among us that we are passing through one of the most critical periods of existence in this country," Walters said. "The race is now facing the question of its complete civil and political rights, and from the struggle it dare not retreat. . . . I have no sympathy with [those] leaders who are advising the negroes to voluntarily eschew politics in deference to color prejudice." The essential reason was one of equity, for "[p]olitics is a legitimate, profitable, and in some respects, honorable business." And black citizens were taxpayers, too; why should only white taxpayers be allowed to share in the "offices and emoluments?" His sharpest words were reserved for the federal government, which he described as "guilty of gross neglect" for failing to protect black citizens from discrimination, disfranchisement, and violence. "[T]he loyal negro, who has helped to make the country what it is, and fought in every war to save it, must be disfranchised because somebody does not like him. This is not only unjust and unchristian, but it is base ingratitude," Walters declared.[33]

The bishop stopped short of threatening a mass exodus from the Republican Party, although he noted that "[s]ome of us have signified to the Democratic

Party our willingness to unite with it wherever and whenever it will make it advantageous to our cause to do so." But without "a consideration in the way of just legislation, and kind treatment," he refused to advocate such a switch. "Until this is done, I do not see how we can consistently help it into national power—and I for one will not do so," he said, drawing "deafening applause" for his efforts.[34] Walters had once again trod a careful line between outright partisanship and pure pragmatism, expressing a clear preference for practical, results-oriented politics. It was a mark of both his skill and a singular determination not to be outflanked by loyalists to either party that he emerged, unbruised, from internal battles over which he so often presided. If his lonely quest to remove active violent partisanship from Council proceedings did not always succeed, he was generally admired, even by those who suspected him of being a "closet" Democrat.

Yet his few public detractors were equally determined. Such a man was Théophile Allain, gadfly of 1899, who now stood up, daringly, to interrupt the convention's tribute to Walters. Allain insisted instead on introducing a resolution aimed at reducing the congressional representation of southern states disfranchising black voters. The recent migrant to Chicago displayed political sophistication born of nearly two decades of Louisiana legislative service. His resolution was a popular, if controversial, strategy, which the Council had discussed previously. His intent, however, was to steal Walters's verbal thunder, laying groundwork for a subsequent challenge to the bishop's authority.

"It is easy to appeal to passion and to sentiment," the urbane businessman intoned, "but you have got to take this matter coolly and deliberately. You have got to reach the heart and the conscience of the American people. . . . You cannot win this fight with bullets nor with bowie knives, nor with your sleeves rolled up in a pugilistic manner." When McGhee asked how Republicans would react if Democrats agreed to cut their political base, Allain sneered, "I should say that the Democrats have performed the first Christian act of their career."[35] Allain's ploy was neatly derailed by the chair, which ruled that all resolutions must first be reviewed by the committee on address and resolutions, not yet appointed. A motion thanking Walters for his address was introduced but sidelined momentarily by a skirmish with Louisiana delegate James Lewis, U.S. surveyor of the Port of New Orleans and an old Allain ally. Lewis insisted on discussing a specific reference in the address first, provoking a furious floor debate between delegates attacking Lewis for impeding parliamentary order and others, notably Fortune, who insisted that Lewis be allowed to continue.

Walters defused the situation by agreeing to allow discussion of his speech later in the session. But the next order of business, selecting the committee on address and resolutions, provoked yet another Lewis outburst, after Walters asked Council permission to ensure committee nonpartisanship by introducing artificial bipartisanship—or selecting members of both parties from any state delegation so requesting. Lewis demanded to see what a black Democrat looked like, prompting Chicago delegate Octavius Royall to demand to hear his city's delegates' names read aloud, since he believed they were all Democrats. The chair assured him this was untrue.[36]

The twenty-two-member committee was finally agreed upon, after some changes requested from the floor, and included at least two known Democrats—McGhee and Crossthwait—balanced by at least one quasi-independent, Fortune. The cumbersome committee represented fully a fifth of the convention's ninety-eight accredited delegates, and while the names were being read aloud, Allain created a new distraction by noisily distributing packets of copies of two *Congressional Record* speeches to delegates. After one delegate complained, Walters ordered Allain to stop.[37]

It was political theater at its most surreal and exasperating. By pure tenacity, Walters had held on to win the first round, but whether he had also plucked the newest thorns from his side remained to be seen.

Money, the most familiar old thorn, was still slow in coming to the Council's treasury, although the Indianapolis convention produced the largest revenue so far: a total of $491.50 from membership dues. Expenses associated with the Indianapolis session amounted to more than $300, mostly for travel reimbursements, leaving about $200 in the general account. Without a larger source of revenue, the Council would continue to struggle to make ends meet each year. But this year's financial picture bore at least one bright spot: the size of the separate fund to finance the Louisiana disfranchisement test case. Thousands of letters and circulars, similar to that sent earlier to Washington, had been distributed by the finance committee, according to Lawson's report, and had generated $391.23 for legal fees associated with the case.

It was a significant amount, if still less than a tenth of the $5,000 needed, George White told the convention. The congressman urged "contributions in liberal amounts" from "all liberty-loving Negroes," after explaining progress thus far on preparing the Louisiana test case. The lawyers intended to present the issue to the Supreme Court in such a way "that the court cannot avoid deciding it clearly." McGhee, director of the legislation bureau, summarized previous similar efforts, arguing that the high court had "always heretofore evaded [the issue] by saying that the records of the cases brought to its attention did not present the question of color as affecting citizenship."[38]

Projecting the total costs depended largely on how many lawyers were hired, and which ones. Booker T. Washington had estimated costs at $2,000 after his March meeting in Washington; White's new higher estimate of "probably $5,000 or more" was nearer the $7,000 that Richmond, Virginia, attorney Giles Beecher Jackson believed necessary after a meeting with Council leaders. Jackson, secretary of the National Council of the Constitutional Rights Association, was willing to help raise whatever funds he could. Emmett Scott was also convinced it was crucial to retain an effective and resourceful attorney "who will command proper respect at the bar in New Orleans," but was concerned at one attorney's excessive rates.[39]

For the moment, all such discussions remained strictly confidential. Louis Harlan says Washington "urged his co-workers never to use his name," preferring his role to be "secret and advisory." To camouflage his involvement in the Louisiana test case, Washington went by the cryptic pseudonym of "X.Y.Z." in Council records, and in written communications from Jesse Lawson, his primary Council contact.[40]

In the end, how best to use the limited funds already raised was not even discussed in Indianapolis, although the convention seemed apprehensive about who would hold the funds until expended. Delegates finally instructed the legal bureau's finance committee to turn the special fund over to treasurer Thompson, who would keep it in a separate account "to be used for no other purpose" than testing the validity of disfranchisement laws.[41]

If Walters had envisioned a peaceful setting for the rumored transfer of power to a successor, his hopes soon proved futile. Three separate incidents, involving three unrelated protagonists—Archibald J. Carey, John Green, and George White—fostered an atmosphere of uncertainty and growing fractiousness, finally boiling over into an explosion of angry accusations. The first incident, more comic than not, was the least significant—or at least the most easily resolved. Who was the Council's current chaplain? The Reverend Reverdy Ransom, more famous for his alleged anti-Washington tirade a year earlier than for his benedictions, had been named Council chaplain in 1899, according to official records—which listed Carey only as director of the bureau of ecclesiastical reform—but not according to Chicago newspapers, or, as it turned out, to Carey himself.

The pastor of Chicago's Quinn Chapel AME Church rose to demand an explanation, and Walters patiently explained: after the Chicago convention ended, "Mr. Ransom and several other gentlemen had informed him that Dr. Carey had agreed to give up the post of chaplain for another office." After Carey "indignantly disclaimed knowledge of such an arrangement," Walters informed him that he could certainly have the chaplaincy. Case closed.[42]

Next came a louder and potentially nastier outburst from Green, who had provoked the "Black Judases" incident in Washington. Having forgotten the embarrassing outcome in 1898—or perhaps under direct orders from party leaders—Green had now returned to the convention, with an even riskier political mission: to swing the Council into an open endorsement of McKinley, despite strong opposition from Council heavyweights Walters and White.

Green's outburst followed an address by Georgia delegate Richard R. Wright, on the subject of industrial education for black youths. Wright, a veteran Republican activist, was president of the State College of Industry for Colored Youth at Savannah. In his opinion, Afro-Americans lacked "ambition," as well as loyalty and unity; many forsook their own race and were "satisfied with doing the menial work of the world," rather than entering the trades and professions. Yet he remained hopeful. "The time is coming," Wright said, "when the Afro-American race is going to take its place in the congress of nations."[43]

At the conclusion of Wright's remarks, Bishop Walters opened the floor to discussion, limiting speakers to five minutes after forbidding "any expression of his personal political views" by any speaker. The *Sentinel* described what transpired next, as follows: Green "stepped out in front of the rostrum at a lively gait and launched off into a political harangue. He was promptly called down by a delegate, whose point of order was sustained by the bishop. Then Green began to cry out at the top of his voice that no man, 'not even a bishop' or set of men, could put him down. . . . in the midst of a mass of his friends, who rushed from their seats to encourage him, he continued yelling at the top of his voice."[44]

Much of what Green said was reportedly "drowned by the hullabaloo he had aroused," but during a moment of comparative quiet, he reportedly "turned about and charged Bishop Walters with having been 'bought up' by democrats." That was more than enough for James Lewis, a "tall, muscular old gentleman" who quickly took a firm hold on Green's arm and led him out into the rotunda lobby "to cool off." Green later returned to his seat, chastened, and "for the balance of the evening behaved himself," observed the *Sentinel*. The more sympathetic *Journal* omitted Green's exit, saying only that "a disagreeable scene was narrowly averted" after Green "was finally compelled to take his seat." Nor did the *Journal* recount Madison Mason's supposed assessment of the events as "a disgrace to the race and an outrage upon the convention and the respectable citizens of Indianapolis."[45]

Black editors reacted in varying ways to the scene, ranging from ignoring it completely—as the local *Recorder* did—to downplaying it in sidebars, the course chosen by the *Freeman*, and headlining its main story with a detailed replay, as Smith's Cleveland *Gazette* gleefully chose. Knox's *Freeman* ranked Green "among the interesting speakers of the convention" and referred only indirectly to the disruption: Green "settled the little difficulty on the day following—they kissed and made up. Bishop Walters versus Green."[46]

Smith, never a friend to his Ohio political rival, printed a front-page cartoon of a weeping Green and accused Green of orchestrating "a disgraceful uproar" by attempting to "make a showing which would please Mr. [Mark] Hanna, chairman of the national republican committee and the president." In glowing detail, Smith described Lewis dragging Green out of the senate chamber, along with Mason's reaction from the podium, where he was waiting to speak. Most men might have shunned additional publicity, but Green insisted on addressing the convention the following day, to correct two misstatements in the *Sentinel*'s morning report: first, that he had been led out of the chamber by Lewis, when in fact they "had simply walked out together," and second, that he was just an "assistant stamp clerk" in the Washington, D.C., post office. In fact, he "had charge of all stamps for the government distributed to about eighty-seven thousand post offices" across the nation.[47]

Delegate Mason was astounded by Green's demand, describing the *Sentinel* report as "so nearly true that no retraction can be consistently called for." Green, unperturbed, went on to explain that his anger had been sparked by the Democratic National Committee's use of a Walters letter—with the writer's consent, Green supposed—but Walters assured him that was not the case. Green had performed his task, however onerous. Delegates heaved a collective sigh of relief. Second case closed.

The Casey and Green incidents had been time consuming, if divertingly frivolous. But what unfolded next was deadly serious and could not be resolved so easily. It involved a struggle of nearly titanic proportions over the future of the Council, in the form of its leadership. George White had bided his time quietly since arriving in Indianapolis, giving only one brief public speech—responding to the welcome at the opening session—and helping prepare resolutions for Convention review on Wednesday night, as one of five subcommittee members entrusted by Walters with writing the actual texts.[48] His only other scheduled appearance on the agenda was on Wednesday afternoon, to present his part of the report that he and McGhee had jointly prepared on the Louisiana test case.

White still expected to be chosen president of the Council during Thursday afternoon's election and would not learn until that morning that Walters "had consented to run for reelection," he later said. But the congressman must have begun to suspect that something was wrong a day earlier, when the bombshell of Jeter Pritchard's impending appearance—also slated for Thursday morning—greeted him. Pritchard's talk was to be entitled "Why the Negro Should Not Be Disfranchised," discussed from the Republican standpoint.[49]

The announcement created "the hottest racket of the morning," according to the *Sentinel*. White jumped to his feet and "sprung a startling surprise:" his intractable opposition to Pritchard's appearance. "In scathing terms he denounced Senator Pritchard" for publicly allying himself with Democratic plans to disfranchise black voters in North Carolina by agreeing to allow state assumption of control over predominantly black counties. The senator had "no right to come before the Afro-American council," White reportedly said, "and for him to now express opposition to the disfranchisement of the negro in the southern states would amount to little more than dry rot."[50]

A thunderous exchange broke out between angry defenders of White and Pritchard, as the convention dissolved into near chaos, ended only by the noon adjournment. Some wanted to appoint a committee "to meet Senator Pritchard when he arrives in this city this [Thursday] morning and ask him directly if he ever uttered the sentiment ascribed to him by Mr. White." Meanwhile, Judson Lyons begged White to reconsider and withdraw his charges, which not everyone present believed were even true. "No sir," said White. "If that man is allowed to speak at this convention, it will be done over my persistent protest. . . . I have quietly borne enough from him already without being forced to sit patiently and hear him exploit his openings upon negro disfranchisement, when he contributed to . . . the present existing conditions of the race in North Carolina."[51]

Round one to White, on a split decision. Inwardly fuming, the congressman soldiered through his afternoon presentation on the Louisiana test case and made no further comment on the Pritchard speech, which he refused even to attend. The furor created by John Green's brief tirade Wednesday night diverted most delegates' attention, and by Thursday morning, the incident might have been forgotten—except by Walters and White, whose previous alliance, badly damaged by the Pritchard announcement, was about to break down completely.

The agenda of the morning session included the executive committee report, formally offering nominees for the Council's officers during the coming year. To the surprise of many, perhaps, that report did not include White's name. To the complete surprise of George White, Alexander Walters was the committee's nominee, for another term as president.[52]

Round two to Walters. According to the *Journal*, which devoted a long section of its coverage for the session to the incident, delegate James D. Miller moved to strike Walters's name and substitute White's name for the presidency. But White immediately "caused another small-sized riot" by refusing to be a candidate under any circumstances, in a speech, which he concluded by "squarely accus[ing]

Bishop Walters of acting with duplicity in the matter of the presidency of the council." Walters had been quoted in newspapers as saying that he did not want to be president of the council another year, but that he did want White to succeed him. "Upon that understanding, I agreed to the use of my name for the place," said White. "But I dislike duplicity, whether practiced by a ward politician or by a bishop. It is my wish that my name be not used, nor voted upon for the position of president of this council."[53]

The congressman's heated remarks "acted as fire applied to powder, and in an instant confusion again reigned in the council," lasting until Walters temporarily resigned the chair and told delegates that an "unfortunate mistake" had occurred. His brother bishops, after complaining that he devoted too much time to the Council, and too little time to religious duties, had suddenly changed their minds and withdrawn their objections. "A large number" of fellow Council members had then prevailed upon him to run again.[54]

It was that simple. "Bishop Walters's explanation was accepted and peace hovered over the body for a time," wrote the *Journal*—at least until after Senator Pritchard's speech later that morning.[55] But if everyone else was willing to give Walters the benefit of the doubt, White remained skeptical. He suspected there was more to the story, and so there was, at least according to an unnamed Council member. The reversal of fortune appeared due as much to money—how much the Council would have to pay White if he were elected—as to anything else. "One of the many reasons why Bishop Walters was wanted at the head of the council was that his church paid him a salary of $2,000 and his traveling expenses," said the *Sentinel*'s new source, compared to paying White "for his time and expenses of going about the states in the work."[56]

That afternoon, Walters would be reelected without opposition, and the story of White's withdrawal would undergo a subtle, mellowing revision, as in the version offered in early September by the *Freeman*: "Congressman White refused to stand for the presidency when he learned of Bishop Walters' reconsideration."[57] Round three, and match, to the bishop, now labeled by the *Freeman* as "the ideal presiding officer" and "justly re-elected." Third case closed.

Before the election could take place, the Council would hear the celebrated—and maligned—Senator Pritchard, whose invitation had provoked so much emotion earlier. For all the buildup, the senator's "eloquent" speech was far from provocative—except to Democrats—and viewed by Harry Smith as "very able, with the exception of one or two distasteful remarks." Yet one bizarre heckling incident marred the presentation. Pritchard had just begun to criticize Democrats for denying voting rights to blacks in the South when "a Democratic negro named

J. T. V. Hill . . . rose to his feet and interrupted the speaker. This breach of the laws of hospitality filled the remainder of the delegates with horror . . . . One delegate, a minister of the gospel, was so indignant at what he characterized as 'a cowardly piece of business,' that he started toward Mr. Hill with arm upraised as if to strike, but was stopped by men with cooler heads."[58]

Pritchard resumed his speech, unruffled. "It is amusing to hear our Democratic friends talk about the 'consent of the governed,' in view of their performance in North Carolina, South Carolina, Louisiana, Mississippi and other southern States, wherein . . . they have denied the colored men the rights that are guaranteed him by the fifteenth amendment," he said. "If we have so much solicitude for [Cubans and Filipinos], who are so remote from us, in the name of common sense, isn't it proper that we should care for those who were born and reared among us? Can we consistently deprive them of the liberty which they have enjoyed for thirty years?"[59]

Far from being oppressive imperialists—as charged by Democrats—the Republican Party's true "record with respect to free institutions has been uniform and consistent from its formation. When it came into existence, its mission was to liberate the slave . . . and preserve the Union, and to-day it stands for the enjoyment of the right to vote by every American citizen, without regard to race, nationality or previous condition," Pritchard declared. "Our Democratic friends are opposed to a republican form of government in many of our own States, but they are very zealous in behalf of Aguinaldo and those who they claim are fighting for the enjoyment of those rights which are denied the colored man by the Democratic party in the South."

Warm applause frequently followed Pritchard's phrases, and at its conclusion he received a standing ovation. His few offending remarks, including one statement that Afro-Americans "ought to rid themselves of the members of their race who commit outrageous crimes," sat better with "the more level headed among them [who] declared that he was right" than with Democrats such as J. Milton Turner, prevailed upon to respond for his party in MacCorkle's absence. The ex-diplomat first attacked Pritchard's entire speech as "from first to last a plain plea for the negro vote," producing a "rank political donnybrook" in a supposedly nonpartisan setting. Turner's "hot shot" then castigated Council planners—by implication, Walters—for bringing a "white Republican . . . across the country to tell the story of the needs of the negro when Congressman George White . . . the last representative of the colored race in Congress, was left on the floor of the convention without an invitation to deliver the 'great speech.'"[60]

Pritchard erred in blaming Democrats for the precedent of disfranchisement, Turner reminded his listeners. "Disfranchisement dated back to a Republican

Congress which took the votes from the citizens of the District of Columbia early in the Seventies, simply to get rid of the domination of the negro," Turner recalled. Pritchard had denounced active disfranchisement with one hand but defended the passive type reflected in North Carolina's statutory law that allowed the state to assume control of local governments and was traditionally used only "to prevent colored citizens from holding office."[61]

The sixty-year-old Turner was usually a convincing speaker, and his political beliefs were strong and sincere, if comparatively recent. As a much younger man, he had served as U.S. minister to Liberia for seven years under two Republican presidents (Grant and Hayes) in the 1870s, before his 1888 "conversion" to the Democratic side. But his activities within Missouri's Democratic Party were generally restricted to election years, and he would leave the party for good in 1903, declaring allegiance to Theodore Roosevelt in 1904.

Yet in 1900 his arguments fell on generally deaf ears. The *Journal* blamed partisan resentment: "The majority of the delegates, it seemed, did not care to hear a Democratic colored man talk politics, and they refused to listen." Turner's performance was flat, said the *Freeman*: "The very brilliant Milton was dumb as an oyster when attempting to answer Pritchard. A different occasion was necessary to stir up a Milton Turner."[62] Perhaps, or perhaps not. The *Sentinel* said that Turner "disposed of the white republican senator's argument in a manner to draw applause even from many Republicans present." But Pritchard was not present, having departed the Indiana statehouse—with almost unseemly haste—as soon as his speech ended, and the babble from the floor was all but overpowering.

It was a tense situation. Before Turner began to speak, the convention had shouted down McGhee, first candidate for Democratic spokesman, and Turner's own speech could barely be heard over the turmoil, yet he persisted. He wanted to warn listeners—including Crossland and Lyon, soon to succeed him in the Liberian posting—that the Council was being "dragged into politics," which he opposed. "I am surprised to find intelligent men, men of the cloth, lending their powerful influence to such a movement," he declared, with an air of obvious resignation.[63]

Men of the cloth would continue to serve as new Council officers, from Chairman Walters to two vice presidents, including a rising star—Ernest Lyon—and one veteran, Bishop Clinton. Clergymen would also serve as the Council's corresponding secretary (Isaiah B. Scott) and chaplain (J. S. Caldwell), in addition to heading four of nine Council bureaus. Yet Clinton and Tim Fortune, now ranking vice president, were the only returning faces on a list now dominated by laymen. Journalists played an increasingly active role, from Georgia's Pledger and Ohio's Harry Smith to Steward, editor of the influential *American Baptist* of Louisville, Kentucky, joining general secretary Cyrus Adams and newspaper bureau director Alex Manly. Pharmacist J. Frank Blagburn of Iowa was named financial secretary, joining New York's John Thompson, perennial treasurer. Other new vice presidents chosen included the Council's first woman— Indianapolis activist Lillian Fox, elevated from the executive committee, Colonel John R. Marshall of Illinois, and O. M. Wood of Missouri.

Three bureau directors were chosen to continue in their positions: Du Bois, reelected to head the business bureau; McGhee, legislation; and J. Madison Vance of Louisiana, legal. Newcomers included W. C. Jason of Delaware, education; W. A. Alexander of New York, ecclesiastical reform; Madison Mason, literary; and the Reverend B. F. Seabrook of Oregon, in charge of emigration.[64]

Ida Wells-Barnett, previously head of the antilynching bureau, became the Council's national organizer, a position first discussed in 1898, but neither listed in the constitution nor clearly defined elsewhere; it apparently involved helping to organize local and state councils. Until now, the organizer had been designated by the executive committee. Wells-Barnett received the post as the result of a change proposed by George White. Relations between the two had been distinctly frosty since 1898, when he refused her request to withdraw a bill awarding federal assistance to the family of the murdered South Carolina postmaster. Wells-Barnett had badgered White personally for five weeks, claiming that the Illinois congressional delegation was willing to introduce a similar bill, one that might actually succeed.

Famous for her sharp tongue and frank language, Wells-Barnett had told White that she knew the South better than he did. (She may have been right— his bill was never voted upon, and no federal assistance was ever given to the Bakers, although the outbreak of war with Spain that spring probably doomed any such effort—but the two activists were never close again. She then declined to support his antilynching bill in 1900.) At any rate, Wells-Barnett's report on the work of the antilynching bureau was well received, according to the *Freeman*, which summarized it in one sentence. "Her greatest point was as follows: 'That a man with a ballot and without a home would always be a poor addition to the citizenship of any country.'" Her sentiments were echoed by special guest Lillian Clayton Jewett, who had traveled to South Carolina in 1899 to rescue surviving Baker family members; Jewett's speech was aptly titled "The Evils of Lynching."[65]

Despite her early active involvement in the Council, and a three-year stint as convention secretary, Wells-Barnett devotes little of her memoir—perhaps a dozen pages—to the Council, barely mentioning Indianapolis and downplaying her own role throughout. What little she says about the 1900 convention amounts to barbed criticism of its most illustrious speaker, the racial leader she considered both ineffective and devious: Booker T. Washington. "Mr. Washington's theory had been that we ought not to spend our time agitating for our rights; that we had better give attention to trying to be first-class people in a jim crow car than insisting that the jim crow car should be abolished," she wrote. "And of course, fighting for political rights had no place whatever in his plans."[66]

If Wells-Barnett publicly scoffed at Washington's philosophy as inimical to her own activism and radical Council impulses, Walters's analysis was far more circumspect. His letter to Washington just before the convention expressed "delight" at the educator's agreement to speak. "There can be no conflict between the Afro-American Council and yourself," Walters wrote. "You are contending for the industrial development of the Negro, while we are contending for his civil and political rights. I am with you in your work and I believe you are with us in ours. We understand that you would take the same stand that we are taking but for your school."[67]

Washington arrived by train from New York just half an hour before his speech and was instantly recognized and greeted "with a storm of applause" that forced a temporary suspension of business. Once on the podium, the educator was introduced by his "intimate friend, T. Thomas Fortune . . . who said that although he himself is a radical and Professor Washington is a decided conservative, he loves Professor Washington and places unbounded confidence in him." Yet if Fortune expected to persuade his mentor to speak on political issues, he was overreaching.[68]

Not so Indiana's Governor Mount, who had come, with others, to hear Washington speak, and whose last-minute appearance provoked an impromptu lead-in to the main attraction. Mount drew enthusiastic applause with his own comments, labeling southern disfranchisement of black voters as "a strange procedure in this country" for "colored men . . . who rallied under the flag of the Union that the Nation might be preserved." Mount also exhorted his listeners to "be worthy of those rights, and then, like men, demand your rights."[69]

Unlike Mount, Washington made no direct mention of politics, save a single reference to a shoeshine man in Washington, D.C., "who does not care whether the Republicans or the Democrats or the Populists are in power in the national administration. He has a way to earn a livelihood." The speaker's attention went instead to the situation now faced by black Americans, who needed "supreme faith, calmness, unity and individual determination" to weather a "season of trial and testing," and the "sacred obligation" white America owed to their Afro-American brothers and sisters.

"I am convinced that nothing can be gained but much lost to the cause of the negro by time spent in the mere badinage of words of blame and censure between the white man North and the white man South," Washington said. "In the same spirit I would add that the negro cannot make stronger his case by aimless railings against the southern white man; neither can the southern man assist much in the solution of the difficulty which is so vital to him by mere condemnation of the negro."[70]

He refused to be discouraged, for his positive personal view of history forecast the inevitable advancement of oppressed peoples who persevered. "In all history of government, I do not believe that in any large degree any race has been permitted to share in the control of government till a large number of the individual members of that race have demonstrated beyond question their ability to succeed in controlling successfully their own individual business affairs," he said. "My own belief is that the time will come when the negro in this country will secure all the recognition to which his merits entitle him to as a man and as a citizen . . . through the natural law of evolution. In a word, we have got to pay the price of everything we get, the price that every civilized race or nation has paid for its position, that of beginning gradually, naturally, at the bottom and working upward toward the highest civilization."

The industrial foundation still promised black America's best hope, according to Washington. "[I]ndustrial training . . . starts the race off on a real, sure foundation . . . . On this industrial foundation will grow habits of thrift, the love of work, economy, ownership of property and a bank account . . . classical education, positions of public responsibility." Without industrial development, however, "there can be no wealth; without wealth there can be [no] leisure; without leisure, no opportunity for thoughtful reflection and the cultivation of the fine arts."

Only economic development would produce "protection to property, security to life, and the right to trial by jury in all cases . . . . We may have to struggle for decades and centuries before we get upon our feet, but out of the struggle we will gain a strength and confidence." If some foresaw a coming race war, Washington saw no such thing. "Race wars have been predicted in this country for three centuries, and the first one has not yet occurred. . . . . The Caucasian in the South needs the negro, the negro needs the Caucasian. The black man has got much from the white man, the white man has got much from the black man. We must teach the white man not to judge us by the worst. This is not an age for pessimism, for doubt, for predicting disaster."[71]

Washington's lengthy speech contained little newsworthy content, to those who had heard this speech before; it was a condensed version of a stock speech, last delivered in Washington in May. Geared to a friendly audience, however, the speech did seem to work; the warm applause given the Wizard at its conclusion lasted for several minutes, according to the *Journal*. Walters then suggested the audience give Washington the "Chautauqua 'salute,' and the fluttering of perhaps a thousand handkerchiefs was a beautiful and impressive spectacle."[72]

But outsiders may not have understood how Washington could win such a reception from an audience widely perceived as "radical." The *Journal* explained that Washington had come prepared to discuss "the thirteenth, fourteenth and fifteenth amendments to the Constitution of the United States, and their violation by white Democrats of the South, but for some reason he did not see fit to read that portion of his speech." The reason given by unnamed "prominent" delegates was "his fear of precipitating another of the unfortunate controversies" that had already occurred at the convention. Once "Washington heard of these squabbles . . . he decided at once to cut out that portion of his speech."[73]

Washington dodged a reporter's question to that effect "with more than the suggestion of a merry twinkle in his eyes." Jesse Lawson later congratulated him for the "excellent taste" of his speech, and "thank[ed] God that you did not fall into the trap that had been set for you." Indianapolis lawyer John Coburn arrived too late to get a good seat and could not hear the speech but found the newspaper account of the speech "every word, to the purpose & excellent." His only objection lay in its abbreviated state ("I fear you made a mistake in not giving us your full address.") Richard Thompson warmly praised Washington's speech, which he said "tempered a highly aggravated condition" and accomplished a "pleasant result." The speech had the additional benefit of "disarming the little band of cheap critics who professed to believe that the National Business League was designed to overshadow or supplant the Council," he wrote Washington privately in early September.

Yet not everyone who heard Washington was impressed with his improvisation. Wells-Barnett, one of Thompson's "cheap critics," neglected even to mention Washington's appearance in her memoirs, stating instead that Washington had "hitherto given us the impression that he could not ally himself with us because we were too radical," and had decided to "steer as far away as possible from the radical group."[74] For the moment, however, almost all eyes remained on Washington.

The Council's resolutions and address to the nation were anticlimactic, and a far cry from the critical tone of the 1899 convention. The resolutions related almost entirely to Afro-American suffrage and lynching and were largely conciliatory: "With thirty-five years of freedom we gladly accept all the responsibilities which civilization and citizenship place upon us, and ask only a 'fair field and no favor.' We plead no excuses, seek no particular privileges, ask no special laws in favor of ourselves or on account of our grandfathers, but we do appeal to the chivalry of the nineteenth century—that if it be too busy to help us, that it will be too generous to push us back," read one.[75]

Another resolution on lynching reaffirmed the Council's dedication to "supremacy of the law," citing more than four thousand lynchings over the past twenty years, and urged President McKinley to repeat his 1899 request to Congress "to enact a law to protect foreigners residing in this country from lynching," but amended this time "to secure the same measure of protection for citizens of the United States which the contemplated legislation will extend to foreigners." Other resolutions approved the goal of domestic emigration of black citizens—from the South and North to the West—and preached education, organization of local Council chapters, and an end to all unjust racial discrimination.[76]

The address to the nation, which Fortune read to the Council, repeated the message in a similar quiet tone, lacking 1899's militant rhetoric, and dealing almost entirely with southern disfranchisement. "We feel it to be of supreme moment to protest against the nullification by fundamental enactment of the suffrage provisions of the Federal Constitution" by four southern states, Fortune read. "We regard it as an immoral and unprecedented construction of the fourteenth amendment to covertly seek to rob a large number of the citizenship of this country by State nullification of the precious rights guaranteed to them by the fourteenth amendment."

While the Council did not oppose "restriction of suffrage rights by any State, by property or educational test, which shall apply to all citizens alike," it believed that the four state constitutions, as amended, "enacted by a minority of the citizens of those States without submission for ratification to the people . . . are immoral in their purpose, in contravention of positive guarantees of the federal Constitution, and in direct violation of the reconstruction acts by which those States were readmitted into the Union. We have faith to believe that revolutions never go backwards, and that the abiding sense of justice in the American people in the North and South, will ultimately impel them to concede to us all that we contend for and which is inherently ours, as inherently theirs," the address concluded.[77]

After the Council's adjournment, a brief routine business meeting concluded the fretful Indianapolis session. Until Philadelphia, management of the Council would be left to Walters, Fortune, and other members of the new operational subcommittee, which bore little resemblance to its predecessor. Cyrus Adams, Pledger, and McGhee, all Council veterans, and four newcomers, Alex Manly, and John Crossland, were joined by new vice presidents Smith and Lyon. Not a single member of the 1898–1900 group was reappointed; gone were such familiar faces as those of White, Lawson, Lyons, and Pinchback. The new group was considerably younger as well, averaging just forty years, with Pledger the oldest at forty-nine. Manly, the youngest at thirty-four, was also the only member living in Washington, D.C., although Crossland, thirty-six, harbored ambitions of spending time there to lobby for a federal appointment.[78]

Described later as "one of those brainy young Afro-Americans who helped shape the policy" of the Council, Crossland headed Missouri's Negro State League and was a member of the Republican State Central Committee. Within eighteen months, he would convince President Theodore Roosevelt to appoint him as U.S. minister to Liberia, vaulting past far better-known candidates in the process. His eventual successor in Monrovia would be Lyon, at thirty-nine the Council's most intriguing new face, a native of British Honduras who had moved to New Orleans as a child, had previously served a large congregation in New York, and continued to take an active interest in that city's race relations. Lyon distinguished himself on the last day by introducing a resolution, adopted unanimously, "extending [to] the negroes of New York city the sympathies and best wishes of the council in their fight against 'mob law and police injustice,' and thanking the metropolitan press for its fair attitude toward the colored people."[79]

The Indianapolis meeting had been the Council's best attended so far, if also the costliest. Travel expenses, mostly for Walters, Fortune, and Miss Jewett, consumed nearly two-thirds of the final costs of $325. For once the general fund was far from empty, thanks to nearly $500 in dues payments, although much of the $200 balance was reserved for legal costs from the Louisiana test case. Jesse Lawson, finance chairman in the legal bureau, was working diligently on that case, as evidenced by his correspondence with Booker T. Washington after the convention. But with a critical deadline approaching, Lawson was finding most of the Council less than helpful. "The National Council, aside from our committee, has done nothing in the matter, but talk. The registration books in La. will close pretty soon, and then we shall have to wait two years before we can get a case," he wrote. Determined not to let that happen, Lawson's group had retained Arthur Alexis Birney, former U.S. attorney for the District of Columbia, but he wanted $500 up front and planned to "work up the case from the beginning. Start it in Louisiana and take it through the U.S. Supreme Court." In Indiana, Washington had reported receiving $100 "from parties in the North to assist in the matter." Could Washington now forward that amount either to Lawson or directly to Birney? Lawson had written McGhee asking for the money, but had heard nothing so far. In any event, Lawson thought it best "for you to keep in the background in matters like the Louisiana case. Your real friends appreciate your position, and will do nothing that is calculated to embarrass you in that work, or jeopardize your standing before the public."[80]

One of those friends, Giles Jackson, had mixed news for Washington on the issue. Jackson had been unable to raise any money for the case and reported that Albert Pillsbury, a preferred Council attorney, now suggested using either North Carolina or Mississippi, not Louisiana, for the test. It was no secret that Jackson was sounding out white attorneys for advice in pursuing disfranchisement rulings before the Supreme Court. In late August, Indianapolis newspapers reported that Jackson's National Council of the Constitutional Rights Association had hired Pillsbury and attorney W. A. P. Breckinridge of Lexington, Kentucky, as counsel to bring a disfranchisement case—relating to "recently enacted statute laws and constitutional amendments in some of the Southern States"—before Massachusetts courts. Breckinridge denied involvement, Pillsbury said nothing publicly, and it was never explained how out-of-state laws could be tested in Massachusetts.[81]

Jackson told Washington he had so far raised less than $10 outside Virginia for his own causes, and his group was broke. He and his colleagues had spent much time and personal money to fight a proposed "Jim Crow Car" ordinance in Richmond but were still willing to "unite with you and other gentlemen in raising the money to test the constitutionality of the 'Grandfather Clause' of the several Southern States." Could Washington come to Richmond to discuss the matter, then accompany Jackson to Washington? "I know a plan by which we can raise all the money necessary but that will have to be done through you and myself and you need not then be publicly known," Jackson wrote in early October.[82]

Already complicated by Washington's need for confidentiality, the money trail became murkier during October. On October 8, Lawson reported receiving two separate contributions—one a postal order from Washington for $100 (half of what Washington promised to raise), and the other a blank check for $250, from McGhee, sent to Lawson on Washington's instructions. Lawson said he had filled in Birney's name and sent it back to McGhee, who promised to endorse it and send it to Walters for his signature. Walters, in turn, would send it to financial secretary J. Frank Blagburn in Iowa, who was to sign it and send it back. The entire transaction might take months, due to the bishop's imminent travel.[83]

"Will also send receipt to the parties contributing the money, if you so desire," Lawson wrote. An additional $150, promised by Washington from New Orleans contributors and noted in a separate telegram, "will just make out the other $250 due Mr. Birney, and will be sufficient to meet our present demands." The committee's long-term needs included another $500 for Birney and an unspecified amount for his associated lawyers. So far, this was Birney's legal plan: "The most important thing to do is to get the case before the [U.S. Supreme] Court in the proper form and on the proper grounds, and that the verbal argument is a thing of less import," Lawson wrote. Birney was corresponding with "a lawyer in Louisiana who has given the case considerable study" and had received a letter from Pillsbury, who could render no assistance until the Supreme Court appeal. Birney "is to have charge and supervision of the case both in Louisiana and at Washington, but he wants the best legal talent . . . and I have agreed to allow him to select that talent," with "full accord" from George White and Judson Lyons. Just how the rest of the money collected was to reach the Council's treasury was not specified, but the treasurer's report later listed the $250 contribution as "from friend of Council," dated October 8, 1900, with a payout of the same amount recorded to A. A. Birney a fortnight later.[84]

As Lawson busied himself with case details, other Council members were far more concerned with a more immediate matter: the U.S. presidential election. Bishop Walters and fifty other members had taken the unusual step after the convention of personally endorsing McKinley for reelection, in a letter released by the *Appeal* on September 29 and reprinted each week until the election. The letter declared that this was "not an action of the Council per se," but a personal act by the group. "The undersigned members of the National Afro-American Council unreservedly endorse the foreign and domestic policy of the National Republican administration, and believe that the best interests of the country at large, and the Afro-American people in particular, will be served by a consistent support of McKinley and Roosevelt in the coming election," read the letter, fashioned on a similar one signed by black editors and released in late August.[85]

Signers included Council officers and a mixture of well-known figures and the lesser-known, many from Indianapolis. Vice presidents Clinton, Lyon, Pledger, and Wood; secretaries Adams, Blagburn, and Harris; treasurer Thompson; chaplain J. S. Caldwell; and sergeant-at-arms John Wheeler all signed. Perhaps the best-known nationally were current officeholders Lyons, highest ranking domestic appointee in the McKinley administration; Green, whose intemperate display in Indianapolis had brought him brief notoriety; and former vice president Dancy, the U.S. customs collector in Wilmington. Subcommittee member Crossland was on the list, along with Republican activists Lewis and Allain. Indianapolis signers included Henderson, Blackshear, Gurley Brewer, and Dr. Sumner Furniss, chairman of the Indiana delegation and younger brother of the U.S. consul to Bahia, Brazil, Henry W. Furniss. The rest were minor Republican loyalists from the convention.

While the letter reinforced the Council's image as solidly Republican, it probably had little effect on the election, which McKinley won handily, improving on his 1896 vote totals against William Jennings Bryan in both the popular and electoral tallies. Yet by helping avert a resolution critical of McKinley in Indianapolis—which would have recalled the unhappy 1899 Council resolution—the letter was still a boon to at least one signer, Cyrus Adams, who had now proved his reliability as a party activist and would soon be appointed assistant register of the U.S. treasury.

Three weeks after the election, a brief notice in the Indianapolis *Recorder* outlined Council strategy for the year. Executive committee chairman Fortune instructed subexecutive members to gather in Washington, D.C., on December 28. "It is of the greatest importance that all members should attend" the group's first session since the convention, he said. Agenda items included the Louisiana test case, "to be further considered in the light of what has been accomplished by the committee having the matter in charge"; a plan of action for dealing with reduced representation by southern states in Congress; and plans for a "more thorough organization of the Council in all the States and Territories."[86]

No mention was made of Council antilynching efforts, although the president's annual message to Congress on December 8 did hand the Council a small victory, of sorts, on that issue. McKinley once again condemned lynching, if only by repeating a passage from his first inaugural address: "Lynching must not be tolerated in a great and civilized country like the United States; courts, not mobs, must execute the penalties of the law. The preservation of public order, the right of discussion, the integrity of courts, and the administration of justice must continue forever the rock of safety upon which our government security rests. This I most urgently reiterate and again invite the attention of my countrymen to this reproach upon our civilization," said the president. As in 1899, he specifically referred only to the lynching of five Italians in Louisiana and offered new regrets to Italy for the inability of the federal or state governments to "inculpate," or punish, "authors of this grievous offense against our civilization."[87]

It was not the long-sought mention of the 1898 Wilmington racial massacre. But at least by mentioning the issue, if not the desired context, McKinley had offered black leaders an olive branch on the issue—as close as he was likely to come—and it would have to do for now. Still, for George White, the president's message was disappointing. The lack of a positive declaration on this issue was a virtual death knell for his antilynching bill, still locked in the House Judiciary Committee. His days as a congressman were quickly coming to an end, and he had hoped that McKinley's reelection might inspire him to speak out more forcefully on the issue, perhaps even dislodging the bill from committee.

This was not a happy winter for White, who was further frustrated by political circumstances blocking him from speaking out in the House on key issues of disfranchisement and proposed reduction of southern representation. House Republican leaders had limited debate on the Crumpacker amendment to the Burleigh reapportionment bill and related resolutions to selected speakers, denying White an opportunity to address the issue on the floor. From Cleveland in early January, the *Gazette* sarcastically ridiculed White's silence. "Our 'great' and only Congressman . . . was conspicuously absent from all debate on the resolution and bills. It was a grand opportunity for him to show that he is really true and loyal to himself and his race. With the exception of Mr. Crumpacker, there seemed to be none to plead for justice." But Harry Smith's sarcasm drew a withering response from White's defender, the *Colored American*, who labeled Smith as "grossly ignorant of parliamentary usage," despite his own legislative service, and dead wrong about White, who had tried repeatedly to gain permission to speak but "was pushed aside" by party leaders, who feared alienating southern Democrats by allowing White to speak. Smith sheepishly acknowledged his mistake, citing "imperfect reports sent local daily newspapers by their Washington correspondents." He had been informed by a reliable source—the *New York Sun*—that White had made "an impassioned speech, resenting the manner in which his race has been maligned" by certain southern congressmen.[88]

On January 8, White had been recognized by the Speaker for that brief statement, as long as he agreed not to refer to the pending bill. He honored his pledge, slyly asserting that he had "sought diligently on both sides of this House to get an opportunity to be heard during general debate on this measure" and "thought it rather strange that the gentlemen managing the two sides of this question" had never "accorded me an opportunity to defend [my people]. God bless Judge Crumpacker, who has taken occasion to stand up in his place as a man, and has said a word in defense of those people who have . . . since their emancipation served their country faithfully."[89]

"We owe Mr. White an apology and take pleasure in making it," Smith wrote in his January 19 editorial. "He is a man of exceptional ability and we believe a loyal Afro-American. It should be a matter of regret . . . that he is not to be a member of the next congress. The great need of his presence there will make us miss him all the more." To White, now busy preparing his "farewell address" to the House, the editorial quarrel was of little consequence. At the end of January, he rose, for the last time in the U.S. House, to offer an eloquent defense of his race and their enduring efforts to prove themselves worthy of full citizenship. "I want to enter a plea for the colored man, the colored woman, the colored boy and the colored girl of this country," he said. "The new man, the slave who has grown out of the ashes of thirty-five years ago, is inducted into the political and social system, cast into the arena of manhood where he . . . is put upon trial to test his ability to be counted worthy of freedom, worthy of the elective franchise." Now, "under conditions but little removed from slavery, he asks a fair and just judgment . . . that he might demonstrate the truth of 'the fatherhood of God and the brotherhood of man.'"[90]

White admitted his frustration at being unable to accomplish what he had hoped to do before leaving Congress. His attempt to protect his race from lynching had been blocked, even though "the arena of the lyncher no longer is confined to Southern climes, but is stretching its hydra head over all parts of the Union." Yet he remained essentially hopeful. "I want to submit a brief recipe for the solution of the so-called American negro problem. He asks no special favors, but simply demands that he be given the same chance for existence, for earning a livelihood, for raising himself in the scales of manhood and womanhood that are accorded to kindred nationalities. Treat him as a man," White pleaded with fellow members of Congress.

"Obliterate race hatred, party prejudice, and help us to achieve nobler ends, greater results, and become more satisfactory citizens to our brothers in white," White asked. "These parting words are in behalf of an outraged, heart-broken, bruised, and bleeding, but God-fearing people, faithful, industrial, loyal people—rising people, full of potential force."[91]

Whether his speech had "electrified the country," as Knox's *Freeman* later said, was speculation. "We hope that able members of Congress and their voices have been lifted up in elective appeal to the conscience of the nation," wrote the *Freeman* weeks afterward. "Mr. White has made himself heard, and he has compelled respect."[92] For the moment, White's turn in the national spotlight was ending. Circumstances demanded that he carry out his continuing battle for civil rights and justice in a new arena, as a private citizen. And despite a personal setback in Indianapolis, and his departure from the operations subcommittee, White remained hopeful that the Council would still play a significant role in his future, and he in its, as well.

His base remained firm. White was still president of Washington's local Afro-American Council branch, with more than a hundred members. He was well known and admired by black citizens, both in the District of Columbia and beyond; a tribute dinner to him in early March would draw three thousand well-wishers. As one of five lawyers preparing the brief, he was deeply involved in pursuing the Louisiana test case through the courts. In the opinion of influential editors like Knox and Cooper, he was certainly of the caliber needed to succeed Walters, if and when the bishop decided to retire.[93]

Only time would tell if a successor to Walters might yet be needed, and if so, whether George White could once again emerge as a truly national leader.

Bishop Alexander Walters was president of the National Afro-American Council from 1898 to 1902 and 1905 to 1908. Reprinted from William J. Simmons, *Men of Mark: Eminent, Progressive and Rising.*

Journalist T. Thomas Fortune was president of the National Afro-American Council from 1902 to 1904. Reprinted from William J. Simmons, *Men of Mark: Eminent, Progressive and Rising.*

Journalist William H. Steward was president of the National Afro-American Council from 1904 to 1905. Reprinted from William J. Simmons, *Men of Mark: Eminent, Progressive and Rising.*

Attorney William A. Pledger was first vice president of the National Afro-American Council from 1902 to 1904 and acting president in 1903. Reprinted from Mifflin W. Gibbs, *Shadow and Light: An Autobiography.*

Attorney George H. White, the nation's only black congressman, was a vice president of the National Afro-American Council from 1899 to 1903. Courtesy of Odessa Spaulding.

Educator Booker T. Washington sat on the executive committee of the National Afro-American Council from 1903 to 1904. Reprinted from William J. Simmons, *Men of Mark: Eminent, Progressive and Rising.*

Journalist Edward E. Cooper was a member of the first national executive committee of the National Afro-American Council in 1898. Reprinted from Mifflin W. Gibbs, *Shadow and Light: An Autobiography.*

Bishop Benjamin W. Arnett was a vice president of the National Afro-American Council from 1898 to 1899. Reprinted from William J. Simmons, *Men of Mark: Eminent, Progressive and Rising.*

Attorney Fredrick L. McGhee was financial secretary of the National Afro-American Council and chaired its legislation bureau. Courtesy of Minnesota Historical Society.

Federal official John C. Dancy was first vice president of the National Afro-American Council from 1898 to 1899. Reprinted from Mifflin W. Gibbs, *Shadow and Light: An Autobiography*.

Journalist Ida B. Wells-Barnett was secretary of the National Afro-American Council in 1898 and later chaired its antilynching bureau. Courtesy of Special Collections Research Center, University of Chicago Library.

Activist Mary Church Terrell was a vice president of the National Afro-American Council from 1905 to 1907. Courtesy of Library of Congress.

The National Afro-American Council's three presidents, shown in Saint Paul (1902): Bishop Alexander Walters (*first row, center*), T. Thomas Fortune (*second row, behind Walters*), and William H. Steward (*far left, second row*). Courtesy of Minnesota Historical Society.

5

Nowhere Else to Turn

Philadelphia, 1901

Two days after William McKinley's second inauguration, a determined Council delegation appeared in the president's parlor to pay its respects and seek assistance on matters of continuing concern to the race: treatment of black southerners, including disfranchisement and violence against them, and recognition of black soldiers during the U.S. Army's reorganization. Walters led the group of twelve, including McKinley's longtime advisor Bishop Arnett and two prominent black appointees—U.S. Treasury register Judson Lyons and Henry Cheatham, D.C. recorder of deeds, as well as Lyons's brand-new deputy, Cyrus Adams. Others included A. T. Arnett, Harry Smith, Jesse Lawson, Fred McGhee, Ferdinand Barnett, Peter Smith, and Dr. Crossland.[1]

This was the third visit by Walters to the White House in as many years and mirrored his quiet frustration with the tradition; little had come of his previous visits, even less seemed likely now. But he persevered—what choice did he have?—asking McKinley this time to continue to use his "potent influence to check the outrages perpetrated against black men and the disfranchisement of them in the south on account of their color. . . . And since the colored soldiers have made such a splendid record for bravery, discipline, and loyalty" in all U.S. wars since 1775, it was only fair to "give to Afro-American citizens in the reorganization of the army increase in representation and regular succession in the line of promotions of commissioned officers."[2]

With regard to the final request, the Council promised the president that "everything in our power will be done to make our people good and capable officers." And while no text is available of McKinley's private conversation with the delegation, his response to their address was characterized by Walters as "entirely satisfactory," including a promise that "he would appoint some colored officers in the new army." The delegation was smaller than originally planned, missing almost half the members appointed by the executive committee just one day earlier: Fortune, Pledger, Ernest Lyon, Wells-Barnett, Charles H. Brooks, H. T. Johnson, Alex Manly, and his boss, outgoing congressman White. Whether all those named were even present in the city is not clear; at least five—Fortune, Lyon, Pledger, Wells-Barnett, and Johnson—were from out of state and may already have returned home. Wells-Barnett's husband took her place.[3]

Fortune's absence from the delegation was predictable, in view of his record of criticizing McKinley. The absence of White—and by extension, Manly—was more difficult to explain, given White's well-known desire for a lucrative federal appointment. He would certainly have regretted missing an opportunity to speak to McKinley, whom he had not seen in person for many months; later that spring, he would attempt, without success, to gain a private audience with McKinley on two occasions.[4]

The bishop's assessment of the meeting was positive, but not all of the news on racial matters from the White House that day was reassuring. The *Evening Star* reported "a strong protest with the President" against reappointing an Afro-American postmaster in Athens, filed by Georgia Democratic representative William M. Howard and citing "unanimous" opposition of white Georgians to "Pink" Martin's continued service. The publicity now given Howard's smug demand was a depressing sign of new political realities, certainly a warning signal to White, whose nominations of black postmasters had once received McKinley's warm support.[5]

Howard's protest notwithstanding, there was cause to celebrate. The local chapter of the Council scheduled a mass meeting of local supporters on Wednesday night, March 6, to commemorate the success of their White House foray. The highlight of the meeting came when Cyrus Adams, Council general secretary, "paid $50 and became the first life member," clearly hoping to inspire others. Even if no other Council member ever emulated Adams, the executive committee had other options, including passing the collection plate at its March 5 meeting. This generated another $100, paid in turn to Jesse Lawson to complete the retainer of the bureau's final new attorney, Armand Romain of New Orleans, not universally popular but willing and available.[6]

Other dues payments dribbled in, but the Council's general fund was on the verge of being depleted by various expenses for travel and printing and would hold barely enough to make the next instalment on legal fees ($125) in late July. Preparing for and holding the executive committee meeting cost nearly $100, and on the eve of the Philadelphia conclave, the treasury showed a balance of just over $30.[7]

Financial problems weren't the only question on Council members' minds as the August meeting drew nearer. Once again, the issue of leadership was being raised and debated widely. The *Freeman*, its ear always to the ground, announced in late July that "[s]peculation is rife as to who will be the next president of the National Afro-American Council," with Bishop Walters drawing at least three possible contenders, notably Fortune, living in New York; McGhee, practicing law in Minnesota; and White, now practicing law in Washington, D.C.

In George Knox's opinion, the name, and even the office itself, were less important than other considerations. "It doesn't matter half so much who is president—as long as he is honest and capable—as that the body is sound in principle, harmonious in action, and sincere in its efforts to live up to the standard marked out," the *Freeman* declared. After leading the group for nearly three years, Walters remained the favorite, yet some members, particularly those in the District's branch, clearly preferred its own president, ex-congressman White, according to the *Freeman*. "The selection is a wise one, as Mr. White is one of the most energetic and reliable leaders the race has today. His friends will urge his name as the logical candidate for the presidency of the national council at Philadelphia [and] a formidable delegation will go to Philadelphia from here the first week in August."[8]

Mindful of the previous summer's events, White carefully avoided an open challenge to Walters until it was clear that Walters would step down. But contingency plans were in place, including maximizing voting strength of supporters by having White represent a separate group in Philadelphia. In July, he was named a delegate from the city's Second Baptist Lyceum, a Council affiliate.[9] So far, White had not publicly agreed to run for anything. Since leaving Congress in March, he had been preoccupied with other initiatives, including his attempt to gain appointment as U.S. Treasury auditor. Almost every Republican House member and a handful of U.S. senators had formally endorsed him, but despite steady support from black newspapers, his candidacy had run into a broad political wall, including opposition from the *Washington Post*.

In mid-April, the *Post* had condescendingly suggested that White return to North Carolina, where he was needed. "He can do much there. He can do nothing here or farther north," read the newspaper's lead editorial, titled "Mr. White's Dilemma." That he desired an "auditorship, or something equally desirable" was no secret, nor was his hope for a quick, favorable decision by McKinley. But the *Post* believed that a "self-respecting colored man of brains, ability and virtue has larger opportunities and wider vistas at the South than at the North."[10]

Two days later, the other shoe dropped. White was one of two former congressmen from the South hoping for a plum in the second McKinley administration, the *Post* reported in a front-page political story; the other contender was W. F. Aldrich of Alabama. Both were eyeing an auditorship at the U.S. Treasury, soon to be vacated, and Aldrich had the advantage, the *Post* implied. "[I]t is not at all probable that Mr. White will be given as good a place as an auditorship, which pays $4,000 a year. Mr. White will be satisfied with a place as deputy auditor, which pays $2,500 a year."[11]

White, a proud and very private man, exploded with a wounded reply to the newspaper's articles, which appeared in print five days later. "Why should I be 'satisfied' with a position of less dignity and salary than any other man situated as I am?" he wrote. "Perhaps the *Post* is of the opinion that I am not properly indorsed, or that I have not sufficient backing." (Even the redoubtable Jeter C. Pritchard supported him.) "On the score of merit permit me to say that I have served faithfully the Republican national party in every campaign during the past twenty-seven years, wholly without reward or one dollar's compensation, or even applying for a government position up to this year," White wrote. "Why should I expect of Mr. McKinley a position of less moment than Mr. Aldrich?"[12]

White's action was imprudent at best, although few could blame him for his anger at the *Post*. Much too long and embarrassingly personal, the letter called unwanted publicity to White's quest for the position, which required confirmation by the Senate, where southern Democrats formed a powerful minority. His refusal to consider a deputy auditorship—a consolation prize that might have led to a later elevation—marked him, however unfairly, as stubbornly unreasonable and, in effect, tying the president's hands. The doors to the White House, once opened so often to the stalwart Republican, were now politely, but firmly, closed to him. His attempts to seek a personal audience with McKinley in May and June were rebuffed, and White was left to endure the indignity of occasional public ridicule.

In an early May letter to the *Post*, J. C. Cunningham, for instance, derided White's "'manhood' and common sense" for rejecting the lesser position. "Such positions don't come to a man of Mr. White's color every day; it matters not what he did during the preceding national campaign. Some loyal white Republican will get the place that he (Mr. White) thinks he is heir to [and] the colored population of this country may rejoice over the fact that he will still remain with us and help us battle for our rights as American citizens," wrote Cunningham. White consoled himself with preparations for the Louisiana test case, which the Council's legal team planned to launch in New Orleans in July. He raised a small sum for the legal battle by speaking at the Capital Pleasure Club, where the "distinguished gentleman was never more witty and eloquent. The rafters shook with applause after his speech."[13]

Even as White pondered his own future, Walters mulled over his organization's purse strings, and how to pay mounting legal bills posed by the Louisiana test case. In late June, Walters resorted to flattery in an appeal to Tuskegee for advice and assistance. "You have won first place on your merit, and I think we all ought to be generous enough to give it to you," he wrote Washington on June 27. "I am greatly pleased with your work and have long ago decided to do all in my power to advance your interest. Believe me when I tell you that I do so cheerfully." That being said, Walters needed two things: Washington's feedback on how best to raise the money to pay Birney, and Washington's assurance that he would appear in Philadelphia. Walters thought he had taken appropriate action by instructing treasurer Thompson to pay Birney another $200, but Tim Fortune had halted the payment and told Walters he would "consult you about the matter. What about it? I am of the opinion that we had better pay the $500.00 and push the case."[14]

Saying that the Council hoped to collect $1,000 in Philadelphia, Walters urged Washington to attend and repeated the urgent request a month later, warning him, "I am afraid that the enemy will use it against us" if Washington was absent. In the meantime, Washington remained the single best magnet, if also the most discreet, for donations to the cause from outside the Council, a fact known to attorneys involved in the test case. Albert Pillsbury, distinguished former attorney general of Massachusetts, was an occasional correspondent with Washington and felt obliged to update Washington in late July.[15]

"It is attended by some difficulties," Pillsbury wrote, "and I think that to reach the root of the mischief we must also bring a [second] suit directly calling in question" a related issue: the legality of the "grandfather clause" itself, which allowed most illiterate whites to vote but not illiterate blacks. It was necessary to persuade the court to attack "the whole scheme of suffrage qualifications," since the court might evade the whole question of Ryanes's disfranchisement by simply striking down the clause allowing certain illiterate men to register and vote, by virtue of having an ancestor who had been registered previously. Ryanes, however, would not benefit if only the grandfather clause were overturned. Even that, of course, would be a "sentimental victory, and may be all that is possible to accomplish," wrote Pillsbury, an active member of the Boston Committee to Advance the Cause of the Negro. "Several of our most intelligent colored men here have said to me that they would be satisfied with this, as it would at least establish equality of right."[16]

No record exists of Washington's response to Pillsbury. The Wizard was preoccupied during the summer of 1901 with the Alabama constitutional convention, and his attempts to produce a compromise to the proposed disfranchisement clause sought by that state's white supremacists. He had spent much of

June writing private letters to white leaders in Alabama; "I am dividing my time pretty nearly equally between that convention and [Tuskegee]," he told Hampton Institute president Hollis Burke Frissell.[17]

Meanwhile, a press release prepared for use by the New York *Evening Post*, while never printed, says much about his view on the subject of disfranchisement. In the mock interview—replacing one he was unable to give the newspaper directly in New York in mid-June—he predicted that Alabama's final plan would produce the South's "most satisfactory Constitution" on the question of suffrage, language he believed would "hold out an incentive for both races to make the best and most conservative citizens." As he told the *Post* in the statement, he was not at all certain of the outcome in Alabama. "I may be disappointed," he said, and he was. When near-total disfranchisement was recommended for Alabama's black voters, Washington maintained a positive face in public, if not in private; he and other black petitioners objected unsuccessfully in a closed session with the chairman of the convention's suffrage committee to both the plan for a board of registrars and the "grandfather clause."[18]

Any publicity given his private actions in regard to the Louisiana test case would have undermined his Alabama efforts, and damaged his familiar accommodationist image, as Pillsbury, no stranger to the Byzantine personal politics within the ranks of educated Afro-Americans, well knew. The constitutional expert would never trade names or reveal his contacts, yet the identities of the unnamed local sources in his July 30 letter are not difficult to guess; they probably included attorney Edward Brown—an active Council member—and Brown's associate Archibald Grimké, who enjoyed his own complex relationship with Washington. A Democratic-leaning independent who sought to prod Washington into a more activist stance on key issues, Grimké is believed to have introduced the Wizard to Pillsbury, while Washington was weighing participation in the Louisiana test case.[19]

Other Boston-area figures in the circle around Grimké included the Reverend William H. Scott, a Baptist minister, and attorneys Clifford H. Plummer, William H. Lewis, and Napoleon B. Marshall, among others. Most were active in the National Colored Protective League, which had roundly criticized the McKinley administration in 1899. If few black leaders in Boston were pro-McKinley, most remained flexible toward the Tuskegeean—most, but not all. Pillsbury almost certainly did not refer to William Monroe Trotter, a close associate of Grimké's but anathema to the Wizard's machine. Trotter would soon begin coediting the weekly *Guardian* with librarian George W. Forbes, catering to the city's small black professional elite, and was a constant, vehement critic of Washington.[20] Trotter himself eventually attended Council meetings but had little policy influence.

For the moment, the Louisiana test case had few critics among Afro-Americans, who generally agreed that a court case was the only way to fight disfranchisement. Two weeks before Pillsbury wrote Washington, the case had taken its final, giant leap toward reality, after a gestation of nearly eighteen months, when it was filed in Civil District Court, for the Parish of Orleans, Division of Orleans, as case No. 65,432. The plaintiff was David Jordan Ryanes, a "member of the African race" who had resided in New Orleans since March 1860 and had been voting there "for the last thirty years or thereabouts." Unable to read or write, he owned no taxable property. On July 10, 1901, Ryanes had attempted to register to vote in "the Ninth Precinct of the Eleventh Ward of said Parish of Orleans" but had been refused by Jeremiah M. Gleason, parish supervisor of registration, because Ryanes did not meet the requirements of the recently added Article 197 of Louisiana's constitution, in effect since May 1898. Because he was illiterate, and because neither "his father nor grandfather were entitled to vote under the Constitution and laws of the State where they then resided, on the first day of January, 1867, or any date prior thereto," Ryanes was not allowed to register to vote.[21]

His attorneys now charged that Article 197, along with the Louisiana legislature's implementing act, violated the Fifteenth Amendment of the U.S. Constitution by discriminating against Ryanes "on account of race, color, or previous condition of servitude." Further, because the Louisiana constitution and laws "were intended to affect poor and ignorant negroes only, and actually to disfranchise only poor and ignorant negroes" like Ryanes, the constitution and laws denied them the "equal protection of the laws" in violation of the Fourteenth Amendment of the federal Constitution.[22]

The suit sought a writ of mandamus as "the only proper remedy which will effectually protect the rights, privileges, and interests of" Ryanes. Such a writ should order Gleason to "inscribe the name of the relator [Ryanes] herein upon the books of his office as a duly qualified elector and voter." Ryanes made his mark upon the petition on July 12, before a notary public, and the case was filed, after which Louisiana district judge W. B. Sommerville ordered a show-cause hearing for August 6.[23]

Attorneys for the plaintiff were Pillsbury, White, Birney, McGhee, and Major Armand Romain of New Orleans, a gifted young lawyer who was local counsel, and probably the only one actually in the courtroom. An active Republican, Romain had graduated from Tulane University at age nineteen, then studied law privately before receiving a Tulane law degree in 1892. A veteran of the Spanish-American War's Santiago campaign, after resigning from the Louisiana senate to accept a major's commission, he had also run unsuccessfully for Congress in 1896.[24]

Romain's presence was certainly useful, although Birney and White apparently directed the case from Washington, with guidance from Pillsbury in Boston and McGhee in Saint Paul.

But for all the flurry of recent activity, the project remained badly underfunded. In late July, Washington's Second Baptist Lyceum, a well-known forum for local black leaders, donated a total of $60 to the Council, after voting to send White and Samuel E. Lacy as representatives to Philadelphia. Fund-raising in Philadelphia would provide the next key test of the case's still uncertain future.[25]

The "City of Brotherly Love" was the nation's third-largest city in 1900, with more than 1.3 million residents. Its Afro-American population that year accounted for less than one in twenty of its residents—62,613 men, women, and children—yet it formed the nation's largest urban grouping of blacks north of Baltimore. Only Washington, D.C., Baltimore, and New Orleans had more black citizens, and among large northeastern cities, only New York's black population was growing faster. Philadelphia's black population had long ranked among America's most prosperous and included the nation's first reputed black millionaire, John C. McKee, whose extensive real estate holdings drew much attention in the press after his death in 1902. In addition, the city was served by a well-regarded black hospital—the Frederick Douglass Clinic, established in 1895 by Dr. Nathan F. Mossell—and a widely read black weekly newspaper, the *Philadelphia Tribune*, edited by Chris Perry, also a former member of the Philadelphia city council. An excellent black school, the Institute for Colored Youth (later Cheyney University), served the city's youth.[26]

Editor Perry had been active in the Council since its inception, having served on the first executive committee, then as vice president from 1899 to 1900. Having the Council hold its annual convention in Philadelphia was a coup for Perry and his local colleagues, as well as a spur to membership in the local council, activated in 1899. Charles H. Brooks was the local president, Hightower T. Kealing secretary-treasurer, and Gertrude Mossell corresponding secretary.[27] The tradition of holding sequential conventions of the Council and the Afro-American Press Association, however, proved less successful. What should have been a perfunctory AAPA meeting on August 6, one day before the Council's convention began, quickly boiled over into heated rhetoric. The next day, East Coast headlines blared excerpts from controversial speeches by Tim Fortune and William Pledger.

Pledger, never one to mince words, advised southern blacks to fight lynch law with rifles. He called "the dollar and cold steel the things the white man respects. Many of them are afraid to lynch us where they know the black man is standing behind the door with a Winchester. But they arrest us and then attack us defenseless in jail." The mob mentality in parts of the South was not helped by the fire-eating rhetoric of men like "Pitchfork Ben" Tillman, U.S. senator from South Carolina, whose recent speech in Wisconsin defended disfranchisement of blacks. Pledger claimed to believe in "the transmigration of souls. It will not be long—I believe I will live to see the day—before the soul of Ben Tillman will be wandering the streets in the body of a 'suck-egg' dog, with no one to throw him a crumb."[28]

Next up was Fortune, who managed to outdo even the gifted Pledger with one memorable phrase. His speech had been entitled "The Press as an Educator," but there was no pretense of diplomatic schoolmaster. "We have cringed and crawled long enough," Fortune began. "I don't want any more 'good niggers.' I want 'bad niggers.'" He might even have paused, for effect, before delivering the clincher: "It is the 'bad nigger' with a Winchester that can defend his home and children and wife."[29]

Both sets of remarks were reportedly "received with enthusiasm" by the listeners, which, for once, did not include Bishop Walters. The *Post* gleefully took quotes from both speeches to former congressman Cheatham, high-ranking McKinley appointee and elder statesman. What did the District of Columbia recorder of deeds think of his friends' statements? "I cannot bring myself to believe that such men as Pledger and Fortune, whom I know to be cool and considerate men, could in all seriousness give such dangerous and mischievous advice," Cheatham said on August 7. "I am inclined to believe they have been misquoted. Fortune and Pledger are hardly the men to make seditious harangues"; perhaps the words had simply "slipped out" during a "very hot debate."[30]

"But be that as it may, I want to say most emphatically that I want to have no part in the new doctrine of the 'bad nigger and the Winchester.' That combination has caused too much trouble already." Cheatham added that he "greatly . . . deplored" lynching, along with "all crime . . . no matter by whom committed or where, or what the crime is." All lawlessness was inexcusable, as was "inciting to crime to check one form of lawlessness. Lynching is no reason for the general arming of the negro. . . . it would be the very worst thing for the negro himself."[31]

The North Carolinian's views on the subject were well known; his dignified, restrained speech in 1898, counseling calm after the "black Judas" disruption, had helped salvage that convention. But three years later, he seemed to have given up on the Council's ability to provide reasonable leadership on critical issues. If two of its best-known leaders could make such inflammatory statements—and risk discrediting the Council—within hours of the convention, what hope was there for the body as an official voice of moderation and prudence?

How Walters reacted to such adverse publicity is not known, but the news certainly did nothing to boost the Council's flagging appeal for conservatives or moderates. Nor did the earlier-than-usual scheduling of the NACW meeting, which had already been held in Buffalo in mid-July. Despite the proximity of Philadelphia to Washington, Cheatham, for one, apparently had no plans to attend the convention. Nor did stalwarts Lyons, Green, and Pinchback—or the one visitor Bishop Walters had so recently begged to attend, Booker T. Washington, who sent Emmett Scott instead. Low turnout rates only recalled the noisy events of Chicago 1899, where Walters and friends of Tuskegee had barely beaten back radical attempts to censure Washington, and had failed to stem criticism of McKinley—not at all what Walters wanted in 1901.

Bishop Walters's opening speech at Odd Fellows' Hall was "largely historical," according to the *Philadelphia Record*, and dealt only briefly with southern disfranchisement. His audience of 135 delegates from thirty-one states was attentive and polite but restrained. Disfranchisement was "subterfuge," Walters declared. The real purpose of those favoring disfranchisement of black voters "is to reduce the negro to serfdom. It is not negro domination that they fear, but negro equality," Walters said. "It remains to be seen whether the Republican party will allow them to carry out their unrighteous design."[32]

Other addresses during the first day were given by such figures as H. Sylvester Williams of London, representing the Pan-African Association, who spoke on the union of the world's negro races; Walter H. Black, who loudly and earnestly condemned disfranchisement and called on God to "vindicate our wrongs;" and AME bishop Charles S. Smith of Detroit, who hailed the "bright and glorious future before us . . . out in Michigan. Every man there is recognized alike." Michigan certainly outranked even favored Pennsylvania in one respect, Smith told his listeners. "You have not one representative in Harrisburg. That is a state of affairs that must change, and in Michigan, it has done so." Indeed, a black representative had represented Detroit in every Michigan state legislature since 1893.[33]

According to the *Philadelphia Item*, in its only major action of the first day, the Council voted to appoint a seven-member commission to attend the planned centennial celebration of Haiti's independence in 1904. Four of those named were officers (Walters, Fortune, Thompson, and Cyrus Adams), joining former vice president Dancy and two future officers, Jesse Lawson and George E. Wibecan Jr. Haiti was the Western Hemisphere's only independent black republic and, despite its unstable political history since independence, symbolized the long-term hopes of many Afro-Americans.[34]

The *Item* also reported the first local rumblings about the upcoming election of officers, to be held on the convention's final day. Easy reelection was predicted for vice presidents Fortune and Pledger, whose speeches earlier in the week had so rankled Washington observers, and for secretary Cyrus Adams. But at least one officer faced the prospect of opposition, however unlikely. "It is anticipated that there will be some objections shown to the reelection of Bishop Alexander Walters of Jersey City as President," the newspaper reported. "Another candidate for this office will be placed in the field," although Walters was expected to win "by a very large majority."[35] The other candidate, unnamed as yet, was George White.

As the convention entered its second day, the level of activity reached a higher level, with adoption of resolutions denouncing lynching and asking the McKinley administration to propose legislation protecting U.S. citizens—specifically, black citizens—in the same fashion that foreigners were protected. This was White's single strongest issue, from his days in Congress, and he was among those pushing the resolution most strongly; others included Fortune, Bishop Grant, and Ferdinand Barnett, whose remarks were the only ones reported at any length. Barnett delivered the report of the Council's antilynching bureau on behalf of his absent wife and described lynching as "an expression of the brute force of the nation, combined with pure love of excitement and race prejudice."[36]

The final wording of the Council's resolution added a new wrinkle to previous calls for national legislation on lynching. The Council's memorial committee, preparing a call to President McKinley, was instructed to prepare "for adoption by several States constitutional amendments which shall give the Federal courts power and jurisdiction to secure the right of trial by jury to every" U.S. citizen. This was part of a refined approach, one that now recognized that Afro-Americans who committed crimes deserved to be punished, but only within the confines of the country's legal system. "We do not even demand that the trial be a fair one," as one delegate put it. "All we ask for now is to be judged by a jury. If we gain only the semblance of law and order we shall have won half the battle."[37]

Another part of the Council's battle for civil rights would underscore the basic right of suffrage, through such efforts as the Louisiana test case. Attorney Charles Brooks, representing the legal bureau, reported on the progress of that case and its goal of testing the legality of the increasingly popular "grandfather clause," emphasizing the continuing need for "ample contributions," from the Council and beyond, for legal fees. According to the *Item*, delegates were told that the Council had accumulated a reserve fund of "nearly $2,000 . . . over and above expenses" for the test case. If accurate, this was certainly good news, but no official confirmation is available. This total was not reflected in the treasurer's records, which showed total collections since 1898 of less than $1,900, with almost every penny of that amount spent. Official legal expenses as of the week of the convention, both itemized and general, had amounted to $625; the rest went toward costs of printing, officers' travel expenses, and expenses related to holding the annual meeting.[38]

Revenue at the session was disappointingly small, with just $340 in membership fees received, against eventual expenses of $267.80. (This included $150 paid to Lawson, for legal fees, on August 9, the last such payment recorded.) By the date of the final entry (June 1902), the treasury would contain just $104.76. Walters was not pleased, but at least he could take some comfort in the Council's adoption of the annual resolutions, which occurred without controversy. One called on the McKinley administration to ensure that "discriminations shall not be made on account of race, color, previous condition of servitude or creed" in the "selection of Americans to represent this government in our lately acquired possessions." Another asked Congress to appoint a commission inquiring into the "status of the Afro-American race in this country and endeavor to promote harmony between the races." The Council selected four representatives—Fortune, McGhee, Emmett Scott, and Ferdinand Barnett—as delegates to the National Negro Business League's August meeting at Chicago, offering an olive branch, of sorts, to the new league, which Barnett's wife and others had criticized a year earlier, and a symbolic tip of the hat to Washington himself.[39]

No election of officers had occurred without incident since 1898, although the recommended slates had been approved, eventually, in 1899 and 1900. From the start, Bishop Walters's firm, almost authoritarian style had rankled a small minority of Council members, if never enough to defeat him for reelection. Only if Walters stepped down voluntarily, most members believed, would there be a new hand at the helm.

Astute politician that he was, George White must have known this to be true. His public humiliation at Indianapolis in 1900, amid his bitter charges on the convention floor of "betrayal" by Walters, could hardly be forgotten by anyone who had witnessed it. George Knox, who recalled the showdown in a later editorial, gave a sanitized recount of it, implying that White had merely misunderstood Walters in 1900 and overreacted to the bishop's last-minute change of heart.[40]

There could be no such misunderstanding in 1901. While many delegates were attending a separate religious meeting at Atlantic City the week before the convention, Walters had apparently gone so far as to declare—to White—that he would definitely not run again.[41] White had therefore come to Philadelphia expecting to run for president, even if Walters went back on his word and chose to stand again, which White hoped would not happen. He might be defeated in a floor fight, but he would not be tricked again by the wily bishop. If Walters chose *not* to retire twice in a row, this time there would be consequences.

And so there were. "The clans assembled with a great deal of pomp and show," with "a great deal of logrolling, bad blood and ambitious office seekers present," wrote Calvin Chase in the *Bee*. Walters ran again and this time defeated White in an open vote, with a consolation prize—the third vice presidency—bestowed upon the loser. Depending on which account one read of the results, the consequences were either comical or alarming. According to the *Bee*, the former congressman "arose in the convention and told the politician Bishop and the convention that he could not sacrifice his manhood to longer remain in such an organization." White's speech "came near breaking up the Afro-American Council," and he "took up his hat and was about to leave the convention" after the vote, until "dozens of delegates got down upon their knees and begged him not to go." Moved, White relented and stayed, for two reasons, he said: "he had the interests of the race at heart, and because he wanted to see the recent case that has been brought up from Louisiana pushed." Yet even if White remained active in Council work, "there is still a bad feeling against Bishop Walters at his action toward Mr. White," claimed the *Bee*, predicting that "the Council will never amount to anything with [Walters] at its head."[42]

The third vice presidency—behind firebrands Fortune and Pledger—was a poor substitute for the position White desired, and there was confusion in the public mind over whether he would even accept it. The *Record* reported that White resigned the office, declaring that "he did not want the position because of the methods pursued in the election, and arraigned Bishop Walters for accepting the presidency after his avowed intention not to be a candidate." The *Baltimore Sun* repeated the claim, under the headline "White Quits in A Huff."[43]

The *Freeman* compared the Indianapolis and Philadelphia incidents at some length, saying a week later that White, "in his extreme provocation, has now resigned his position as vice president. It may be that he has washed his hands of the whole business for all time." Yet at least one newspaper, Cooper's *Colored American*, believed otherwise and found a silver lining in the affair: "George White's manly course in remaining in the vice presidency and continuing to cooperate for race development has made him many friends. He went out of the session a stronger man in the organization than at its opening."[44]

Cooper even held out hope for the future. "Some day [White] may yet, if he so desires, achieve his honorable ambition to be president of the Black congress, and should that day come he will find in the membership as loyal supporters of his administration as are they now the supporters of the present one." In Emmett

Scott's opinion, the election was "the only unpleasant feature of the Convention," but White actually deserved what he got. "White was a candidate & was slaughtered, & I think for the best as he only wanted it to use as a weapon to help him politically," Scott wrote Washington the next week. Little of note had been accomplished in Philadelphia, except that at least "it served to emphasize the opposition to the disfranchising schemes."[45]

In October, White would report to the Second Baptist Lyceum on the Council's activities and the convention's outcome, delivering an "eloquent, logical and clean-cut discussion entitled 'The Times in Which We Live.'" According to the *Colored American*, White described "with the keen eye of a statesman the tendencies of the age—the principles that move men in the political, commercial and social world."[46] Even out of office, his enthusiasm for political activity had certainly not waned. By then, the tragic death of his former mentor William McKinley had ended his hopes for a lucrative federal appointment. Would the Council ever need his statesmanlike leadership?

Friday night's closing banquet, which White did not attend, provided opportunities for a wide range of speakers, some of whom had not yet been heard in that year's Council meeting. Tim Fortune, who had said little since his well-publicized press association tirade, offered an intriguing response to the toast, "Hanging Together," which caught the ear of the local *Item*.

"Whenever the law of humiliation touches one person, it touches another," Fortune said. "This is so all over the world, and it is more so in this, the so-called Land of the Free and Home of the Brave. But I tell you, you haven't got the public opinion right here in Philadelphia that you had before the War of the Rebellion, and you haven't got the public spirited men, either." It was a less than subtle slap at the unenthusiastic response to the national Council by many of Philadelphia's independent black citizens, but Fortune declined to pull his punches. Not enough money had been raised for the cause, either—certainly not the $1,000 Walters had hoped for. "We ought to get right here in Philadelphia, the City of Brotherly Love, the necessary amount to test the validity of the laws of the Southern States, which are utterly disfranchising our people."[47]

Equally disheartening to Fortune, however, was the second-class social treatment Afro-Americans regularly suffered in the South. "There is not a woman here to-night who can travel two miles below Washington without having her dignity lowered," he added. "And I tell you a man who will not defend the women of his race is a cur and worse than cur. Every white man desires to protect his women, and we certainly ought to have manhood enough to protect ours."[48] Most of those in the audience were residents of the City of Brotherly Love, including newly elected vice president Gertrude B. Mossell, and few were accustomed to such negative outbursts. As first vice president, Fortune was now Walters's heir apparent—if indeed, the prelate ever retired—and nervous applause, no doubt, greeted Fortune's expressive but unhappy thoughts.

Perhaps some expected Bishop Benjamin T. Tanner, the evening's main speaker, to restore a positive air. But Tanner instead took the American church—particularly in the South—to task for its complicity in allowing segregation, discrimination, and second-class treatment of black citizens, and in not demanding an end to the evil of lynching. "If you would depend on the Christian church, and if you would do what is right—that which is just and should be done—my wife, your wife, my children and your children would not have to ride in the 'Jim Crow car,'" Tanner said, to warm applause. "I lay at the door of the Christian church all these battles to be fought. If it were in any way moved by Christian spirit all our battles and burdens would cease."[49]

"The Church can strain her eyes to see anything but the equality of the negro. . . . the average American pulpit can see nothing wrong with [lynching]. Had the clergy of the South been true Christians there would have been no war of the rebellion," Tanner concluded. Other speakers included William H. Jones, former U.S. minister to Haiti John S. Durham, Mrs. E. W. Moore, Sylvester Williams, Jesse Lawson, Dr. W. H. Brooks, and Chris Perry. Last, but not least, was Walters, whose talk was, appropriately, "The Origin, Growth, and Future of the Afro-American Council."[50]

The bishop's text, not given, was undoubtedly positive, since he rarely missed an opportunity to beat the organization's drums loudly. Yet beyond Walters's personal vision, the future of the Council was cloudy. No real mandate for action seemed to exist, and little had been accomplished here. The Louisiana test case, while discussed at length, was being carried out by a small group of paid lawyers. Walters would continue to hold most of the cards between sessions, assisted by Fortune, Pledger, Clinton, and Cyrus Adams. Still, an interesting mixture of old and new blood now marked the Council. New officers elected included vice presidents George W. Lee of Washington, D.C., and Charles Brooks of Pennsylvania, joining White and Mrs. Mossell, financial secretary Wibecan, corresponding secretary Lawson, and national organizer Ernest Lyon—stepping down from his vice president's slot to replace Ida Wells-Barnett. New bureau directors included Emmett J. Scott, business; Chris Perry, newspapers; Dr. Walter H. Brooks, ecclesiastical reform; and Dr. A. L. Brown of Massachusetts, emigration.

Questions abounded for Walters, and those around him, as the fall approached. Were new faces enough to spark a renewed interest in the Council mission among general membership? Could fund-raising be accelerated? Would

McKinley, comfortably situated in a second term, finally respond to Council pleas for assistance? Would the Louisiana test case succeed? And, most urgently, perhaps, what role would Booker T. Washington now play?

Of all the events between its conventions in Pennsylvania and Minnesota, none would have a greater impact on the nation or the Council than the shooting of William McKinley in Buffalo in early September 1901. McKinley's death a week afterward, when most observers were confidently predicting his complete recovery, provoked an outpouring of national grief not seen since Lincoln's murder nearly four decades earlier.

Like their white counterparts, black newspapers poured out tributes to McKinley for weeks after his death in eloquent, heartfelt editorials and long stories. Many editors felt that the race had lost a true friend and fatherly protector, who had once fought for their emancipation as a young officer in the Civil War and never forgotten their cause. Even churlish ones like Fortune, who had so often jeered at McKinley, were suddenly respectful. For the Council, McKinley's death was a sadly dark reminder of the new politics, and of the lily-white faction in the Republican Party. For all his recent backpedaling on racial issues, McKinley had remained the best political friend of black Americans in the nation's history, appointing more blacks to federal office in his first term than almost all predecessors combined. His successor, Theodore Roosevelt, had far less interest in dealing personally with black leaders; Roosevelt's past comments had even led some to accuse him of holding racist views. Worse, he seemed more at home with lily-whites than with the reformers.

It did not help that Roosevelt's first instinct was to call in Booker T. Washington, whom he later described as "the most useful, as well as one of the most distinguished, members of his race in the world." That Roosevelt had canceled a planned trip to Tuskegee in the days after McKinley's death, and a week later asked Washington to come to the White House instead, was a suspicious sign to many black leaders, who felt trumped. The explosion of negative publicity given his October meal with Roosevelt only raised the level of nervousness elsewhere in Afro-American ranks, especially since it later served to strengthen their relationship.[51]

McKinley had never confined his contacts to a single gatekeeper, preferring to maintain a wider circle of advisors. Since his days as a congressman and Ohio's governor, McKinley had especially valued advice from Arnett and other Ohio black leaders, heeding their requests and suggestions. During his first term, black ministers had been appointed to Haiti and Liberia, and to a number of consuls' posts; black appointees had continued to receive the two highest domestic offices reserved for them, the D.C. recorder of deeds and the register of the U.S. Treasury. Black postmasters had been named, at least until 1899, on a scale almost unimaginable before 1897 in some southern states.[52]

The Council's leadership had been welcomed into the White House on at least three occasions, despite occasional outbursts of militant criticism from some members. Until his reelection, at least, McKinley had often called in Congressman White and his high-ranking black appointees—Cheatham and Lyons—for consultations and had privately reassured them of his support for their hopes and goals. If McKinley had accomplished little else in the way of legislative enactments favorable to Afro-Americans, few black leaders tended to fault him personally (beyond Fortune and a handful of black Democrats), and most never gave up trying to convince him to act. They sensed, however unhappily, that political circumstances tied the president's hands—if sometimes too easily—on issues like lynching and disfranchisement. His desire to make inroads among Democratic southern voters, and the cautious advice of political advisor Mark Hanna, had precluded any truly daring moves, especially in a leader disinclined toward political risks.

Roosevelt was entirely different: outspoken, abrupt, charismatic, tempestuous, and stubborn. Adjusting to his style would require skill and patience on the part of Walters and his own advisors. It was a different political world, suddenly, and the Council would have to adjust rapidly to the new reality if it wished to remain a player on racial issues. That would mean establishing a stronger relationship with Booker Washington—a savior to some, anathema to others—and, perhaps, ceding cherished authority over the Council's agenda to Tuskegee.

For Jesse Lawson, the Council's new corresponding secretary, it offered an opportunity to burnish his own personal image with the Wizard. He wrote President Roosevelt to congratulate him for inviting Washington into the White House ("Your act in honoring him was a masterly stroke of statesmanship—worthy of the best minds this country has produced") and sent a copy to Tuskegee. "Of course, you knew nothing about my sending it and cannot object now that it has been sent," Lawson wrote Washington, diplomatically. Indeed, Washington saw nothing wrong with Lawson's action and promptly included him at the top of a short list of candidates for civil magistrate in the District of Columbia, a list recently requested by Roosevelt. Lawson did not get the job—it went instead to Robert Terrell—but the good impression was long remembered.[53]

For Fortune, the first months of the Roosevelt administration brought less favorable reviews, probably dooming already slim chances for a high-status appointment. The Council vice president was known for a drinking problem, which many friends blamed for his notorious speech attacking McKinley in December

1898. His all but incoherent address to the sophisticated Bethel Literary and Historical Association in December 1901, however, astounded influential members like Francis Grimké, who left in disgust, and Council members Dancy and Pledger, who tried but failed to sober Fortune up before he spoke. Two confidants soon relayed "Fortune's spectacle" to Booker Washington.[54]

Whitefield McKinlay, one of the Wizard's most prolific reporters in the capital, warned of possible consequences. "You must cut diplomatically loose from these fellows [Fortune and Calvin Chase] and that at once. Several very strong men have recently expressed surprise that you should associate with F[ortune]," McKinlay wrote. "You must pardon me for being so frank but . . . this matter unless heeded will sooner or later cause you endless embarrassment." A pained, frustrated Washington replied that he had "warned Mr. F. before he went to Washington about the class of people he would meet and the temptations to which he would be subjected, and he made a promise that he would not be led astray." But Washington could not jettison Fortune or Chase, or, for that matter, any black editor, without making it "impossible to use the press for the purpose of educating our people." Nor could he afford to "shake off at once the old time men and old time influences" who "stood manfully in the earlier and darker days."[55]

The so-called "old crowd" deserved better, along with those through whom Washington still hoped to be able to work, like Fortune, and even those who resisted his approach, as Chase now began systematically to do. Angered that Washington refused to support him for the position Lawson sought and Terrell received—on grounds of Chase's poor reputation, not the technicality of his criminal record—the editor now emerged as a biting critic of Tuskegee, as well as a vocal sniper at the Council.[56]

Fortune desperately wanted to be U.S. minister to Haiti but enjoyed little political clout. The job was also encumbered—by New Jersey's perfectly adequate William F. Powell, another McKinley holdover—whom Roosevelt saw no reason to replace. Worse, Roosevelt disliked Fortune personally, while Fortune's erratic behavior made it all but impossible for him to obtain necessary recommendations for any federal appointment, whether as New Jersey collector of internal revenue or even as postmaster in Red Bank.[57] Fortune's drunken speech at the Bethel Literary meeting endeared him to no one; only the Wizard, who regarded Fortune as a wayward son still worth redeeming, stood by him in his latest hour of need. While he could not yet recommend Fortune for any appointive position, he did foresee a useful role for the journalist. The coming year would amply demonstrate Washington's plans for the future of Tim Fortune—as well as his long-term strategy for the Afro-American Council as it slowly developed into a more useful instrument for the Tuskegee Machine.

6

Fortune at the Helm

Saint Paul, 1902

Ordinarily, Council leaders paid a New Year's courtesy call on the White House, respectfully reminding the president of their loyalty, their influence, and their pressing issues for the year ahead. But with McKinley's death still fresh in their minds, Walters and his court held back in January 1902. Theodore Roosevelt's sympathies for their cause were, at best, of questionable depth, and his solid alliance with Booker T. Washington an increasing obstacle to their own agenda. How to establish a competitive, productive relationship with the new president was the question on everyone's mind, and there was no easy answer.

Roosevelt had been chief executive for scarcely three months when he was faced with a pressing need for two major black appointments—one scheduled, one unexpected. If both of the men Roosevelt eventually selected—John Dancy and John R. A. Crossland—had strong ties to the Council, their membership in the group was a secondary consideration for the new chief executive. What seemed a timely opportunity for Walters and the Council to emerge as major players in the new president's selection process, however, soon proved illusory.

Acting primarily on advice from Tuskegee, and seeking none from Walters, Roosevelt selected Dancy, a veteran of the Harrison and McKinley administrations, and newcomer John R. A. Crossland, to fill two of the top four posts traditionally held by black appointees: recorder of deeds for the District of Columbia and U.S. minister to Liberia. Both men were Republican activists. Both appointments also augured well for the prestige of the Council, at least, since Dancy had served as its original vice president and executive committee member, Crossland as a recent member of the subexecutive committee.[1]

Henry Cheatham had seemed a safe bet for reappointment as recorder of deeds, until mid-December, when a potentially damning scandal involving the former congressman suddenly threatened to overshadow all else. While details were never made public, at least one newspaper reported that the U.S. attorney general was contemplating federal charges in the case. For Cheatham, who had served nearly five years in the post and had just remarried, the unexpected furor was devastating. Gone was his strong backing by U.S. senator Jeter Pritchard of North Carolina, along with a careful recommendation by Booker T. Washington, who had heard rumors against Cheatham but was not convinced they were true ("Cheatham on the whole is as good a man as Dr. Crossland and is much more widely known throughout the country among our people"). After one of Cheatham's former clerks—Henry Y. Arnett, son of the venerable McKinley advisor and onetime Council vice president Bishop Benjamin Arnett—brought new details to Roosevelt's attention, the nomination collapsed.[2]

Other supporters, including Senator Pritchard, seemed surprised at Roosevelt's decision, although Pritchard was soon "very much mortified to learn the facts" behind the charges and "wanted to crawl out but did not see his way clear," according to Whitefield McKinlay. The *Washington Post* soon reported that unspecified legal charges were possible, in the opinion of U.S. attorney general Philander Knox, for Cheatham's actions "disregarding the provisions of a federal law." Cheatham was doomed.[3]

The joint father-son campaign against Cheatham appeared to reflect Henry Arnett's relentless personal ambition, perhaps tinged by animosity and his father's stubbornness. Why the Arnetts had pushed Crossland as a replacement was never clear; the younger Arnett had traded on his father's name for years and may have expected Crossland to retain and promote him. If so, their strategy misfired. Dancy, a familiar, trusted appointee, was a faithful party warhorse and a known quantity; Crossland, passed over, was then tapped for Monrovia—yet even this created hard feelings in some quarters, due to his more or less naked display of ambition and presumptiveness, which particularly offended the influential William Pledger. Much of Pledger's resentment centered on Booker T. Washington, who had inadvertently raised Crossland's stock in President Roosevelt's eyes with a cursory endorsement ("Dr. Crossland, so far as I can get information, is a clean high toned man of ability"), an opinion specifically solicited by the secretary of the interior in November. Emmett Scott assured Pledger of Washington's innocence in the matter, saying Washington had assumed he was vetting candidates only for the D.C. recorder's post.[4]

As the months passed and spring approached, Dancy took up his new position, and Crossland prepared to set sail for Monrovia, while Cheatham retired to North Carolina in disgrace. Only Dancy remained active in the Council; Cheatham, perhaps depressed by his lack of support during the affair and already disillusioned with Fortune's headstrong rhetoric in Philadelphia, now cut all ties to the organization. (Both Arnetts, for reasons of their own, were also inactive after this.)

As the Cheatham scandal lost its newsworthiness, Council leaders turned their attention to preparations for the next annual session at Saint Paul. For George White, that included a round of speeches, in his role as president of the Council's largest local branch. For Walters, the plans included continuing overtures to the Wizard, but this time through his virtual deputy, Emmett Scott, who was now directing the Council's business bureau.

"My Dear Friend," Walters wrote Scott on April 2, using Council letterhead, "Inclosed find the part of my address which outlines the duties of the bureaus. I have appointed you a member of the program committee. Mr. F. L. McGhee is the chairman. He will communicate within a few days if he has not already done so. I hope you are well and succeeding nicely with your work. Yours sincerely, A. Walters." McGhee had, in fact, already written Scott a lengthy letter, offering his thoughts upon the duties of the business bureau, whose function he compared to the National Negro Business League, and expressing his delight at Scott's appointment. In due course he would write another letter to Scott's boss, Booker T. Washington, regarding the convention, set to open July 9 in the Minnesota state capital.[5]

As overall chairman of Saint Paul's local committee, McGhee was already working steadily on all convention arrangements. It was a rare opportunity for the city to draw the national spotlight onto its small but flourishing black population—under 2 percent of its population of nearly two hundred thousand. (Almost as many black citizens lived in the larger "twin city" of Minneapolis, ten miles west and certain to send a large delegation.) Though the smallest city so far to host the Council's convention, the city had "no color line," boasted the local black weekly, the *Appeal*, "and every hotel will receive Afro-Americans." One of the main reasons that the city had been selected, Walters said later, was "to create more enthusiasm in the work of the Council in the West," where its organization was still comparatively weak.[6] Few westerners had journeyed to Philadelphia in 1901, and Walters hoped to remedy that.

McGhee predicted that the Saint Paul session "will be the greatest convention the race has ever held" and would deal with "many very important questions," he told John P. Green by letter toward the end of June. He begged Green to attend, so "that we might have your earnest zeal to the end that right effects be the result."[7] But McGhee's cordial plea apparently fell on deaf ears; Green, well remembering his humiliation in Indianapolis in 1900, had skipped Philadelphia in 1901 and made no effort to appear in Saint Paul. Whatever actions the Council might now take, he would not be involved.

Regardless of turnout, Saint Paul would serve as a proud showcase for the achievements of Minnesota's prosperous black population. The convention was to be held in the senate chamber of the Minnesota State House, where attorney J. Frank Wheaton, now transplanted east to New York, had served as the state's first black legislator in 1899. The city also boasted two of the Council's hardest working members: McGhee, forty-one, and John Quincy Adams, fifty-four, copublisher of the weekly *Appeal*. Both had moved to Saint Paul in the mid-1880s, McGhee as the state's first black lawyer, Adams as a reporter for the *Western Appeal*, which he later purchased. Both had been active in the Council since its inception, and only their politics divided them when it came to promoting either their city or the Council. McGhee was a fervent Democrat, while the older brother of Council secretary Cyrus Adams was an equally avid Republican.[8]

The *Appeal* was a rarity among black American newspapers, a self-contained chain publishing regional editions in five other cities—Minneapolis, Chicago, Washington, D.C., Saint Louis, and Adams's hometown of Louisville, Kentucky. It relentlessly promoted the upcoming Council convention and that of the Afro-American Press Association for weeks in advance, devoting nearly every column to the organizations and their officers and other members. By the time Bishop Walters's call for the meeting was issued, few readers in those five cities, at least, could have claimed ignorance of the events. His letter went out "To the members of the National Afro-American Council, Delegates from National Councils and Affiliated Organizations, such as Churches, Colleges, Benevolent Societies, Newspapers and other Race Organizations," touting the gathering as "the largest and most potent for good of any which the Council has ever held," and adding that "the citizens of St. Paul are preparing to entertain the Council in first-class style and the trip promises to be a delightful one."[9]

Among the subjects to be debated was continued work on the Louisiana test case. "We have just received notice from our Chief Counsel at Washington, D.C., A. A. Birney, Esq., who informs us that although subject to many delays and complications, arising from local and legal causes, the Louisiana test case is now in a fair way to reach final adjudication," Walters wrote. "There is urgent need for more money to carry on this legal contest, which we hope will be cheerfully contributed by our race." Local councils were reminded of the $5 "annual tax" for each accredited delegate. Affiliated organizations ("Religious and secular organizations which have for their aim and work the mental and moral elevation of the race") could send no more than two delegates each, while "editors of Afro-American newspapers," school principals, and college presidents could also attend and vote, by paying the tax.[10]

Walters left the listing of proposed major speakers to the *Appeal*. Among them were the governor of Minnesota, Samuel R. Van Sant, and Saint Paul's veteran mayor, Robert A. Smith; Josephine Silone Yates, of Kansas City, Missouri, president of the National Association of Afro-American Women; Tim Fortune; W. E. B. Du Bois; Isaiah B. Scott; Josephine St. Pierre Ruffin; James H. Guy, county attorney in Topeka, Kansas; and George White, slated as the final speaker on Thursday night.[11]

Not listed on the programme, but universally expected to speak if he attended, was the Wizard of Tuskegee. McGhee wrote Washington on April 5, reiterating his hope that the educator would make the journey to Minnesota. "I appreciate how that you need to be careful lest you become indirectly if not directly involved in some wrangling, but those who would cause such will hardly come to St. Paul," he reassured Washington. "We are free to arrange our programme so that you will not be placed under any embarrassment from that source. . . . You are free to say what will satisfy you best and also make any suggestions that may occur to you."[12]

So far, ex-congressman White remained the feature attraction, though what he might have to say was anyone's guess. He had spent the past six months promoting his new real estate development in New Jersey, as well as addressing various groups in Washington, D.C., and New York, often touching on favorite themes. In early February, he delivered a talk entitled "Our Children" to the People's Lyceum, "dwelling on the necessity of firm character, thrifty habits, and practical education." Sometimes his remarks were more personal than philosophical, as on Lincoln's birthday, when he told listeners in Brooklyn that "I'm too poor to smoke cigars, too poor to drink and too poor to go on excursions. [But] If battling day in and out will make it easier for my son and daughters, I'll keep on battling."[13]

At other times White was more statesmanlike. In mid-March, he gave a "ringing address," as president of the local council, at the Second Baptist Lyceum's celebration of "Afro-American Council Day." In April, he addressed the Personal Liberty League on suffrage, then served as orator of the day at the fortieth anniversary of slavery's abolition in the District of Columbia. At the end of April he delivered to the Bethel Literary and Historical Association one of his regular serious talks, "What of the Future?" calling for "a footing in the soil, investments in the great enterprises of the country, possession of homes, education that can be utilized at once," and sounding far more like Tuskegee than the outspoken critic of social and racial injustice he had once been in Congress.[14]

Indeed, his perspective seems to have begun to shift subtly in matters political since leaving office. A brief essay he wrote for a collection compiled by Daniel Culp, titled "What Should Be the Negro's Attitude in Politics?"—and written as a counterpoint to a similar essay by Tim Fortune—sounded distinctly, and uncharacteristically, bipartisan. The black voter "should identify himself with that political party which proves to be the most friendly towards him. There is very little in a name. Results should be sought, and the Negro should never waver until they are obtained. This will necessitate a division of the Negro vote."[15]

His thoughts were admittedly utopian, White said. And if he remained a true Republican himself—as he most certainly did—he no longer believed that all black voters should join him there. Freed from seeking election after a twenty-year career in public office, the onetime politician now began to sound more like the closet Democrat and consummate pragmatist Alexander Walters, who had twice betrayed his trust. Was White finally moving to the moderate center, or was the aging political warrior simply executing a pragmatic dance step to confuse his enemies?

Before the Council could meet, the nation's black editors gathered for their own annual session on July 7. Always lively, the editors disappointed no one, from Tim Fortune's first morning grumble—at the lack of black members on the commission to the upcoming Saint Louis Exposition—to that afternoon's annual address by AAPA president Cyrus Adams. "We should revere the memory of this noble band of men who sacrificed themselves upon the editorial altar for the race," Adams said of John Russworm and Frederick Douglass, among others—"They were poor in pocket but noble in spirit"—and also had warm praise for President Roosevelt: "It should be gratifying to us to know that we have in the White House a man who is President of all the people, who is broad enough to take counsel with Booker T. Washington, and who is courageous enough to denounce lynch law and mob violence."[16]

Dancy offered a brief historical lecture on the black press, as a longtime religious journalist in North Carolina. Black journalists, he said, were doing much to educate their people, "as well as to obtain for them a hearing before the public," and his remarks were well received. But another curious observation by a prominent local white speaker, Harlan Page Hall, that "the enfranchisement of the negro, at the time it was undertaken, was a national mistake," brought Fortune to his feet for a second time, fairly exploding in denunciation of the sentiment. "If the suffrage had not been conferred when it was declared, it never would have been conferred," Fortune all but hissed. "Does the gentleman see any sign in the South which points to enlarged political rights for the negro, either in the present or future? He has not properly considered the volume of illiteracy among the Southern whites. The negroes of the South are taking better advantage of the schools than their white neighbors."[17]

New Orleans attorney J. Madison Vance countered with the argument that despite recurring outrages against southern blacks, "the better classes of Southern whites are eager to protect" law-abiding, industrious blacks. "The colored race must learn the serious lesson that its only road to independence and prosperity is by work, and not by living on its wits," Vance warned. "The negro must work out his own salvation, and not expect to have it worked out for him by the good people of the North."[18]

The election of officers for the upcoming year underscored traditionally strong ties between the press group and the Council. Cyrus Adams, reelected president, was Council secretary; the press group secretary, Fortune, was ranking Council vice president; and treasurer Steward and vice president Dancy sat on its executive committee. In addition, the new executive chairman of the press group was Emmett Scott, director of the Council business bureau and secretary to Booker T. Washington. In its only other major action, the group did manage to produce a revised resolution, one acceptable to the querulous Fortune, on the proposal to "cordially indorse" the 1904 Saint Louis exposition. After mentioning the lack of a black commission member and the absence of a proper exhibit "of the thought, skill, and industry of the Afro-American people," the resolution noted that "there is still time to remedy this omission" and called on exposition managers to do just that.[19]

Now all that was needed was the arrival of Booker T. Washington, the race's acknowledged leader in the eyes of most, but not all, the members of the Council. Washington "holds first place by reason of his work for his race and the prominence which has lately been given to him by the fact that President Roosevelt took counsel with him in regard to Southern problems," wrote the *Saint Paul Pioneer Press* the day the convention opened. Yet, as William Monroe Trotter's group of anti-Bookerite delegates was only too happy to point out to the newspaper, that viewpoint was not unanimous—and Washington's arrival would trigger more than enthusiastic applause.[20]

The Council convened on Wednesday in the Minnesota senate chamber, with welcoming addresses by Democratic mayor Smith and Republican governor van Sant, midway through his single term as the state's chief executive. Van Sant praised Afro-American progress in education and civic development, before recalling his own notable experience as a Civil War private: "When the order of Lincoln that the negroes should be armed was read, I stepped out and proposed three cheers," the governor said. "There was not a response from my regiment. A short time after a black brigade saved that regiment from annihilation. Then there were cheers for the negroes and they were given with a will." Four decades later, van Sant felt no less fulsome but cautioned, "We rejoice at the progress you have made, but let me tell you there is just one way to secure and maintain the place you want among the citizens of this country, and that is by work. It is the price that all must pay for advancement."[21]

Similar themes would echo throughout the next three days, as the Council continued its pendulum-like swing away from 1899 radicalism toward the conservative social philosophy of Tuskegee. In his annual address, Walters expounded upon his own twin themes, melding social justice and civil equity with moral development. "What can the negro do for his own protection and uplifting, and to cause the white man to recognize his rights?" he asked his audience. "I answer, first, promote education; second, stand firm in demanding the rights guaranteed by the laws of this great republic; third, cultivate thrift and accumulate wealth; fourth, develop character, promote morality, put down loafing and idleness; fifth, be a man, be proud of his country, and take part in all its duties and responsibilities."[22]

He saw no problem with voter registration carrying "an educational restriction," so long as it was "reasonable and reasonably enforced upon all alike, without regard to race or color." But in order for this to be accomplished, black citizens had to exert unified political pressure on Congress. "If the present congress will do nothing for the inforcement of our rights, then we should see to it that men are sent to congress that will force that body to act in behalf of the lives and property and manhood of all classes of citizens. The negro asks nothing that the law does not grant to every American," he said. He endorsed the principle of the Crumpacker bill, aimed at reducing southern representation in Congress, as well as the establishment of a commission to inquire into the conditions of the colored people of the South. He also gave considerable attention to the Louisiana test case, before concluding with a call for a government inspired effort to persuade black Americans of the advantages of remaining in healthier rural areas, rather than crowding into U.S. cities where their death rate was "about double that of the whites." Among those present to mull over Walters's thoughts was Booker T. Washington, earlier escorted to the platform with widespread applause. He would shortly be appointed to the convention's significant committee on resolutions, joining such familiar heavyweights as Dancy, Fortune, Cyrus Adams, and Du Bois.[23] It was the first official role the Wizard had ever played in Council activities; it would not be the last.

Following Walters onto the platform were the tag-team headliners from Philadelphia's 1901 press association, Pledger and Fortune. If neither saw fit to repeat the memorable catchphrase from that meeting—"bad nigger and a Winchester"—both echoed subtle reminders of their brief notoriety. Despite close friendship with Washington, Fortune relished the occasional opportunity to distance himself ideologically from his mentor and now dissented from the Tuskegeean's declaration of sympathy with both white and black men in the South. "The negro's first duty," said Fortune, "is to protect himself and his colored sisters from scoundrels like Benjamin R. Tillman." Pledger, whose 1901 attack on Senator Tillman as a promoter of lynching had prompted Fortune's turn of phrase, was also more circumspect this time, but the underlying implication was clear. "No man black or white who does not look after his family and see that it is cared for . . . can expect to hold the respect of the community in which he lives," Pledger declared. "If the colored man wants the white man to respect colored womanhood, he must be ready to defend, with his life if necessary, the woman under his own roof."[24]

Mrs. Yates, principal speaker at the Wednesday evening session, charmed her listeners with a literary discourse entitled "The Twentieth Century Negro and His Opportunities for Success." A "remarkable chain of events has been preparing the negro for a higher evolution" for nearly three hundred years, she said. "We have now the opportunity in the twentieth century to take the next step and learn the value of well-directed competition. . . . Let our development be full, free and unimpeded. Let us seize each opportunity in time."[25]

Booker T. Washington must have smiled inwardly at these words, for he could not have put it better himself. He had, in fact, seized another's opportunity—previously granted to George White—to become Thursday night's keynote speaker. White had withdrawn from his trip to Minnesota for personal reasons—perhaps even under pressure from McGhee—and Washington wasted no time filling the slot. Warned a week earlier by Peter Smith that "the 'Guardian' folks are going to use every effort to have the Afro-American Council denounce you," the Wizard had decided to attend and had taken McGhee up on his offer to be added to the programme.[26] It was part of Washington's developing plan to transfix—and transform—the Council.

Booker T. Washington's speech to the assembled Council delegates on Thursday night was a tour de force. "The great negro leader was at his best and for more than an hour held the attention of his hearers alternately by his humor and by his hard sense," wrote the *Appeal*, in part through his now familiar "stories of

Southern life and reminiscences of his struggle in building up the Tuskegee Institute for negroes." But Washington gave subtle hints of the future paths he hoped the Council would take. He would never underestimate the problems confronting his race, yet it was easy to be an armchair critic. "Such organizations as this should bear in mind that we cannot by ourselves help forward the race in any large degree by fault-finding, condemning or criticizing," he warned. "We must bear in mind that destruction is easy, construction is difficult; but it is by construction that the ability of a race is measured, rather than by destruction or fault-finding."[27]

Such a positive outlook mandated working closely with "strong, helpful white friends" in the South, Washington declared. He recalled how white men in Tuskegee once "took hundreds of dollars out of their own pockets and loaned it to me without a guaranty that it would be returned, in order that that institution might be built up for the benefit of our race. Such white men are not enemies to the negro." In a strategically veiled jab at militant opponents, Washington said he would be "a coward and a traitor" if he showed "that kind of ingratitude."[28]

The proof of his vision was in the achievements of a small but increasing number of prosperous southern blacks. "The object lesson of one negro succeeding in every community as a wealthy, prosperous farmer, or as a contractor, or as a banker, or as a cotton-mill owner, is worth scores of more abstract speeches," he said. "With all her disadvantages, there is an opportunity for industrial and business development by the negro in the South that is scarcely presented in any other part of this country. The great lesson which we as a race want to learn at present is that the negro must now learn to work. There is a vast difference from being worked and working. Being worked means degeneration, working means civilization," he said. "I want to see a large proportion of our educated young men and women planting themselves in the fundamental and wealth-producing industries."

George Kennan, "the great Russian traveler, who has traveled extensively through the South," had compared progress made by American freedmen to that of Russian serfs, freed at about the same time. Serfs had been given land, while Afro-Americans had been compelled to buy theirs, yet "the progress of the negro in the South is to-day equal to or greater than that made by the Russian serfs," Kennan concluded. This was borne out by statistics compiled by Du Bois in Georgia, where "the negro owns 1,400,000 acres of land and pays taxes upon property valued at over $15,000,000."[29]

Were relations between the races "more strained now than ever," as some critics repeatedly charged? Washington saw no evidence of such deep-seated racial tension, only of inevitable social friction as black citizens assumed their place in a still-transforming society. Farsighted black leaders owed it to their race to ensure that each man "must work for the common good." Council efforts to encourage this were praiseworthy, said Washington. "I am glad to see in this council so many evidences of the fact that we can sink the individual preferences and unite our efforts in the one direction of uplifting the race."

The vast majority of America's black citizens still resided in the South and would probably remain there for all time. If black observers elsewhere could not always understand the motivations of their southern brothers, that did not make regional barriers inevitable. "We who live in the South must not become estranged from those of our race who live in the North," he said. "You must not take it as a sign of cowardice if some of us who live in the South are gleams of hope and encouragement for the race in that part of the country which you up in this section cannot always see. We must not become discouraged or disheartened as a race. I see nothing from which to grow hopeless," he concluded. "The influence of property, education and high character are universal, are everlasting, and these influences cannot be nullified in any part of our country."[30]

Adams's *Appeal* gave little indication of reactions by individual Council delegates, but at least one listener, Emmett Scott, believed Washington had scored a complete triumph. "It was wonderful to see how completely your personality dominated everything at St. Paul," Scott wrote his employer the next week. "From the moment that you reached there you were the one center of interest, much to the chagrin and regret of our friends, the Barnetts—especially." Scott's assessment of the Barnetts' feelings was undoubtedly accurate, although Ida Wells-Barnett mentions the 1902 convention only briefly in her memoirs, calling it simply "a fiasco." If she was unhappy at losing the post of convention secretary, which she seems to have held since the Council's formation in 1898, she remained antilynching bureau director, although she grew gradually less active in the Council, not recorded as attending another annual meeting. She remained nominal head of the antilynching bureau until 1904; upset by the snap election, she reportedly attempted to step down at Saint Paul, but the delegates refused to accept either her resignation or that of Nelson Crews, emigration bureau director.[31]

But even years later, her bitterness toward "Mr. Washington's theories of industrial education" and his manipulative strategies remained almost tangible, nearly as strong as her growing ideological identification with Du Bois or her growing disappointment in her onetime friend Fortune. She never indicated her feelings about the slate of officers elected at the "fiasco," but like Trotter and other critics, she could hardly have favored a slate controlled by Washington—the man Trotter soon called, "in reality," the new president of the Council.[32]

In reality, perhaps, but not in name. After four years as Council head, Walters was finally stepping down as president, although he would remain head of the executive committee. Fortune was the new president—a questionable choice, in many eyes—and his selection would provoke some of the strongest criticism of the Council yet, both for his own erratic behavior, and for the persistent belief that he was simply a puppet of Tuskegee. Chicago's J. F. Taylor, writing in the *Broadax*, ridiculed "old bat-eyed Tom Fortune" as an "old drunken immoral reprobate," resurrecting a year-old story about Fortune's alleged inebriation during an appearance at a meeting in Chicago. "This is the creature whom Prof. Washington chooses for President of the Afro-American Council." By mid-1903, even Wells-Barnett's *Conservator* would begin sharply criticizing her onetime friend.[33]

Trotter may not have known all the details but reacted with incredulity to Fortune's victory, calling it "about as bad a calamity as could have befallen the organization." Fortune was "a politician, pure and simple, a perennial office seeker," and "only a 'me too' to whatever Washington aspires to do," said the *Guardian* just after the convention ended. They had "long since turned themselves into one twain in their dealings with the Negro race, Fortune providing whatever brain the combination needs, and Washington the boodle," Trotter sputtered.[34]

For all his bluster, Trotter was spewing most of his venom straight at Washington, not Fortune ("ordinarily, this would not be such a bad choice"). Yet Fortune had certainly invited the limelight by agreeing to take over the Council, which he had helped create but never wanted to run. For all his brilliance as a writer, Fortune had never displayed any real aptitude for leadership or for inspiring others to carry out directives, even when sober. Why he agreed to take the post at this point is not clear—perhaps to burnish his own image for a much-desired federal appointment, although it was inevitably perceived as doing the Wizard's bidding. Two years later, Du Bois recounted the election to Oswald G. Villard, claiming that the logical successor to Walters in 1902 had been Isaiah B. Scott, "a man of sterling honesty." (Whether Scott, a loyal Washington supporter, even knew he was being considered for the position is not known.) Fortune had been Washington's handpicked candidate, Du Bois learned in Saint Paul, and he had pleaded with Washington not to force Fortune upon the Council, "because I knew the selection would kill the Council among decent Negroes."[35] Washington's response was "non-committal," Du Bois wrote, but the wily strategist had other plans.

The publication of insurgent plans to bolt the council if Walters was reelected seems to have spurred the calling of a snap election. Walters was allegedly allowing the Council to be "used for political purposes in the interests of a faction friendly to the officers," wrote the *Saint Paul Pioneer Press* in a lengthy article in its July 11 edition; Walters's faction "has made political capital at Washington," by claiming to "represent the united sentiment of the colored people of the country" and attempting to oppose Roosevelt's unacceptable appointments in the South. By quickly forcing a vote on the nominating committee's report (proposing Fortune as the new president and Walters as executive chair) ahead of schedule during Thursday's noon hour, "when a majority of the members were at dinner," the leadership prevented any possibility of an unfriendly floor fight; in any event, fewer than twenty delegates actually voted. Du Bois blamed the plot on a joint effort engineered by Washington through Pledger, who presided over the election, and Emmett Scott. Du Bois, in despair, never attended another annual meeting.[36]

On Friday, a few angry delegates challenged the validity of the election but without success, winning only a technical victory: Walters's election was set aside, temporarily, until the executive committee itself could meet. (It elected Walters on its own.) The storm had largely blown over, and "Harmony Seemingly Reigns," observed the *Pioneer Press* on Saturday. But not everyone was mollified; Wells-Barnett and Du Bois left the Council in a huff, followed more slowly by McGhee and, almost inexplicably, by Edward Cooper, among the Council's most fervent supporters, and a longtime Tuskegee ally. The convention had been a "roaring farce," Cooper wrote in the *Colored American* after Fortune's election.[37]

Fortune's public distaste for Cooper was no secret, and Cooper's reaction to the Council election may well have been tinged by reflected animosity. But he was certainly not alone in questioning Washington's enigmatic motivations. Why had he engineered Fortune's election? The Wizard was far too shrewd a judge of character to believe Fortune could become either an enthusiastic or effective leader, puppet or otherwise. He could hardly have expected to control the Council through Fortune, given the journalist's headstrong nature, erratic personal behavior, and continued financial difficulties, which worried him greatly. Indeed, no one had yet mastered the unpredictable Fortune, although Washington had come closest, emerging as the only true father figure in the orphaned journalist's life. Those who manipulated Fortune most effectively in the past—like Calvin Chase—had simply undermined his credibility by capitalizing on his alcoholism, something to which the prim, prohibitionist Wizard would never stoop.

His plan was more likely a devious master stroke: to co-opt the Council by neutralizing Walters, installing an easily controlled replacement, and preventing the Council from either criticizing Roosevelt or emerging as an independent counterweight to his own National Negro Business League, while secretly funding the Council's only constructive project: the Louisiana test case. Hardly foolproof, the plan would require constant attention, both from Washington and trusted lieutenants among the newly amenable lineup of officers and executive committee. New officers included vice presidents Dancy, Isaiah Scott, H. T. Johnson,

Edmund H. Deas of South Carolina, Charles W. Scrutchin of Minnesota, Mrs. Jeffrey, and White, who remained inactive. Cyrus Adams and John Thompson were reelected secretary and treasurer, respectively, while Bishop Clinton succeeded Lyon as national organizer. McGhee became financial secretary, while Fannie B. Williams of Illinois—wife of Samuel Laing Williams, a Washington supporter—was the new corresponding secretary. Peter J. Smith of Massachusetts chaired the newspaper bureau, Emmett Scott ran the business bureau, and William T. Vernon of Kansas, the education bureau.

Most of the members of the executive committee were congenial moderates; only the Barnetts of Illinois were likely obstructionists. Technically, Washington was only an executive committee member from Alabama, but even Scott believed he now controlled the Council. "Fortune is President. Pledger, whom we can hope to hold, is 1st Vice President," Scott crowed. "Bishop Walters is Chairman of the Executive. Adams is Secretary. . . . Most of our friends compose the Executive Committee. Steward, of course, will be a dominating factor at Louisville and is one of the Vice Presidents and a potential character."[38]

Steward, among others, would soon have the opportunity to help Washington maintain control of a more compliant Council. For now, as chairman of its resolutions committee, Steward was responsible for overseeing the issuance of as mild a statement as possible in the Council's annual address to the nation. The *Guardian* sneered that "there was not a word stronger than a feeble regret in the instrument," which carried the strong imprint of Washington's philosophy, if not his signature.[39]

The address paid strong homage to the importance of education, religious development, and business enterprises among Afro-Americans—three of Washington's favorite themes—before lodging a mild protest against disfranchisement, calling it "poor encouragement for the sacrifices we have made;" a somewhat stronger protest against separate-car laws; and a carefully worded call for enactment of laws against lynching. "Despite the progress made along all lines, and the removal of objections to the exercise of the franchise on account of the acquisition of education and wealth, the disposition to disfranchise the race by legislative or constitutional enactments seems to be on the increase in some sections of our country," the address declared. "This is indeed poor encouragement for the sacrifices we have made in the equipping of ourselves for citizenship. We do not object to any reasonable qualification for the exercise of the suffrage, but we do insist that the requirements be such as will apply to all citizens alike."[40]

"Prejudice appears to be on the increase, and legislation of every conceivable character to crush out and humiliate manhood and womanhood of the race is being enacted," including the separate-car laws, "unchallenged except by the manly efforts made by members of our own race acting upon the part of the National Afro-American Council against them. Such legislation is unjust, unwise and unnecessary" and paid only lip service to requirements for "equal and exact accommodations." The laws' basis lay in "a bitter and stern prejudice which bodes not good to a common people in a common country."

The address reserved its sharpest language for lynching, which it described as "a species of lawlessness and violence that is still too prevalent in our country, and must be suppressed." The Council's own studies had found that "most" lynching victims "are only charged with misdemeanors and minor felonies, and in many cases are entirely innocent," but were regularly being "hung, shot, and burned" by "enraged men" without a jury trial. The Council praised President Roosevelt and governors Longino of Mississippi and Yates of Illinois for their "strong and vigorous denunciations of mob violence," hoping that such leadership would "create sentiment in the right direction" and impel "the enactment of such laws as will punish those that engage in the business of taking human life without the sanction of law."[41]

That Congress had so far failed either to investigate suffrage abuses in the South or enact "the Irwin inquiry bill . . . looking to a thorough investigation of the conditions of the Afro-Americans" since the Civil War was regrettable, as was the "deplorable disposition manifest in the federal congress during the past four years to ignore all matters of legislation in which the rights of Afro-Americans are concerned."[42] It was a toned-down version of previous addresses, covering all the same bases, perhaps, but in far less combative language than before. The Wizard was now at the helm.

The Saint Paul gathering ended on Friday, July 11, with a gigantic banquet and reception staged in the armory on the Minnesota State University campus, open to those attending any of the three major meetings of the week. Among those attending, more than one hundred persons were named in the *Appeal*'s account of the event, which ranked among the most lavish ever arranged by the Council, at a cost of $364.50. Overall, the Council's meeting had been the most expensive in its history, with expenses of nearly $900. Travel expenses and accommodations amounted to more than $318, while printing and miscellaneous expenses had cost another $116. Yet the Council had taken in considerably more than usual—more than $1,000 in dues and individual tickets—and managed to end its fourth year with a small balance on hand of $159.40.[43]

No specific accounting was given of the separate fund-raising for the Louisiana test case, although Jesse Lawson of the Council's legal bureau did discuss the bureau's progress on that project and other initiatives, including a proposed amendment to the federal law on interstate commerce "prohibiting common carriers from discriminating against passengers on account of race or color." Perhaps in deference to Washington, the test case and its progress—or lack thereof—seems to have been downplayed in Saint Paul, or at least in coverage provided by black newspapers. Legal bureau director Vance addressed the Council on its final day, reviewing the history of Afro-Americans' legal status and the effects of various U.S. Supreme Court decisions interpreting the Reconstruction amendments. The *Appeal*'s account gave no Louisiana specifics; the *Pioneer Press* called Vance's speech "noteworthy" but cited only "the cases brought to test the validity of the constitutional amendments to those Southern states which have practically disfranchised the negro."[44]

Washington's role in helping finance the Louisiana test case remained a closely guarded secret. The Wizard had recently undertaken an even more secret role as backer of an effort to test disfranchisement efforts in Alabama and may have engineered a lower-key discussion of the Louisiana case, for fear his own involvement in either case might leak out. But there were other factors at play, notably the increasing dissatisfaction of Walters and Fortune with at least two of the other major Louisiana players, White and Lawson. Three months later, Walters offered Washington a frank, presumably confidential assessment of the situation:

"Mr. Fortune and I find it utterly impossible to work harmoniously with Hon. George H. White and Mr. Lawson, chief factors in our Legal Bureau located in Washington," Walters wrote, without specifying the reasons for their disagreement. Would Washington please chair an emergency steering committee to address the situation? Members might include such men as Cyrus Adams, Dancy, Robert Terrell, Pledger, Bishop Abram Grant, and Judson Lyons, Walters, and Fortune—or other "persons who have more influence with the Administration than those named."[45]

George White's fall from grace was part of a complicated realignment of strategies, both within and without the Council, since McKinley's death. White's political influence had all but disappeared after Roosevelt's ascension, due in part to Roosevelt's alliance with Senator Jeter Pritchard, whom White had attacked in Indianapolis in 1900. Despite reelection to a vice presidency at Saint Paul, White was increasingly less active in Council affairs, and his devotion to the Louisiana test case was his last strong connection to the national group. The former congressman's personal relationship with Walters had deteriorated since Indianapolis and had worsened since his defeat by Walters in Philadelphia.

If White had no real reason to trust Walters, he was almost certainly unaware of Walters's campaign to have him removed from the Louisiana test case team, or of Washington's own involvement in this scheme. For better or for worse, White still trusted Washington, whom he had asked in late 1901 to intercede on his behalf with the president. Washington had blamed Roosevelt's unwillingness to appoint White on Pritchard's opposition; in his 1902 response, White characterized Pritchard as "an evil one . . . who takes delight in misrepresenting and speaking disparagingly of me."[46]

In the Byzantine world of racial politics, Washington may simply have preferred to keep White dependent on his future benevolence. White, ever dutiful to colleagues, penned a recommendation at year's end for Richard Thompson, seeking a Tuskegee position, whose past indiscretions—whether real or rumored—forced him to submit good-character references as penance. Thompson sought to leave government service and the *Colored American* staff to become Emmett Scott's assistant. Yet neither Thompson nor White would benefit from the latter's gracious gesture. Thompson would remain in Washington, where he would soon found the National Negro News Bureau. White, whose recent letter castigating Pritchard in Chase's *Bee* had stirred up vivid memories of the 1900 face-off in Indianapolis, gained no points in Roosevelt's estimation. Meanwhile, his financial situation grew daily more difficult, as he struggled with his less-than-lucrative law practice, his expensive real estate development, and his wife's mounting medical bills.[47]

How much income White actually derived from his work with the Louisiana test case cannot be documented; almost all of the payments mentioned in Council records or other correspondence were intended for outside counsel. Walters's comment about White and Lawson must have puzzled Booker Washington, who, according to his biographer, was growing gradually more disenchanted with the entire legal team and reports of its internal strife. But if he had also grown weary of subsidizing the test case, no record exists of it or a response to Walters.[48]

What was clear was that Walters wished to reassert his diminished influence over the Council—with Fortune soon to be sidelined—while burnishing his own image with Tuskegee. Not coincidentally, Walters's October letter dealt with another substantive issue: his recent meeting with President Roosevelt on the nettlesome "lily-white" Republican faction, and its effect on black appointments. Walters and Council representatives Clinton and Corrothers had met with Roosevelt and top advisors General James S. Clarkson, who handled black appointments for Roosevelt, and Postmaster General Henry C. Payne, Roosevelt's longtime friend. Walters, Clinton, and Corrothers aimed to protest appointing a "lily-white" Republican as U.S. attorney in Alabama.[49]

The *New York Times* publicized the meeting in some detail, noting that "if the President gave them an unfavorable reply," Walters and his colleagues had been prepared to issue "a long advisory document to negro voters throughout the country suggesting that negroes vote independently in the coming Congressional elections." They need not have worried. "To-night President Roosevelt gave a black eye to the movement to establish a 'white' Republican Party in Alabama" by choosing an acceptable Democrat instead, the newspaper wrote, further telling the delegation that "he did not believe a man's color should operate against him anywhere, and that in all appointments," an applicant's reputation in his community "would be the first consideration." Walters then "informed [the country] of the attitude of the President." Two weeks later, Walters assured Washington that he had first cleared the visit with "our mutual friend, Mr. [Richard] Thompson," who had told him that such a visit would not "interfere with any of your plans."[50]

The Wizard's larger plans, never known in great detail to Walters, included a new position for Tim Fortune. It had not been easy persuading President Roosevelt, who had been unwilling to dispatch Fortune to a Caribbean diplomatic post, despite Washington's gentle pressure, without support from New Jersey's senators. But Roosevelt had responded enthusiastically to an innovative proposal in October by Fortune, who wished to study labor conditions in Hawaii and the Philippines, where he believed Afro-Americans should move.

The proposal, transmitted by Clarkson to Roosevelt in late October, was approved quickly; Roosevelt had described this "special agency" as "a mission that might result to the great good of the country," Clarkson wrote Washington in mid-November. There was one caveat: Fortune "must keep himself strictly in the middle of the road," a delicate reference to his penchants both for drink and flights of verbal hyperbole. This was "his opportunity" to prove himself worthy; his reward might be "a place for himself as the head of some bureau." But Clarkson depended on Washington to "talk to him more plainly than I have any license of friendship to do. . . . He must realize that in standing sponsors for him, we have taken such a responsibility as he will take a gentleman's delight in honoring."[51]

Fortune had already taken Clarkson's advice to heart. In early November, he had told Washington of his decision to stop drinking permanently, in consultation with a local physician. "You need have no further fears on that score. I have none, I am very glad to say." Fortune then wrote Washington again from San Francisco on December 10, as he set sail for Honolulu, promising that he was "living absolutely up to your parting advice at the Grand Union."[52]

He would be off the continent for nearly six months, during which time the Council would be entrusted to the care of his friend and first vice president, William Pledger. But the Council and its effectiveness, or its lack thereof, weighed heavily on his mind. In a letter written during the first week of December 1902, he advised Council members that one of his major drives would involve reorganizing the Council to strengthen grass roots appeal among ordinary black citizens. "The main difficulty with and drawback to the . . . Council today is that it has no substantial basic organization. The masses of the people do not belong to it or support it with their sympathy and money," Fortune wrote. Delegates to the conventions paid their $5 and effectively disappeared between summers, making the Council's official board "the only membership . . . from the adjournment of one annual convention to the assembling of another."[53]

Fortune wanted to change that radically, increasing the base membership to "at least five hundred circles [local councils] reported and represented" at the July convention in Louisville. At a minimum of ten members per local council, that meant attracting 5,000 dues-paying members. Assuming at least one delegate from each council, his proposal also envisioned annual revenue of at least $2,500, more than four times the amount received in Saint Paul. Fortune's plan encouraged the formation of separate local councils for women, although he offered no rationale for this part of the plan. "I am reasonably certain that the women of the race will take hold of the work," he said mildly.[54] If the national records showed fewer than fifty women members—all either as executive committee members, a handful of officers, and bureau directors—Fortune must have hoped to interest large numbers of female members who had not previously found the male-dominated Council an appealing outlet for their energy and money.

The number of local councils in existence in 1902 is not known with any certainty, nor are their membership numbers. Local councils can be identified in larger cities, where the annual conventions were held—Baltimore, Chicago, Detroit, Indianapolis, Louisville, New York City, Philadelphia, Rochester, Saint Louis, Saint Paul, and Washington, D.C.—and official references exist to those in other cities that made dues payments to send official delegates, including Atlantic City and Trenton, New Jersey; Cambridge and Springfield, Massachusetts; Clarksdale and Mound Bayou, Mississippi; Des Moines, Iowa; Evanston, Illinois; Kansas City, Kansas; Milwaukee; Nashville; Portland, Oregon; and San Francisco among others. State councils, technically supposed to exist only when ten or more local councils already existed, are nowhere listed, although credible references exist to state councils in Indiana, Iowa, and New York.[55]

Fortune's vision was thus exceedingly optimistic and dependent on the success of others, notably Pledger, who would preside at the next semiannual meeting of the executive committee in late January. If all went according to plan,

Fortune would return to the mainland in late spring and assume the nominal reins of power once again, just in time for Louisville. But all would not go as hoped. Instead, with Fortune absent, the fretful opposition to Booker T. Washington—now the real power behind the Council throne—and to Fortune himself would regroup, growing far bolder and more determined than ever.

7

Dueling Portraits

Louisville, 1903

The struggle for control of the Council had seemingly resolved itself in Saint Paul, but only for a moment. As the winter of 1903 unfolded, the old struggle entered a new, more intricate phase, with old players jockeying for position and new players waiting for strategic opportunities. Tim Fortune's absence from the scene was both a blessing and a curse for Council leaders and aspirants alike. Walters, concerned at the lethargic pace of preparations for Louisville, had begun testing the waters for a possible campaign to regain the presidency, though with little encouragement, while names of other potential candidates were also being floated, among them acting president Pledger, who admitted interest but refused to challenge his good friend Fortune.[1]

Fortune was still halfway around the world, completing his temporary official assignment in the Pacific, and more concerned with Hawaiian and Filipino labor trends than with domestic political intrigues. But an ominous strategy loomed on the home front, as William Monroe Trotter and a small band of restless northeastern radicals dreamed of wresting control of the Council from its Tuskegee-centered orbit. Trotter, Ferris, and Forbes—"the Boston crowd," as Washington called them—were among "various groups of our people [who] are agitating the calling of all kinds of conventions," the Wizard wrote his protégé in mid-February. "As far as possible I am trying to stem the tide . . . and directing the attention of the race to the importance of standing by the Afro-American Council with a view of letting it be the medium through which our battles are to be fought."[2]

Washington's private thoughts coincided with the public sentiments of Cyrus Adams in the March issue of *Colored American Magazine*. Adams said the Council's aim and hope was to "incorporate all existing social, religious, political and benevolent organizations into the body of its membership," but without interfering with their independent existence, and thus into the great struggle of "the uplifting of the Afro-American people."

The Council's mission was idealistic: to "ameliorate so far as it can intelligently, wisely, and practically do so, the deplorable industrial and political position of a large portion of the Afro-American people," most of them in the South, "in the shadow of a condition which they did not create and from which they would gladly emerge if encouraged by the Afro-Americans of the North." But its strategy was pragmatic—essentially a modern public relations campaign, and hardly radical: "There is a battle to be fought, not with swords and guns on bloody fields, but in the arena of public opinion. The combat must be fiercely contested with skill, courage and intelligence, and must be persistently waged until a healthy public sentiment is created."[3]

The text of the executive committee's January address reiterated the Council's Minnesota assessment of the situation now facing Afro-Americans during "one of the most critical periods of our existence in this country." The address was issued at a Washington mass meeting, where activist lawyer James H. Hayes of Richmond delivered a fiery address on disfranchisement, discrimination, and the need for Afro-American resistance, telling an overflow crowd at Lincoln Memorial Church that the black citizen "must fight—not theoretically, not intellectually, but with his hands. . . . If this oppression in the South continues, the negro must resort to the sword and torch. . . . the Southland will become a land of blood and desolation." Declaring himself "a man without a country" in his own Virginia, Hayes called on his listeners to "start something, and keep it up until the white people stop something. We don't intend to be oppressed any longer."[4]

If Hayes's angry metaphors alarmed Walters or presiding officer Cyrus Adams, neither showed it in their public words. Walters urged Afro-Americans to "be more radical in fighting for their rights" and "ridiculed the idea of industrialism solving the problem," a thinly veiled jab at Booker T. Washington's educational philosophy. Other speakers concentrated on the work of the Council. Adams, for instance, chose to praise the Council's "edifying" work on behalf of the race; Lawson and Dancy explicitly endorsed Washington's stand as the best solution.[5]

Echoing Lincoln's famous "half slave and half free" phrasing, the Council's address was less apocalyptic than Hayes's. It warned, nonetheless, that disfranchisement and state-sanctioned segregation threatened the foundations and future of democracy: "It follows as a necessary corollary that the manhood of no state can with safety be divided, in nearly equal parts, into voters and non-voters." The South clearly intended to reduce Afro-Americans to "a position of absolute subserviency in all the relations of life. Even college graduates and men of business and wealth have been denied the right of franchise." But the right of suffrage, conferred on citizens by the federal government, "is the basis of the individual sovereignty of the American citizen, which in turn is the basis of the sovereignty of the whole body politic." To help combat disfranchisement, the Council pledged its "moral and financial" support to "the Afro-Americans of Virginia, Alabama, Louisiana . . . seeking redress through the courts of the land."[6]

The Council also denounced lynching, the resurgence of virtual peonage on southern farms, and "unfair practices in the transportation of passengers in Southern states, discriminating unjustly against Afro-Americans; requiring of them the highest rates for travel and providing in return the poorest accommodations in carriage." It appealed for federal assistance and asked Congress to appoint a commission of inquiry into the condition of Afro-Americans. Perhaps the most surprising clause of the address singled out Theodore Roosevelt for specific praise. "We heartily endorse the deliverances of President Roosevelt with references to the fitness for appointment to office, and the attitude of the Federal Government toward all of its citizens, regardless of race or color," the address stated. "He has imparted new life and vigor to the time-honored principles and traditions of human rights, and has given hope and inspiration to a people struggling heroically beneath the burden of hate and proscription."[7]

In fact, Roosevelt's performance had disappointed almost every black leader outside Tuskegee's reach. His demonstrated reluctance to appoint more than a few blacks to high federal office—indeed, to any federal job—brought headlines in April, confirming what most black leaders knew. Compared to his predecessors, the "Rough Rider" had much more in common with Harrison and Cleveland than with McKinley, reported the *New York Times*. During his first eighteen months in office, Roosevelt had made just fifteen black appointments, compared to McKinley's record-setting pace "extending to almost every department of the Government," including the so-called "top four." McKinley's early ardor for black appointments—179 during his first six months—had cooled considerably by the second half of his first term, coinciding with the rising influence of "lily-white" Republicans and reflecting misplaced hopes of carrying southern states in his 1900 reelection bid. Roosevelt had displayed no comparable early enthusiasm.[8]

By April 1903, Roosevelt had replaced just two McKinley holdovers—Cheatham and Smith (twice)—with black appointees, in addition to Fortune's commission. Roosevelt's decision in January 1903 to name Dr. William D. Crum as U.S. collector of customs at Charleston marked his first major black domestic appointment outside Washington, and it had provoked a bitter struggle with the U.S. Senate.[9] Later in 1903, Roosevelt did name Boston's William H. Lewis as assistant U.S. district attorney. Harvard-educated, and a former state legislator, the comparatively radical Lewis had once alienated Washington, yet the highly selective Wizard shrewdly took credit with Lewis for the appointment—and by so doing, converted a critic into a long-term ally. Roosevelt's dependence on his black gatekeeper strengthened the Wizard's public image in the short term, though even Washington sometimes failed to sway the president, and the Council clearly reflected Tuskegee's wishes by paying homage to Roosevelt's halfhearted record. But Washington's heavy-handed tactics still fanned flames of resentment.

Occasional political hiccups also tarnished Roosevelt's overall image in matters racial. Scandals in early 1903 over the forced exile of black Mississippi postmistress Minnie Cox, and replacement of Samuel H. Vick, longtime black postmaster in North Carolina, with a white man did not reassure nervous observers about Roosevelt's long-term intentions. Meanwhile, his appointment of former senator Pritchard, "lily-white" Republican leader, as judge of the supreme court of the District of Columbia seemed pure heresy to such black leaders as George White.[10]

In early February 1903, Walters sent a revealing letter to Tuskegee, hoping to sound out Washington's opinions on political activity among Afro-Americans while reinforcing his own position. Rumors had lately begun to circulate that Roosevelt and Washington were in agreement that black appointments of all types should be scaled back, perhaps sharply. The New York *Journal* had just described Washington as being "against Negroes holding office," and only a statement to the contrary from Tuskegee could overrule that, or so Walters thought. "If you could issue a statement denying this, and in some way assure the public that you stand for the civil and political rights of the Black man, it would greatly relieve the situation. . . . A word from you in this crisis will spike their guns."[11]

Walters had just returned from a trip to Boston, where he had dared to visit the weekly *Guardian*, the Wizard's brand-new tormentor, and met with editors Trotter and Forbes, "but I could not get them to agree to anything that is reasonable." Trotter and Forbes, among others, "know of your influence among the white people and they are taking advantage of it to advance their interest by misrepresenting you." In the absence of "an expression from you it will be utterly impossible for me to control the Boston meeting. Can't you send me a letter to be read there which can be given to the press?"[12]

Walters knew that offering to help Tuskegee carried mixed advantages and risks. But he was also confident of the outcome. Washington was unlikely to issue the statement he recommended, but Walters could boast—confidentially, to the right people—that he had tried to warn the Wizard of the consequences of not doing so. For those Council members worried that Fortune was too dependent on Washington, Walters was a sensible alternative. His flurry of correspondence with Washington that spring, and at least one face-to-face meeting—in early April—underscored his shrewd plan to trump his friend and colleague Fortune in Louisville. It was Walters, for instance, who whispered to Washington that Pledger was seeking the Council presidency, thus forcing Pledger to disavow any such hopes when Washington wrote him. Washington, no stranger to such backstage intrigues, ignored Pledger's wounded pride and warning ("What you want to do, is to keep the Bee out of old man Walters' Bonnet").[13]

The series of run-up meetings that Walters and others attended and reported on during the winter and spring included a pro-Washington rally in February at the Bethel Literary and Historical Society in Washington, at which Jesse Lawson read a paper defending Tuskegee philosophy. "Our friends were out in force . . . and saw to it that the salient points were greeted with acclaim," Richard Thompson wrote Emmett Scott the next day. Pro-Washington speakers included Walters and Judge Terrell, while anti-Tuskegee speakers included Lafayette Hershaw and Ferris, who had attacked Washington at a similar meeting in January.[14]

Thompson painted the most favorable picture possible of the Bethel meeting. "I believe the expressions of approval that punctuated Lawson's speech . . . gave us several shades the better of it," he declared, despite a disappointing turnout and the ominous silence "rivaling that of the tomb" from such invited "heavyweights" as Dancy, White, Kelly Miller, and John Green during the spirited debate. "You can place upon it your own construction," Thompson said, blaming their hesitation on rumors of a still-gestating "patronage committee," that Walters denied existed but which many believed was about to spring from his forehead, fully armed. Walters asked Thompson "to assure Dr. Washington of his absolute loyalty to his leadership. . . . He wants the help of Dr. Washington at Louisville. . . . He wants harmony."[15]

Washington included the bishop on a select list of leaders to attend a private New York conference he had tentatively planned for the end of March and, a week later, began distributing letters to Walters, Du Bois, Bishop Grant, and others, requesting their attendance. The group should "consist of twelve or fifteen of our best men, representing every phase, if possible, of Negro life and activity" and would meet for two or three days "concerning the present condition and future of the race."[16] But schedule conflicts and competing meetings interfered, and by month's end, Washington decided to concentrate on making a strong showing in Louisville in July, advising Walters to do the same. (The New York conference was delayed for nearly a year, while Washington sought funding for it and reworked the list of possible attendees.)

Walters had sought Washington's help after the Cooper Union gathering, which had endorsed the Council and chosen fifteen representatives to Louisville. Cooper Union "was a great success," one that had thwarted Trotter's tactics, yet Trotter was still bent on recruiting Walters, or so Walters wished Washington to believe. How should he most effectively deal with "a deceiver whose object is to build himself up at the expense of others," Walters wanted to know. "Bend all of your energies in the direction of advertising the Louisville meeting and get our papers to do the same thing," Washington responded, advising him to work closely with Cyrus Adams. "You can depend upon me to do everything possible to promote the success of the Louisville meeting; it is in the hands of good conservative men and a body that really represents the race." A separate meeting planned by Trotterites in Cleveland should be ignored, and never mentioned by Walters or any black newspaper. "To fight it openly will simply mean to advertise it all through the country," warned the Wizard. "If you can get the colored papers to completely ignore the *Guardian* and Trotter and his crowd the sooner they will die."[17]

Washington did have reservations about Walters's agenda, as he later told Emmett Scott after one New York meeting. "I think it is rather clear that Bishop Walters is going to try to be president of the Council again, though he promised [Cyrus] Adams and myself to support Fortune," he wrote on April 6. "He is laying a great deal of stress on the opposition which he seems to have found throughout the country against Fortune."[18]

Having located the opposition, Walters carefully stoked it under the pretext of maintaining regular contacts with such non-Council activists as Hayes, president of the National Negro Suffrage League. Under Walters's prompting, Hayes had written to reassure the Wizard of his personal respects in February. "The work we are trying to do [the Virginia suffrage cases]," he wrote, was not "intended to criticize you. . . . I couldn't harm you if I would nor wouldn't if I could."[19]

For now, Hayes remained a useful conduit to those outside the Tuskegee orbit. Walters's presence on stage with Hayes at the Council's January meeting had imparted a new legitimacy to Hayes's image, and the meeting had chosen Hayes as national organizer for the Council. Yet Washington's confidant Charles W. Anderson clearly did not trust Hayes and believed that he and Walters were in league—against Washington—with such disgruntled former Council officers as Bruce and Wibecan.[20] But Hayes's letter to Washington raises interesting questions. Why did he write it? How much, if anything, did Hayes know of Tuskegee's secret support for other disfranchisement lawsuits in Louisiana and Alabama? And if he did know, was he signaling Washington of his willingness to pretend ignorance and play along? What did he hope to gain?

It was a risky game for all concerned. Walters would have known better than to reveal secret details to Hayes or anyone likely to publicize it; doing so risked permanent estrangement from Washington. But Hayes was playing into the hands of Anderson, who gleefully reported to Tuskegee the essence of Hayes's barbed attacks on himself and on Wilford Smith, Tuskegee's secretly subsidized attorney in the Alabama cases.

"Just how Mr. Hayes arrived at the conclusion that I am against his movement, I do not know, but I have a rather sneaking suspicion that Mr. Wibecan is responsible for it," Anderson wrote. In a private conversation with Anderson, Wibecan had admitted his strong preference for Hayes over Washington, after which Anderson suggested calling attention to alleged fund-raising irregularities by Hayes and the League. Wibecan went straight to Hayes with the threat.[21]

Washington, at his most devious when facing possible double agents, blunted Hayes's leadership on the suffrage question by publishing a lengthy statement on the subject in the Philadelphia *North American*, calling disfranchisement laws "unjust" for discriminating almost exclusively against poor, illiterate blacks while furthering the continuation of illiteracy among whites. He had promised Archibald Grimké to do this in early June, and Grimké thought it "wise to do so." The Wizard would soon act to co-opt Hayes completely, in the face of Fortune's strong opposition, by formally anointing him as the Council's national organizer.[22]

Despite a recurrence of his chronic malaria, Fortune had rushed home from the Pacific in May to attend the Council's annual meeting. Embroiled in a dispute over government per diem payments, and ignoring doctor's orders for a complete rest, the always frail journalist insisted on presiding at the convention a week after his arrival home.[23]

Louisville was the southernmost city to host a Council convention so far. Its selection had been mildly controversial when suggested a year earlier by Dancy. J. Madison Vance, head of the Council's legal bureau, had objected to holding the convention in any city with a "Jim Crow" law, but national organizer George Clinton had assured delegates Louisville had no such regulation and argued that the Council owed it to the South to convene there. "This is the ground on which our great battle is to be fought," Clinton had said in 1902. "It is time we stopped dodging around the South. . . . There is nothing this Council needs to say which cannot be said in Louisville."[24]

Another plus was the city's proximity to Bardstown, Walters's hometown. Nearly forty thousand black citizens lived in Louisville, almost a fifth of the city's population, making it the nation's seventh-largest urban environment for Afro-Americans. And while not a state capital, like Indianapolis or Saint Paul, an old, established metropolis like Philadelphia, or a major commercial center like Chicago, the prosperous Ohio River port still boasted an elegant charm and abiding sense of history, dating back to Revolutionary days. Its small Afro-American college, a Baptist institution called the State University of Louisville, had proudly offered liberal arts courses and theological training since 1879.[25]

The *Appeal* published a regional edition in Louisville, hometown of publishers John and Cyrus Adams. Their father had been a free Baptist minister there before the war. More than one-fourth of the city's antebellum black population had been free, and racial attitudes were still comparatively relaxed; residential segregation would not be officially introduced until 1915.[26]

All in all, the Council and its leaders were well received by Louisville citizens, who tendered a lavish closing reception and banquet at the city's Liederkranz Hall, hosting five hundred persons. A public speech given by Booker T. Washington at Macauley's Theater during the three-day convention also drew an overflow crowd of some three thousand, encouraged from afar by the flattering editorial attention of the *New York Times*. "Whatever hope there is for the negro in this country lies in the faithful application of Mr. Washington's ideas," wrote the *Times*.[27]

Yet not even the *Times*—perhaps eyeing the coup attempt planned for Louisville by Trotter and others—expected everyone to follow Tuskegee's lead. "It is, of course, inevitable that Booker Washington should incur misunderstanding and prejudice and excite some not altogether worthy opposition among his people," the newspaper cautioned.[28] The "Boston crowd," infuriated by Washington's friendly Minnesota takeover, had no illusions about the task before them. With assistance from newcomer Hayes and a handful of Council veterans like McGhee and Madison Mason, the New Englanders now plotted their course.

Washington was taking no chances. An alert from Peter Smith had warned him of rumors to this effect as early as February ("Trotter has said he will spend all his own money and everybody's else's he can get to kill you"). As detailed by Harlan, the Wizard carefully drilled his troops all through the spring and summer, even arranging for paid transportation for those unable to pay. By late June, he believed that up to a dozen Bostonians would attempt to storm Louisville, and he cautioned Fortune—back from the Philippines—to give "a calm, conservative" opening speech. Under no circumstances should either Walters or Hayes be given "an excuse for going against us."[29]

Walters is barely mentioned in Louisville newspaper accounts, indicating that he did not fit into the well-choreographed plans for Fortune's triumphant reelection. On opening day, July 1, the stage at Odd Fellows' Hall contained large pictures of Booker Washington and of the Tuskegee Institute to frame the entire proceedings, although floor protests forced the immediate removal of Washington's picture, at least. Protesters were "largely from New England," according to the *Courier-Journal*. Few dissidents were yet active in the Council, but many newcomers represented Hayes's suffrage organization and had gained admittance through a compromise arranged by the credentials committee—part of a "peace movement," as described by the *Louisville Herald*: "those dissenters were admitted . . . upon the payment of $1 apiece, the regular fee being $5." Most of the newcomers "have the idea that the negro should assert himself, and not stand in the background. They are enemies of Booker T. Washington because they think he makes the negro looked down upon by the whites."[30]

A slightly different scenario, advanced by the *Colored American*, claimed the "New York delegation"—led by Bruce, Wibecan, and Fred Chew—refused at first to enter the Council convention in a dispute over the $5 fee, before reportedly adjourning to another auditorium to meet and elect Wibecan president and Chew secretary. (Bruce later claimed that all the New York members had paid the $5; that their plea had been on behalf of other "indigent" attendees; and that all attended the Council.)[31]

Elsewhere in Louisville, the Afro-American Press Association had just adjourned its own meeting, reelecting Cyrus Adams as president on June 29, although poor attendance prompted AAPA members to switch to biennial sessions in the future. It was clear that of the three groups in town—the Council, the AAPA, and the National Suffrage League—the Council was the biggest draw. More than 1,500 persons attended the Council's Wednesday night session at Quinn Chapel church, and for the evening, strategic quarrels were laid aside, as the crowd heard addresses by a series of "representative colored men on the race question."[32]

But resentment over Washington's picture lingered, provoking a major confrontation between Council leaders and suffragists the following day. On Thursday, literary bureau director Fannie Williams delivered her annual report, with warm words for Washington's educational work. As she concluded, a man stepped forward from the wings of the stage, carrying a "picture of Booker T. Washington in a gold frame and painted in oils" and setting off howls of disapproval. Fortune quickly adjourned the session, but the clamor resumed at the next opportunity, as delegates Ferris and Trotter angrily denounced Washington and demanded to know why his likeness was on stage. "For a time it looked as if blows would be exchanged," wrote one local newspaper, while "Washington was called 'a traitor to his race' in the excitement." Fortune's weak rationale for the new portrait—allegedly "painted by a negro woman of Louisville"—convinced some, but not Ferris or Trotter, who "began speeches against Washington, saying he had done more to pull down colleges for the higher education of the negro than any other influence. Washington's friends hissed the speakers and the others applauded." Only the sudden appearance of another picture—one of Dr. Joseph C. Price, late founder of Livingstone College and the original Afro-American League's president—quieted the uproar.[33]

An even noisier reaction greeted release of the nominating committee's report, which contained two slates—one with Fortune as president and Cyrus Adams as secretary, and a minority report listing Isaiah Scott and A. B. "Corey" for those offices. Both slates apparently retained Bishop Clinton as national organizer, not attorney Hayes as promised. Clinton resigned, Hayes was substituted, and the amended majority report was ordered adopted as a whole, over the angry protests of McGhee—who was himself reelected financial secretary, but who believed the process employed was unconstitutional, since no floor nominations were allowed.[34]

Presiding officer Pledger ignored McGhee and declared the slate carried and the new officers elected. The delegate vote was not even close—101 votes to 16—but Ferris still rose once again to make a sarcastic observation: that black men from the North were being disfranchised in a black convention called to protest southern political disfranchisement of black men. Two years later, McGhee told Du Bois that Washington had sabotaged Scott's election in Louisville by paying the dues of "new voters." Du Bois refused to attend the Louisville conclave but quoted McGhee in a letter to Oswald Villard: "We had them easily beaten and would have elected Bishop Scott president, when a lot of new voters qualified . . . It must have cost Washington over $300 to carry the organization." McGhee's account, however unlikely in this case, at least served to confirm Du Bois's deepening suspicions of Tuskegee tactics.[35]

But for McGhee, president of his local council, it was the last straw. He had left Minnesota determined to rescue the national Council from the grip of Tuskegee, as he had strongly implied in a speech delivered in late June, and to expose the Council's poor record on business affairs and its financial mismanagement. "We have pursued a path of humility only to be trampled on the more," he told a Saint Paul audience, and the implication was clear: the nonpartisan Council must be reclaimed from the Republican Party and Booker T. Washington. McGhee had written Trotter in mid-June, asking him to send as many men as he could "to help overthrow the present officers of the Council." Defeated and humiliated, McGhee never attended another national Council meeting.[36]

Among those he had watched be elected were six new vice presidents, including Washington's new supporter William Lewis, Minnesota's John Q. Adams, New York's Granville Hunt, Louisiana's James Lewis, attorney James Guy of

Kansas, and R. J. Griffin of Oregon. Lewis Jordan was named chaplain. Those reelected included Pledger, Steward, and Mrs. Jeffrey, vice presidents; secretaries Cyrus Adams, McGhee, and Mrs. Williams; and treasurer Thompson. Named to the executive "board" were several sitting officers—Steward, Cyrus Adams, Jordan, and Guy—and one reluctant newcomer, Trotter. The list as published by the *Courier-Journal* omitted one familiar name—Walters—but the wily bishop, as outgoing executive committee chair, remedied the oversight by simply having himself reelected by the group. Walters's action was an underhanded move, at best, and illegal at worst. Fortune later complained to Washington: "Bishop Walters took snap judgment on me in my absence by calling the executive committee together and getting himself elected chairman. *He was not a member of the committee* and had no right to call the new committee to order," Fortune insisted (emphasis in original). "What should be my attitude in the matter?"[37]

By contrast, Friday's session was far quieter, almost anticlimactic. The northern protesters had been soundly vanquished by the Tuskegee Machine, and all but Trotter had begun leaving. Nashville attorney James Napier, active Republican and former congressional candidate, suavely chastised them for their violent attitudes toward whites. "You cannot make people do what they have made up their minds not to do. I would rather have the good will and friendship of my neighbors, when absent from home, than a whole army a thousand miles distant to fight for them," Napier noted. "Shotgun advice is not the thing needed. I admire the gospel of peace, and that is what is going to settle these great questions."[38]

"What the negroes want to do in this country is to make friends with the people," Napier added. "These young men who come from Boston with their high notions of life, with their bloodthirsty speeches, would make it better for visiting the South [by] knowing something of the condition of their people, and preaching to them the gospel of peace. Passing laws will not bring about the desired results." But Napier's final point was obscured in the Council's own resolutions, two of which called for congressional action—one denouncing disfranchisement and demanding that President Roosevelt recommend federal laws restoring the franchise to black southerners, another asking Roosevelt to ask Congress to "make secure the life and constitutional rights of the citizens of color, along with other American citizens."[39]

The third resolution had nothing to do with legal actions, instead praising the "lofty and patriotic attitude and expressions of President Roosevelt" and assuring him "of our unshaken confidence in his principles and policy of an open door to all American citizens." Trotter fumed and sputtered, waving copies of his own failed resolution criticizing Roosevelt, but his final efforts were ignored. "He has given but one office in one hundred to colored Americans in a section where colored Republicans outnumber the white Republicans two hundred to one," Trotter had charged, and "has shown so little confidence in the negro as to put the patronage in the hands of white Democrats."[40]

Isaiah Scott, resolutions committee chair and, briefly, presidential candidate, read the Council's address to the nation aloud on the final day. Its tone was practical, clearly reflecting underlying Tuskegee themes, yet with an edgy undertone not characteristic of Washington's public addresses. More than ever, the address seemed aimed directly at white America, weaving together both conciliatory phrases and occasionally provocative statements. "We, the representatives of 10,000,000 American citizens of African descent . . . recognize with pleasure the friendly relation that has all along existed between the best people of the white race and our own, and we sincerely desire that nothing may be permitted to intervene to mar this relation," the address declared, echoing Washington phrasing. Yet in too many eyes the race was judged only by its worst examples, not by its best. "We declare this standard of measurement to be unfair to our people, and believe that fair-minded citizens of the entire country will agree with us in this view. These do not indicate our capacity, either for present or future citizenship."[41]

Such a standard was no fairer than judging whites "by those of their number who have assassinated Presidents or been guilty of treason or have betrayed and murdered innocent women. Judge us . . . as you judge yourselves, not by the worst, but by the best products time and opportunity have enabled us to send forth to take their places among their fellows." A gratifying recent decline in mob violence against blacks was offset by the increasing triviality of crimes punished by lynching. "It is not an unusual thing to read these days of negroes being lynched for impudence, refusing to obey, striking a white man, etc. . . . lynching for any cause is destructive of law, is demoralizing. But to subject persons accused of or even guilty of such trivial offenses . . . to unlawful punishment and death is to make the negro the marked man of the nation," the address continued. "Whatever the crime, the accused is in your hands and must be tried by your law, and surely he could not be more completely at your mercy."

In another section, the address candidly dealt with white perceptions of black attitudes, particularly those exhibited by modern, educated Afro-Americans, rarely "as humble and self-forgetful in all things as . . . 'the old negro.'" Postwar race leaders, especially those born after 1865, could not apologize for assertiveness, for they "breathe an entirely different atmosphere. Nevertheless, we allow no man to be more polite, more considerate of the rights of others than we. We make this a leading principle of our daily life and teach it to our children as well."[42]

But in many states, educated black citizens had been punished simply for being black. Disfranchisement of illiterates, a legitimate social course, had "been broadened and strengthened" and "now includes almost all negroes" in many southern states, where "thousands of qualified men are denied positively and absolutely the right to vote. In such States taxation without representation prevails as truly as it ever did when England held control over the American colonies." Such unjust discrimination subjected southern blacks to the "mercy of a class of officials who themselves do not always represent the best thought and blood of the community" and was bound to provoke resentment and civil strife among the race. Yet the Council contended "not for special but equal privileges. We have no desire to dominate, but we believe the ballot a protection to the citizen."

While black leaders were "willing to leave our interests on this line in the hands of the justice-loving people of this country," many feared the consequences: "We have reason to fear there is some danger from this source. Nevertheless this will serve to place the friends of the race on their guard and to remind them that 'eternal vigilance is the price of liberty.'" Reliance upon God and a crusade for universal literacy should be accompanied by commercial diligence and continued acquisition of property by the race, which already controlled half a billion dollars in U.S. property.[43]

For all its understated eloquence, the Council's address drew far less national attention than the speech given by Washington, whose heartfelt tribute to his native South was balanced by an uneasy realization of the "regrettable . . . recent events" that had, ironically, done so much to "simplify" the region's race problem by transcending local and sectional boundaries and turning the problem into a national one. Washington was glad to attend a Council meeting in the South, for "It is in the South that the great masses of our people dwell, and will abide . . . . It is fitting that this body should have its hearing, and perform its work in the section of our country where the negro race lives . . . in the midst of the white people who are most directly concerned about the future of the race." He was convinced that racial progress was likely, with two prerequisites: "open, frank discussion and a sympathetic cooperation between the highest types of whites and the same class of blacks." Despite pessimism in some quarters, Washington was hopeful, believing that a "class of brave, earnest men at the South as well as at the North . . . are more determined than ever before to see that the race is given opportunity to elevate itself."[44]

If the Afro-American race was indeed "passing through a very serious and trying period of its development, a period that calls for the use of our ripest thought [and] our most sober judgment," history was nonetheless filled with examples of similar struggles. "Almost without exception, every race or nation that has ever got upon its feet has done so through struggle, and trial, and persecution, and that, out of this very resistance to wrong, out of the struggle against odds, they have gained strength, self-confidence and experience, which they could not have gained in any other way."[45]

But nothing could be more harmful than "extremes of utterances or action." Descending to "the level of the mob" was to be avoided at all costs. "In advocating this policy I am not asking that the negro act the coward," he insisted. "We are not cowards," for the military bravery and commitment of black soldiers was "sufficient evidence of our courage, when the proper time comes to manifest it." The persistence of lynching—or what Washington called "outbreaks of government by the mob"—held lessons for both blacks and whites across the country. Blacks had no choice but to stamp out "idleness and crime" among their ranks, to remove any excuse for whites to "label any large portion of the race as idlers and criminals." Whites, in turn, must realize that lawless treatment of blacks was a dangerous precedent. "If we break the law where a helpless negro is concerned, it will not be very long before the same law is disregarded where a white man is concerned."

If only for simple economic reasons, the nation much strive to keep its supply of black laborers "happy, contented and prosperous by surrounding and guarding it with every protection and encouragement of the laws," for "nothing is more costly and unsatisfactory than discontented, unhappy and restless labor. Few people are wise enough to learn the economic value of justice." Washington chose the metaphor of a tree to compare the prewar and postwar racial situations. "Before our freedom a giant tree was growing in the garden which all considered injurious to the progress of the whole nation. The work to be done was direct and simple. Destroy the hurtful tree," he said. "The work before us now is not the destruction of a tree, but the growing of one. Slavery presented a problem of destruction; freedom presents one of construction. This requires time, patience, preparation of the soil, watering, pruning and the most careful nursing."[46]

And while protesting injustice was every citizen's right, only complaints made "in a conservative and simple manner" would succeed. "We shall make a fatal error if we yield to the temptation of believing that mere opposition to our wrongs, and the simple utterance of complaint, will take the place of progressive, constructive action, which must constitute the bedrock of all true civilization," he said. "Whoever North or South, black or white, by word or deed, needlessly stirs up strife, is an enemy to both races, and to his country." The most effective appeal of all, he said, would always be to "the community and State in which we reside." Because both races must reside together permanently, black citizens "should lose no opportunity to cultivate in every straightforward, manly way the greatest harmony between the races. . . . Let us hold up our heads and with firm and steady tread go manfully forward."[47]

Washington's speech remains one of his most memorable discourses on the future relationship between the races. It was covered at length by both local and northern white newspapers and was reprinted in at least one anthology in 1932. But whether Washington actually delivered all of the prepared text is not clear, since contemporary versions printed in newspapers differ in length, both from each other and from the authorized text. He had been known to change his mind at the last minute, as in 1900, when he disappointed Indianapolis listeners expecting to hear his thoughts on politics. One three-hundred-word section of the prepared text—in which Washington dealt with the percentage of cases of lynching involving allegations of interracial sex or rape, and called for execution of rapists of either race—did not appear in Louisville papers. But in a speech the *Courier-Journal* described as "characteristically sensible," local editorial censors may have preferred not to risk causing an outcry by condoning even his measured thoughts on such an explosive subject.

The *New York Times* also printed only selected portions of the speech, but was apparently disturbed by nothing its correspondent heard, including in its account about half the language not carried in Louisville. Washington's *Evening Star* printed none of the text but described Washington's speech in an editorial as "advocacy of his well-known opinions on the subjects of the black man's duty and his opportunity. It is to him and such as he that we are probably indebted for the council's wise and conservative deliverance on questions of much difficulty and moment."[48] What Washington was at least prepared to say on lynching is as follows (with *Times* excerpts in italics):

> . . . and that we show ourselves as anxious as any other class of citizens to bring to punishment those who commit crime, when proper legal punishment is sure.
>
> *We should let the world know on all proper occasions that we consider no legal punishment too severe for the wretch of any race who attempts to outrage a woman.*
>
> *The lesson for the other portion of the nation to learn is that, both in the making and the execution, the same laws should be made to apply to the Negro as to the white man. There should be meted out equal justice to the black man and the white man whether it relates to citizenship, the protection of property, the right to labor, or the protection of human life. Whenever the nation forgets, or is tempted to forget, this basic principle,*

> *the whole fabric of government for both the white man and the black man is weakened and threatened with destruction. This is true whether it relates to conditions in Texas, Indiana, or Delaware.*[49]
>
> To show how far we have already been led astray by those who disregard the majesty of the law and would insult governors and judges, by those who would uphold the law in one case and trample it under foot in another, we have but to call attention to the lamentable fact that the most careful and systematic investigation into the subject of lynching that has ever been made in this country shows that only thirty-five percent of those lynched have ever been charged with violence to women. To attempt to say that all these thirty-five percent were guilty would be to argue that the judgment of the mob is more unerring than that of the court. We cannot, and should not, escape the punishment for our sins of commission or of omission.[50]

Washington's statements, however measured, were risky in the racially charged southern atmosphere of the day. Similar sentiments had brought down a storm of angry criticism, primarily from white newspapers, upon George White three years earlier, when the congressman had introduced his antilynching bill in the U.S. House and claimed that, based on his own 1899 study, "fewer than fifteen percent of the lynchings in this country were for assaults upon women." But in his speech, White had also taken the issue a step farther—too far, perhaps, for most southern white listeners—by explicitly reminding them that "assaults . . . were also committed by white men upon black women, as evidenced by the great number of mulattoes in the Southland." Both kinds of assault were equally heinous, the former prosecutor declared, and any man—white or black—who assaulted a woman should be executed, but by legal means.[51]

The situations and settings, however, were quite different. White's statements had been twisted almost beyond recognition by his critics and injected into a heated political campaign, one won eventually by white supremacist Democrats. He had retired from Congress that same year, rather than seek reelection. Washington, a respected educator with national stature and a solid reputation for moderation, had little to lose politically by addressing the topic in a nonpartisan setting in racially moderate Louisville. But the debate over lynching, and allied themes of racial justice and judicial equity, remained dangerous issues for any black leader to raise openly in the South, regardless of his audience.

Black newspapers, meanwhile, were divided over how to assess the Council's effectiveness. Some were adulatory, others negative or indignant. Chase's *Bee* had little good to say about the Council or its new benefactor, calling the Council "a national fraud," headed by "toadies who are dancing to the music of demagogues and political tricksters." What had the Council done, he wanted to know, with the "thousands of dollars [collected] under the guise of protecting them in their civil and political rights"?[52]

By contrast, attorney Hayes "has done more and created a more healthy sentiment among the people than all the negro councils combined. The *Bee* is compelled to say that the editor of the *New York Age* has at last become the obedient tool of the principal of Tuskegee," Chase added, while *Atlanta Age* editor Pledger "has at last lost his power of speech and today is the willing slave of apologistic measures." The Council should be abolished and replaced, Chase declared. But the *Colored American*, long friendly to Tuskegee, called the Council "an intelligent body of men and women bent on a close scrutiny of the problems affecting the race to-day." Edward Cooper printed excerpts of Washington's speech, which it called "great" and "characteristically sensible." But the accuracy of his coverage of the convention, less than favorable to the suffrage delegates, was disputed at length by former Council officer turned dissenter John Bruce.[53]

From Cleveland, former vice president Harry Smith dismissed the Council as irrelevant. "Much as we regret to say it, the Council seems to have outlived its usefulness and clearly indicates the fact in its largely political official staff," wrote Smith's *Gazette*, blaming the Council's decline on widespread objections to "the questionable methods of the 'Wizard of Tuskegee' and his anti-citizen and anti-civil rights propaganda for the purpose of popularizing Booker and raising funds for his school."[54]

Weeks later, Smith continued his critical comments against Tuskegee's philosophy. "Messrs. Washington and company may believe that they conserve the best and most lasting interests of our poor people by truckling to southern feeling," he wrote. "We are entreated and enjoined to make terms with the southern whites . . . . But when we see that those terms are to be gained only at the price of chains, humiliation, and slavery, we prefer rather to die protesting against outrage and wrong than live a race of menials. This is what men of the Afro-American Council are asking us to do, this is in spirit what they would have, and by the God of heaven, we declare our eternal opposition."[55]

Indianapolis editors differed on the subject. The *Recorder* worried aloud that "as long as designing politicians are in control, we cannot hope for very much, but we do expect harmony. Objections to Booker T. Washington's picture or to any other race leader's picture is indeed small play for men to indulge in." George Knox's *Freeman*, however, claimed the Council "has more than justified its existence and the work it is doing deserves the encouragement and support of every race loving Negro man and woman."[56]

The debate over Washington's influence over the Council would grow far shriller as Washington ventured north into hostile territory and encountered the opposition in person. The so-called "Boston riot" was a watershed in the widening schism between conservatives and radicals, helping nourish the Niagara Movement and producing an "enemies list," on which Trotter, Du Bois, and both Grimkés, among others, figured. Described at length by Harlan, the "riot" was little more than a public brawl—with or without Maude Trotter's infamous hatpin—but quickly became sensationalized. Briefly, the facts: Trotter heckled Washington as he prepared to deliver a scheduled speech at a black church in Boston on July 30, before some two thousand listeners. Anticipating unrest, Boston policemen were on hand. Trotter was ejected from the hall but returned. Fist fights broke out inside the church, and a group of women surrounded policemen, who threatened to use clubs unless they dispersed. Maude Trotter was arrested for assaulting a policeman with a hatpin (those charges were soon dropped). Her brother and two companions were arrested and charged with disturbing the peace; Trotter and Granville Martin were convicted and sentenced to thirty days in jail.[57]

Washington completed his speech without further incident and left for Illinois after making light of the situation to reporters. But over the next few months, he compiled a secret blacklist of those sympathetic to Trotter. Their offenses seem comparatively minor: Du Bois and a fellow Atlanta faculty member wrote letters to the *Guardian* defending Trotter, the Reverend Francis Grimké a personal letter of support to Trotter. Archibald Grimké served as chief witness for Trotter during his trials and addressed a small crowd celebrating Trotter's release.[58]

Publicly, Washington remained statesmanlike. Behind the scenes, his behavior was increasingly vindictive, his actions and those of his close friends often petty. And even though some of the "enemies" were invited to attend the upcoming Carnegie Hall conference, their relationships with the Wizard, or with the Council he controlled, were never again quite the same.[59]

The Council's foremost dilemma in late 1903 seemed to be what action to take on the Louisiana test case, while awaiting a ruling from that state's highest court. Meanwhile, legal team members wrangled over possible grounds for appeal to the federal courts. The five lawyers "spent more of their time squabbling with each other than in prosecuting the case," according to Harlan, and Washington despaired of the team's chances of success, at least in working together. The Louisiana case had not gone well so far in state courts, having already been filed twice, and denied twice, at the local level; it seemed lost in the labyrinthine appeal process to the Louisiana supreme court. Washington was far more interested, personally, in the progress of Alabama's Giles cases, on which he maintained a steady correspondence with Wilford Smith in 1903 and 1904. It was not an easy path, and Smith had his hands full; each time a court ruled against Giles on technical grounds, observers blamed him "for carelessness or incompetence," although Washington maintained faith in his abilities, according to Harlan.[60]

Washington was less interested in the Louisiana case than in pushing the Council to endorse Roosevelt. He did not attend the December 1903 meeting of the Council's executive subcommittee, but his influence over its decisions remained clear, from the resolution endorsing the Roosevelt's controversial nomination of Dr. Crum—still stuck in the U.S. Senate—to its ringing endorsement of Roosevelt himself. "We take this opportunity to express our gratitude to President Roosevelt for daring at all times to stand up for impartial justice and the manhood rights guaranteed by the Constitution and the law based thereon," the subcommittee declared. "We have never asked special consideration in any matters affecting the common rights of citizens, and we have never asked for more and will not be satisfied with less. By announcing that he would not submit to the closing of the door of hope to us, he played the whole gamut of principles for which the nation stands, and for which the founders dedicated their lives, their fortunes, and their sacred honor."[61]

Although no official list is available, at least six members attended: executive committee chairman Walters, president Fortune, vice presidents Pledger and Steward, treasurer Thompson, secretary Adams, and at-large member Walter Cohen. The group finalized the site and dates of the Saint Louis meeting and designated a Council committee "to present an argument before the platform committee of the Republican National Convention urging . . . a vigorous position . . . by the party looking to a rectification of the malignant suffrage abuses known to exist in certain states of the Union." But a plan to reduce "Southern representation in the Republican National Convention" was strongly opposed as "unjust to the loyal men who were risking their fortunes and very lives by their open support of the policies of the party," as was recent action by certain state parties in "drawing the color line" within convention delegations.[62]

The subcommittee selected attorney Alfred Cosey of New Jersey as new national organizer, succeeding James Hayes, whose sudden departure ended a brief, amicable coalition between the Council and the Suffrage League, which held its own tumultuous convention days later. Judge Terrell was named "counselor for the District of Columbia," a position whose function was not explained. According to the *Freeman*, "The attendance at the Washington session was representative of the best purposes of the Council and the deliberations were presided over by Bishop Alexander Walters, chairman of the national executive committee." Walters then led a delegation—including Fortune, Steward, Cosey, Adams, Thompson, Cohen, and W. T. Andrews of South Carolina—to the White House for "an exceedingly pleasant meeting" with President Roosevelt.[63]

With that, the Council's leaders adjourned and prepared for Saint Louis, described as an "eminently satisfactory" site, allowing visitors to see the scheduled Louisiana Purchase Exposition while attending the convention in an auditorium furnished at no charge. The September date, later than usual, would facilitate attendance at the National Negro Business League convention at Indianapolis in August.

Days later, the Council's short-lived merger with Hayes's National Negro Suffrage League collapsed. Walters attended part of the league's Washington convention, as did George White and a few other speakers, but little was accomplished, except to attract unusual numbers of District police to preserve the calm. Calvin Chase, chairman of the league's executive committee, proved inept at maintaining order at the chaotic meeting, which failed to endorse Roosevelt, threatened to censure Booker T. Washington, and generally invited public ridicule. The league's virtual disintegration as a cohesive body all but removed it as a strategic challenger to the Council, which the *Evening Star* described as "the strongest organization of a political nature the Afro-Americans have ever had and . . . growing stronger each day. It embraces the leading negroes in the country."[64]

From Saint Paul, New Orleans, and Washington, D.C., the legal-legislative bureau announced plans to raise funds for the antidiscrimination battle pursued by the Reverend H. T. Johnson, editor of the *Christian Recorder*, whose case the Council hoped to take to the U.S. Supreme Court. Johnson's order for breakfast on a Pullman-operated dining car, while traveling on the Seaboard Air Line Railroad, had sparked the suit. A subsequent favorable verdict in May and a $500 damage award from a federal jury in New Jersey had been set aside by the judge, according to a circular printed in the *Appeal* throughout the fall of 1903.[65]

On the surface, all seemed well for the Council, but new, hidden dangers lurked just ahead. Within two weeks, vice president Pledger was dead of tuberculosis at fifty-two—a shock to all his friends and colleagues, but a devastating blow to close ally Tim Fortune. Within three months of Pledger's death, Fortune would resign as Council president, after an unfortunate quarrel with his mentor, and the Council would enter a long twilight period, from which it seemed unlikely to emerge.

8

Enduring the Interregnum

Saint Louis, 1904

The Carnegie Hall conference called by Booker T. Washington in January 1904 was to be a private brainstorming session for prominent Afro-American leaders, where issues might be discussed discreetly and solutions proposed to problems involving race. Washington had begun planning for it nearly a year earlier, notifying Walters and other leaders but doing little else until after the Boston incident, when he resurrected the dormant plan and pushed it forward energetically. By December, after lengthy negotiations with W. E. B. Du Bois, all plans were finalized, with one major exception. Washington wrote President Roosevelt after Christmas, announcing that twenty-five "leading colored men . . . represent[ing] the educational, political, moral and sociological forces at work for the elevation of the race" would attend. He planned to call on Roosevelt on January 5, just before the conference opened, to discuss any "suggestions to put before the conference."[1]

What advice Roosevelt had for Washington is not recorded. Indeed, much of what is known about the conference was written down much later by a few participants, sworn to secrecy. What is known is that conferees resembled a cross-section of America's most successful black men, though no women—lawyers, ministers, politicians, and educators, handpicked by Washington; that conservatives and moderates loyal to Tuskegee outnumbered radicals; and that the result was the memorably named Committee of Twelve for the Advancement of the Interests of the Negro Race. What is rarely noted, however, is the solid representation at Carnegie of those with ties to the Afro-American Council. From current officers Fortune, Lewis, Steward, and McGhee, and executive committee members Bishop Walters and J. C. Napier, to former vice presidents Abram Grant, Elias Morris, Hightower Kealing, and Isaiah Scott, and onetime executive committee members

Judson Lyons, George Knox, and P. B. S. Pinchback, Council experience was perhaps the single most common characteristic shared by those at the conference.[2] Nearly half of those invited had already served as national officers, and almost all had some Council ties; even Du Bois, no longer active in the Council, had once chaired the business bureau, while Washington had served on the executive committee in 1902.

Washington already knew these men well, both from the Council and through other dealings. And if the Carnegie gathering had little practical impact on later Council actions, the meeting did produce one proposal long on the group's wish list: establishing a "strong national Negro paper which will unify the race," as Washington told potential donor William H. Baldwin Jr.[3] Council leaders had approved the idea in 1898, at the urging of Atlanta editor William Pledger, who had raised commitments for about one-fourth of the $50,000 capital envisioned for the newspaper before the plan was dropped. Ironically, the newspaper proposal was resurrected at Carnegie Hall the week of his death.

The loss of his good friend and co-militant was depressing news for Tim Fortune, who had been unable to visit Pledger just before his death—despite a telegram from Atlanta pleading with him to come—and he brooded aloud for weeks. In mid-January, Fortune left New York for a nationwide fund-raising lecture tour on the Council's behalf, but the tour failed to raise either his own spirits, despite Washington's encouragement, or enough cash to pay for traveling expenses.[4]

"They came out to applaud to echo," he wrote Emmett Scott later that month, "but put pennies in the case." The lecture tour cost him $50 more than he could raise, wrote Thornbrough, and he returned, badly dispirited, to New York, preparing to leave journalism for a life of privacy—if he could just sell the *Age*. Otherwise, he still dreamed of a federal patronage job to relieve financial pressures and approached both James Clarkson and Washington about an appointment. Before the appointment could be sorted out, however, Fortune's relationship with Washington took a decided turn for the worse. Washington's acquaintances informed him that Fortune had been given to "boasting of his intimacy with Washington" and had mentioned the Alabama suffrage cases—and Washington's involvement, a closely guarded secret. Furious, Washington chastised the indiscreet Fortune, who wrote Scott in late March that "There is hell in the camp between me and the Wizard."[5]

Without Washington's support, Fortune had little chance of surviving as Council leader. The hapless journalist saw no recourse except to resign as president and promptly drafted a long letter to this effect to his next-in-command, Steward, the ranking vice president since Pledger's death, and another letter to Scott. Steward, dumbfounded, sought guidance from Washington, who instructed him to ignore the letter ("The fact is that [Fortune] has not been acting properly for the last ten days, and probably wrote you in a fit of temper") and simply to write Fortune with good advice.[6]

Fortune did not change his mind but instead released his letter publicly, forcing Washington to write Steward again with different advice. "On the whole, I believe it is as just as well to let the resignation stand and for you to take charge of the Council as President," the Wizard advised Steward. "If you desire it, I feel quite sure that you will be elected permanent President at the St. Louis meeting."[7] Fortune's departure seemed to reenergize the despondent journalist. For a time, he continued to chair the executive committee of the National Negro Business League and would still enjoy a cordial relationship with his former mentor, if one without the trusted access of years past. Relieved of the burdens of office, Fortune supported the Council's progress and goals from his newspaper's pages, but his days of national influence, aside from his editorial page, had largely ended.

Steward, editor of the *American Baptist* weekly, had little executive experience—a shortcoming he shared with Fortune—but willingly acceded to Washington's directive. The onetime letter carrier in Louisville soon became acting president of the State University of Louisville, a small Afro-American school whose board he also chaired. But lacking the ambition of Walters or the passion of Fortune, he left little mark on the Council during a nondescript term. The Council's interregnum—eighteen months during which it all but disappeared—had commenced.

At the turn of the century, Saint Louis had been America's fourth-largest city, a bustling center of transportation and manufacturing on the Mississippi River with nearly six hundred thousand residents. Its Afro-American population—35,916 by the 1900 census, or just over 6 percent of the city's total—formed the nation's ninth-largest black urban community, larger than that of Richmond, Virginia, and was served by one black weekly newspaper, John Wheeler's *Palladium*.[8]

Missouri's black population was continuing a long, slow relative decline, down from 10 percent before the Civil War to just over 5 percent in 1900, as its influence in statewide politics gradually withered. Once a heavily Republican bastion, the state's black voters had begun drifting toward the Democratic Party in recent years, mustering a concerted effort to defeat a "Jim Crow" segregation law in 1903 by browbeating urban party bosses. Yet black Missourians maintained a proud presence in national organizations like the Council. Wheeler and J. Silas Harris of Kansas City had been among the Council's original officers, elected assistant secretary and sergeant-at-arms respectively, at Rochester in 1898. O. M. Wood of Saint Louis and Crossland had been Council vice presidents, while

Nelson Crews of Kansas City had directed the emigration bureau in 1902. Cecile Rodney now served on the executive subcommittee.

The state's powerful delegation had influenced previous conventions, finally persuading Council leaders to visit Missouri in 1904. Familiar to many as site of the 1896 Republican National Convention, Saint Louis was slated to host two remarkable international events that would draw millions of tourists. The Louisiana Purchase Exposition (April to November) attracted an estimated twenty million visitors. The five-day Olympic Games of 1904, the first to be held on American soil, were far smaller—almost a sideshow—but still attracted almost seven hundred athletes and many onlookers into a thirty-five-thousand-seat stadium, in August and September.

Afro-American visitors to the city encountered an unfortunate but pervasive resistance to equal treatment, especially on the World's Fair grounds. Emmett Scott, who journeyed there before the Council opened, reported that "the spirit of color-prejudice has wide sway on the Exposition ground," especially in purchasing food and beverages. Wilberforce University professor William Scarborough, there on academic business, found that "sentiment in this city is avowedly anti-Negro," with lodgings available only in hotels managed by Afro-Americans.[9]

It was in this setting that hundreds of Council visitors appeared, largely lost in the late-summer tourist onslaught, as the Council's seventh convention convened on September 6. Calvin Chase, who chose not to attend, sent a bouquet of acid instead from the pages of the *Bee*, titled "A Dead Corpse":

> The Afro-American Council is to meet in St. Louis, Mo. That is, three men who are supposed to represent this defunct organization will meet and attempt to speak for the entire negro race. For monumental gall, we are of the opinion that we can find more of it among certain so-called negro leaders than within any race of people upon this earth. What is this council and who does it represent? It is without a head and was never born with a body. . . . At its birth, it was deformed, and it has continued ever since to walk on crutches. . . . A few men have gotten together under false pretenses and when the election is over about a thousand bogus claims will be presented to the Republican administration. And should Mr. [Alton B.] Parker come in, the Afro-American Council will be enlarged and every member will declare that he was never for President Roosevelt. . . . Now, let this bogus Council rest in peace, because if it is resurrected we have no idea what kind of disease it will bring forth.[10]

News accounts out of Missouri defied Chase's prediction, describing the gathering—even in Chase's *Bee*—as "a large and successful meeting." Those attending the opening session in Central Baptist Church enjoyed speeches by Steward, C. H. Tandy, Walter M. Farmer, Peter H. Clark, and the Reverend D. P. Roberts. Bureau reports "showed a decided increase in the work of the Council," while the group's treasury continued to show only a small balance, with just under $700 collected and more than $600 spent during the past year. Public meetings of the Council at Music Hall and Saint Paul AME Church produced "immense crowds of people" to hear speeches that "aroused considerable enthusiasm." An estimated 2,500 persons turned out to hear Louisiana's veteran politician James Lewis, Indianapolis editor George Knox, former Memphis prosecutor Josiah T. Settle, Mississippi bishop Evans Tyree, and recent Yale graduate William Pickens, whose prize-winning oratory on Haiti had angered Trotter and the *Guardian* into a libelous fit earlier in the year.[11]

Newspaper coverage of the event provided a study in unexpected contrasts. The local *Daily Globe-Democrat* covered the meeting in depth, from interesting minor details, such as the singing of an opening hymn composed especially for the meeting (the "Afro-American Hymn") by a Charlotte, North Carolina, minister, to the full text of the annual address to the nation. Yet only limited coverage was offered by most black newspapers, including the *Palladium*, which had announced the meeting a week in advance but offered only cursory accounts of Council actions. The Kansas City, Missouri, *Rising Son* failed even to mention the meeting, before or after.[12]

Outside Missouri, few mainstream newspapers carried any news of the session. Among national black newspapers, the *Appeal* carried a comprehensive record—a version probably written by publisher John Adams, and carried in Washington's *Bee*—but neglected to mention its resolutions. The only major black newspaper to do so was Knox's *Freeman*, which printed the text of one resolution offered by S. Joe Brown, on the simmering issues of disfranchisement and reducing southern representation in Congress. Adopted unanimously, Brown's resolution cited the Fourteenth Amendment, "which provides for the reduction of representation of those states that have disfranchised a large portion of their male citizens over twenty-one years of age for reasons other than those authorized or permitted by law," and reminded voters of both races of their best course of action. "We advise all Negroes and all white persons who are not in sympathy with . . . so-called constitutional disfranchisement to support no candidate for member of congress who refuses to openly declare himself as favoring the enforcement of said clause by appropriate legislation," it read.[13]

The controversial issue of reduction of representation had split Afro-American leaders for years; Fortune, for one, had always opposed it as counterproductive. But Knox's printing of it carried subtler political undertones. The Indianapolis editor was busy collecting signatures on a petition to run as an independent congressional candidate that year, a course that Washington and others were trying diligently to persuade him to abandon, for fear of hurting Roosevelt's uncertain electoral chances in Indiana. Knox saw the resolution as a clear warning to Republican candidates who might try to avoid raising the issue, and an indirect appeal to Indianapolis blacks to vote for him instead of the Republican candidate.[14]

Despite the adoption of Brown's resolution, the mood among Saint Louis delegates was clearly pro-Roosevelt, and, as it turned out, anti-Knox. The only other resolution noted in any account was offered by J. Madison Vance, "commending in the highest terms the administration and personal character of President Roosevelt," and was "adopted by a rising vote," said the *Globe-Democrat*, clearly a slap at Knox. *Palladium* editor Wheeler recounted what transpired the first night: "Many speeches were made by men who constituted a part of the old guard, better known as the true Republicans. These speeches were all complimentary to the republican party and our next president, Theodore Roosevelt. [Then] our old friend and Brother George L. Knox saw fit to give vent to his views and charge that the council were not honest in their actions."[15]

Knox's "vacillating" speech lacked a clear focus, and many listeners soon lost interest. "He said we should vote for the best man, regardless of his politics," Wheeler wrote. "Knox said that Lincoln, Grant, McKinley, and other good republicans were gone and we must make some other friends." To Republican stalwarts, who attacked Knox vigorously, this was political heresy; the Indiana editor was laughed out of the meeting. His feeble attempt days later to explain his true meaning—an opportunity granted by Steward, ever the diplomat—fared no better. "After about twenty minutes talk [Knox] failed to convince any one that he was misunderstood. He advised that we as negroes should vote for the best man, let him be democratic or republican. It is no use to try to deny his true meaning."[16]

Steward's yeomanly patience was soon rewarded. As Washington promised, the Kentucky editor was unanimously elected president in his own right, thanks to diligent advance work by Tuskegee operatives. Months earlier, Emmett Scott had enlisted Charles Anderson's assistance, emphasizing his preference for Steward. "It would be most satisfactory for us to work with [Steward] as President of the Council, rather than with the Bishop, who plans, if possible, to use the Council in promoting his own ends." "The Bishop as you know, is only Chairman of the Executive Committee," Scott wrote. "Steward is a strong, resourceful man, and will resist any encroachments which have been made by the Bishop" since Fortune's resignation.[17]

Yet Walters was not completely handicapped by pro-Steward forces. He easily won reelection as chairman of the executive committee, which also reelected Cyrus Adams as secretary. But Fortune's departure, Pledger's death, and Steward's elevation had provided the opportunity for a mass replacement of officers. Just three vice presidents were reelected—John Adams, James Lewis, and Mrs. Jeffrey—and only two other officers were returned: treasurer Thompson and secretary Cyrus Adams. The new leadership, with a distinctly midwestern flavor, included vice presidents Walter Farmer and F. F. Scott of Missouri, Settle of Tennessee, Theophilus B. Morton of California, J. Douglas Wetmore of Florida, and Allen Allensworth of Montana; Kentucky's Wallace Gaines as financial secretary; and Missouri's Cecile Rodney as corresponding secretary; S. Joe Brown of Iowa as sergeant at arms; and the Reverend D. P. Roberts of Missouri as chaplain.[18]

Interim national organizer Cosey was replaced by outgoing vice president James Guy, while corresponding secretary Fannie Williams shifted over to the literary bureau. Almost all bureau directors were replaced, except for Emmett Scott at business and Vance at legal. New bureau directors included J. R. Morris of Texas (education); the Reverend Robert T. Pollard of Alabama (ecclesiastical reform); Matthew M. Lewey of Florida (newspapers); Missourian Dr. D. W. Scott (vital statistics); and, almost improbably, George Knox at antilynching.[19]

Despite Wheeler's wishful thinking, Booker T. Washington did not attend the convention. Nor did former president Fortune, conveniently busy in New York. Absent from the speaker's podium this time was Missourian J. Milton Turner, who had previously attended to defend his Democratic loyalties, but who had switched to a pro-Roosevelt stance as the fall election approached. Also unable to attend was former Council vice president Crossland, home recovering from gunshot wounds in Saint Joseph; the onetime U.S. minister to Liberia, sent home in disgrace in 1903 after a spicy scandal in Monrovia, had been faring no better in his home state, victim of yet another jealous husband. Off to Africa were two other notable absentees: Ernest Lyon, replacing Crossland in Liberia, and new bishop Isaiah Scott, recently posted there as a missionary.[20]

Among those able but unwilling to come was McGhee, Minnesota's iconoclastic financial secretary—a post he soon relinquished—and active on the Council's legal bureau, which he continued to serve diligently. A maverick—an ardent Democrat publicly committed to supporting Roosevelt's election—McGhee had always preached Council adherence to its nonpartisan mission and, for the moment, remained on cordial terms with Washington. Yet he was alarmed by the overtly political activities of the Council of late and was drifting toward the orbit of Du Bois.[21]

McGhee may have had little encouraging to say, in any event. In late April, the Louisiana supreme court had denied the Ryanes appeal, citing the U.S. Supreme Court ruling in the first Giles case (*Giles v. Harris*, 189 U.S. 485). The state's ruling left no apparent room for appeal, dismissing the suit for lack of jurisdiction under terms of the 1898 constitution and offering no ruling on the claim that Louisiana's disfranchisement provisions violated the U.S. Constitution.[22]

The only option left seemed to be to refile the case a third time, alleging the level of monetary damages required by the court's ruling for purposes of appeal; yet its chances of success seemed marginal. The U.S. Supreme Court had since dismissed the second Giles case (*Giles v. Teasley*) on separate technical grounds—the plaintiff's failure to claim in state courts that his rights as a U.S. citizen were denied. For every new suit, a new loophole seemed to appear; after four years' work, it seemed hopeless to start over again with the Ryanes case, and to raise new funds. But neither the news of the Ryanes ruling nor of any debate over future options was widely publicized, either in Saint Louis or after, leaving many contributors to wonder how prudently funds previously raised had been spent.

As more and more old Council leaders simply drifted away, the question rankled some more than others; Harry Smith would still be bitter over the issue years later. If few of the Council's old leadership remained active delegates in 1904, Booker Washington's unseen presence had amply filled the resulting vacuum. Nowhere, perhaps, was his spirit felt more than in the Council's address to the nation, signed by Steward and a dozen other Council leaders, yet bearing Tuskegee's unmistakable imprint. The annual address condemned crime, denounced lynching, and spoke to the consciences of all Americans for racial justice—mainstays of previous addresses—but appealed, for the first time, to the nation's ministers to join the crusade against injustice and racial discrimination against Afro-Americans, trends described as "running riot" in the United States.[23]

In part, the address read as follows:

> We the representatives of more than 10,000,000 of Afro-Americans feel that we have a cause that ought to have a fair and impartial hearing at the bar of public opinion. . . . We therefore appeal to all patriotic and fair-minded citizens of all creeds and nationalities to give our cause a fair, unprejudiced and patient hearing, and render us that justice which we merit at the hands of the American people."

Moreover, the Council asked

> the people of the United States, the pulpit and the press, the state and national legislatures, to encourage crystallization of such a public sentiment and the enactment of such laws as will absolutely prohibit the perpetration of these outrages that blacken every page of the history of this country's civilization and places us in bad repute at home and abroad.
>
> We wish the American people to understand that we join hands with the best people of the country in emphasizing our condemnation of any crime against the womanhood of the land and have no sympathy for any wretch who commits such a crime [the address declared, echoing Booker Washington's "lost" words from 1903]. In the South, because of intolerance and race prejudice, a great many of its peaceful and law-abiding citizens are denied their civil and suffrage rights solely upon the ground of their color.

The continuing addition to state law of "mean, proscriptive and humiliating legislation" was decried.

> We view with alarm the rapid spread of race prejudice in this country. For a number of years an active and aggressive campaign has been waged, which seeks to arouse a spirit of race hatred in all sections of this land. Whatever may be the motive actuating those engaged in this unholy work, we wish to show our countrymen that we are the innocent victims of an unjust and an unmerited attack. . . . No one can wrong his brother without injuring himself and a community in which the moral sentiment of the people is not strong enough to restrain organized lawlessness is in danger of being engulfed.[24]

Even the backdrop for the address—the dazzling World's Fair—offered a darker moral lesson for the nation: "Here in this great city are assembled all the nations of the earth. The various races of men are coming in contact with each other. . . . This spirit of good will is shown by the kindly attention bestowed upon the Filipinos and naked Igorrotes and other dark races at the World's Fair" but denied to Afro-Americans, either in exhibits or as tourists. "Refinement and culture count for naught when the individual has African blood in his veins. Many of the Afro-Americans are stockholders in the great Louisiana Purchase Exposition, yet they are refused at many of the public places of accommodation."

Only "a quickened public sentiment" could check such rampant discrimination against the nation's black citizens. "We therefore call upon the Christian ministry everywhere to lift up their voices against this growing evil . . . . We implore the press of the country to stop magnifying our vices and say something of our virtues." Yet the Council, mindful of Tuskegee dicta, did not forget its own. "We call on every Afro-American man and woman in this broad land to teach their children moral rectitude and the practice of thrift and economy. Let us inspire respect for the law and condemn those whose lawless conduct and vicious tendencies bring shame and humiliation to the Afro-American people."[25]

Without Fortune at the helm, the Council as a group was certainly calmer, less disposed to frantic swings and unexpected bursts of activity. But if Fortune's penchant for hyperbole and provocative statements had vanished, Steward's calm restraint and diplomatic oversight bordered on lethargy. By year's end, the Council was almost invisible, in a landscape now filling with new challengers for supremacy in the volatile world of organizations concerned with civil rights and social justice for black Americans.

John Elmer Milholland's Constitutional League of the United States, for one, offered one of the nation's first truly biracial organizations, recruiting other white liberals, radicals, and a core group of talented black lawyers. The New York millionaire had amassed a fortune in the pneumatic mail-delivery business, then dabbled in newspaper publishing before becoming a racial justice advocate. During the winter of 1903 to 1904, Milholland and Andrew B. Humphrey created the Constitution League, although it only assumed a national character during the uproar over the Brownsville affair in 1906, when President Roosevelt summarily dismissed 167 black soldiers on suspicion of involvement in a Texas racial incident.[26]

Another putatively biracial organization was the National Sociological Society, founded by Jesse Lawson and others in 1903, which sought to study the condition of Afro-Americans and suggest plans for the improvement of those conditions. Lawson, the first president, and George White, executive committee chairman, convened a three-day conference in Washington, D.C., in November 1903; many of its participants paid a brief courtesy call on President Roosevelt after the conference.[27]

The only other organization with true national potential, the National Suffrage League, had begun a gradual decline after its disastrous convention in December 1903. While James Hayes maintained a cordial relationship with Washington, and sought his advice after a meeting with Roosevelt in December 1904, before pursuing an unspecified disfranchisement case, the organization was mentioned less and less.[28] William Monroe Trotter's separate New England Suffrage League, a regional magnet for anti-Washington radicals, never gained enough traction to achieve a truly national following.

The Committee of Twelve, created by Washington and Du Bois after the Carnegie Hall conference in January 1904 and underwritten by philanthropist Andrew Carnegie, struggled to establish itself as a moderate-to-conservative counterweight to Trotterite radicalism by "turning the attention of the race to the importance of constructive, progressive effort" and "emphasizing . . . points of agreement, rather than points of difference amongst us." But the Committee soon—predictably, perhaps—became simply another Tuskegee vehicle, a sort of sociopolitical counterpart to the National Negro Business League, tackling just one major civil rights project, fighting Maryland disfranchisement in 1905. Harlan calls it "a still-born racial organization."[29]

Fortune and at least four active Council members were selected as "safe" members of the Committee of Twelve, which had been announced in July. They included bishops Clinton and Isaiah Scott, the Reverend Elias Morris, and Hightower Kealing, editor of the influential *AME Church Review*. Its few "radical" members—Du Bois, Archibald Grimké, and Charles E. Bentley, with Kelly Miller as a somewhat unlikely fourth—were outvoted from the start. Du Bois resigned almost immediately, while Grimké also resigned but then changed his mind. Conspicuous among those who might have hoped to be named, but were not, was Walters.[30]

It was a blessing, perhaps, for the volatile prelate. Alarmed at the stultifying effect Washington's grip was having on the Council, the bishop now contemplated the most unorthodox move so far in an often perplexing career. More than anyone else in the Council leadership, Walters longed to break the Council free from a decaying orbit and restore both its original stature and its fading promise, as an all-inclusive group—activist if less brazenly partisan, and this time productive, but this time with himself as restored leader. Over the winter of 1904 to 1905, the once and future president daringly opened his arms to Du Bois and his emerging band of impetuous intellectuals, soon to be known as the Niagara Movement.

His strategic dance began with an overture to longtime Council critic Calvin Chase, editor of Washington's *Bee*, and ended with a virtual coup d'état nine months later in Detroit.

9

Walters Redux

Detroit, 1905

Steward's lethargy was tonic to Alexander Walters, who stepped up his campaign to reclaim Council leadership as 1904 drew to a close. His December speech before a mixed-race audience in North Carolina was followed by an informal conference of black leaders in Washington, where he embraced an emerging viewpoint on disfranchisement: that the federal government, through Congress, should force southern states to apply suffrage restrictions equally to both races. "What the negro wants and what he contends for is that his franchise be restored to him," Walters told listeners in Edenton. "If that cannot be done, let the Federal Government see that the revised constitutions in the South be applied to both the white man and the negro."[1]

It was a jarring change of both direction and tactics for Walters, who had endorsed restricted suffrage, if reasonably applied, as early as 1900, but had always pushed the threat of reduction in representation—allowed under the Fourteenth Amendment, and proposed in the Crumpacker bill. Reducing southern representation, long the preferred remedy among most black leaders, remained a tool, as he told one white questioner. But by implication, it was now a secondary goal, to be sought only if southern states refused to eliminate discriminatory rules like the hated "grandfather clause." The Fifteenth Amendment offered a different route, barring any discrimination against voters on account of race. Originally enacted to remove the Fourteenth Amendment "loophole," under which states refusing to enfranchise black voters could simply accept reduced representation instead, its provisions could legally be enforced by Congress with "appropriate legislation." (States retained the right to define and restrict the franchise, so long as race was not a criterion.)[2]

Theoretically, Congress could order southern states to stop discriminating against black voters, and if they refused, then reduce representation. Yet problems existed with this approach, which Walters presumably did not detail. While considerable (though not majority) support existed for punitive reduction in Congress, simply allowing a state to accept reduced representation was problematic. The South might declare moral victory, since disfranchisement would then be sanctioned as acceptable. No federal election laws existed, the last ones having been repealed in 1893. And state suffrage restrictions, such as the "grandfather clause"— distasteful at best and arguably immoral (or unconstitutional) at worst—would remain on the books; the Supreme Court openly viewed them as "political," and beyond the judiciary's reach.

Walters amplified his view in Washington, where he analyzed President Roosevelt's position on the question. "The South is endeavoring to flirt with and deceive the President," Walters told one hundred "representative colored men" in Calvin Chase's law office. "The time has come for the negro to act and define a policy that will be effective." Walters's strategic movement toward the Fifteenth Amendment may have pleased some listeners. It certainly should have pleased Fortune, who had long argued that reducing southern representation was counterproductive. For different reasons, it should also have pleased those to whom Walters was now reaching out: the emerging Niagara Movement, whose members still advocated reduction of representation under the Fourteenth Amendment.[3]

But it may not have sat so well with conservative Council members, including Washington, who, whether publicly or secretly, much preferred court lawsuits, and the noble sanction of a definitive ruling, to reduction of representation—or by extension, to any punitive legislative action, perhaps fearing a white backlash against reinstated black voters. The Council's annual messages had typically accepted reasonable suffrage restrictions but insisted (as in 1902) that restrictions "apply to all citizens alike." The Council's legal challenges to disfranchisement had generally been couched in language asserting that state actions violated the letter and spirit of both amendments, as in the cases in Alabama and Louisiana—by denying equal protection of the laws (Fourteenth) and by discriminating on the basis of race (Fifteenth).

In his letter to the *New York Age* in early January, Walters went farther to distance himself from the existing Council by announcing that Congress must pass legislation forcing disfranchising states to apply their laws to both races. While he had once favored punishing states who passed such restrictive laws by "reduction of Southern representation in Congress," he had now—apparently just since December—changed his mind. "After serious thought I was convinced that the Fifteenth Amendment was passed to strengthen, if not supersede, that part of the Fourteenth Amendment which refers to the franchise of Afro-Americans, and I came to the conclusion that for Congress to reduce Southern representation would legalize our disfranchisement and in the end would prove ruinous to the race," Walters declared, all but quoting Tim Fortune.[4]

"The duty of Congress is to pass such legislation as will make the law apply to white and black men alike in the States where there is a restricted ballot," he continued. Only if this did not happen should representation be reduced, "for they ought not to be allowed to retain their seats forever on a false representation basis." With this letter, Walters had staked out controversial stances on two important issues and indicated his unmistakable desire to resume control of his old organization—and the civil rights movement. In a second letter, dated in January but printed by the *Age* in early March, he made clear that this foundering vehicle would be reborn as a broad, center-left coalition, with room for moderates and conservatives—but freed from Tuskegee's imprint.[5]

How Tim Fortune came into possession of the circular appearing in the March 9 *Age* he never explained. Its contents were no secret to anyone watching events among the fairly small sphere of anti-Bookerites headed by Trotter, and newsworthy only to those not informed by Tuskegee's network of spies and tipsters, like Fortune. The once-close alliance between Washington and Fortune was fraying, although the editor remained faithful on most issues. Yet why he printed this letter at all—and why he chose the date he did—are far less clear; he probably acted impetuously, and alone. Certainly Walters did not put him up to it, and Washington would hardly have suggested it, for it served no useful purpose to either man.

In his brief preface, Fortune claimed that the letter vindicated his position on reduction of representation in Congress by southern states who had disfranchised black voters. "It is chiefly interesting as a revelation of the fact that certain people who have been rabidly advocating a reduction of Southern representation as a remedy for disfranchisement seem to have been for some time of The Age's opinion that such action would be suicidal, and to have been convinced that any action taken should be based on the Fifteenth Amendment," Fortune wrote.[6]

"The Age is gratified that its campaign . . . is being recognized more and more as wise and farsighted, and will heartily back up any action along the lines indicated in this letter." Self-congratulation, so necessary to Fortune's massive ego, was a shallow reason for dredging up a cold story. The circular, signed by Walters and Professor Kelly Miller, was dated January 13, when the two had met with a group of anti-Washington dissenters in Trotter's Boston office. That was old news, as was Walters's conversion to the Fortune position on disfranchisement remedies, already announced in his January 12 letter.[7]

The only timely information, in fact, lay in Walters's public announcement that a "committee of representative men should visit the President and present broad lines of policy which we desire him to pursue concerning the colored race," selected strictly from the ranks of men with no personal agenda ("It is thought best not to include any known office seeker or office holder on the committee"). This White House meeting had not yet occurred, pending Roosevelt's March 4 inauguration. But this was no secret, either; Washington, New York, and Tuskegee had been abuzz for weeks over plans for the Walters-Miller preparatory conference.[8]

As to just what the delegation would propose to the president, "three definite propositions have been suggested," Walters wrote. The first concerned the use of the Fifteenth amendment by the U.S. Attorney General as the basis for "cases that may be brought in the Supreme Court, testing the constitutionality of the Revised Constitutions of the South." The second envisioned asking Roosevelt's administration to wield its influence "to carry out the Interstate Commerce Clause of the Constitution affecting interstate traffic, including the passenger service," combating the growth of "Jim Crow" railroad cars. A third concerned national aid to education "in the most needy States." Although in line with original Council goals, the new group's stated objectives should also have sounded familiar to members of the New England Suffrage League, mirroring that group's resolutions approved at its organizational meeting in October 1904.[9]

By mid-February, the requests had gone out to Roosevelt, Whitefield McKinlay told Tuskegee after meeting with Miller. "I got the following names without [Miller] suspecting my object," McKinlay wrote. "Bishop [Abraham] Grant will probably attend the Conference at [Miller's] home tho he did not sign the memorial which has been sent to the Presdt." McKinlay was invited, as were Trotter, Du Bois, Corrothers, Archibald Grimké, John W. E. Bowen, the Reverend H. T. Johnson, and D. Augustus Straker.[10]

True to his word, Walters had included no political appointees—even excluding such Republican stalwarts as Dancy, Terrell, Lyons, and Pinchback—but McKinlay promised to "do all in my power to have Pinchback there" as a backup. Nor was Fortune to be invited. Walters's March 9 wish list in the *Age* had envisioned "about fifteen or twenty men to make up the conference," including those McKinlay named plus a dozen more: Samuel G. Atkins, Harry Smith, Josiah Settle, George Jackson, John Clifford, J. Douglas Wetmore, G. N. Grisham, and several ministers, the best-known of whom was the Reverend Owen M. Waller. Walters and four others—Du Bois, Miller, Brown, and Bishop Grant—would handle arrangements, joined by volunteers from the field.[11]

They were the nucleus of what Walters secretly hoped would become the "new" National Afro-American Council. Surprisingly, or perhaps not, few active Council members were asked to be present at the creation; less surprising was the exclusion, except for Miller, of any sitting members of the Committee of Twelve. Grimké and Du Bois had resigned from that committee almost immediately, although Grimké had repented briefly, and Du Bois had left the Council in disgust in 1902. Of those on the new Walters list, only Settle and Wetmore were active Council officers, as vice presidents, elected in Missouri. A few others, now inactive, had once held Council offices—Harry Smith, George Jackson, and the Reverend H. T. Johnson—and Clifford had served on the executive committee as late as 1903.

Walters's daring experiment would not succeed; little was heard of his memorial, and there is no evidence that the Roosevelt meeting ever came off. Tuskegee continued to hold its singular position at the White House, refusing to be supplanted as Roosevelt's black think tank by any self-appointed committee, especially one including the ill-tempered Trotter—or the blasphemer Du Bois, whose sensational new charges of hush-money payments to the press by Tuskegee had just aired in January, in *Voice of the Negro.* Washington denied the charges, but his credibility was damaged nonetheless.[12]

But Walters had given notice of his intentions, and as the next meeting of the Council drew nearer, he quietly consolidated his position. In mid-July he sent out an unusual letter to more than six dozen Afro-American leaders, many of them former Council supporters who had fallen away. Some, like Bishop Arnett, Daniel Murray, Lyons, and Dancy, had probably felt ignored for too long and stopped attending meetings; others, like White, Lawson, and both Barnetts, had been shown the door by circumstance and were unlikely to return. A few, like Chase and Francis Grimké, had criticized the Council almost from the start, while McGhee and others (including William H. Lewis) had once been members of the faithful in-house opposition.

The bishop was careful to throw his nets wide, to cover all bets and offend no one—except reckless members of the new Niagara Movement, of whom McGhee was the only member invited. The first names on the list were those of former president Fortune and Washington, and the letter sought to reinforce Council ties with Bookerites Samuel Laing Williams, Charles Anderson, Walter Cohen, and Isaiah Montgomery. Yet almost inexplicably, some—not all—current officers were included, such as vice presidents Mrs. Jeffrey, Wetmore, and Settle, national organizer Guy, and bureau directors Williams and Lewey.

Most of its former national organizers—Wells-Barnett, Clinton, and Cosey—were recruited (Ernest Lyon and James Hayes were omitted), along with former chaplains (J. S. Caldwell, Walter Brooks), vice presidents (Gertrude Mossell, Elias Morris, George Lee, bishops Holsey and Harris), and bureau directors (Pinchback, Madison Mason, J. C. Jason, William Vernon, and Bishop Turner). Almost everyone who had ever attended a Council meeting, from former officers to onlookers, received a copy. Almost anyone likely to help—and some who were unlikely—was named; some had more than one reason for inclusion. For instance, invitations went to half the Committee of Twelve (Grimké and Miller, plus Anderson, Fortune, Kealing, and Elias Morris), as well as to some on Walters's abortive January list (Bowen and Clifford, plus Corrothers, Grant, and Waller). On this later list, prominent political appointees were featured: Judge Terrell, Crum, Anderson, and Lewis.[13]

Walters asked these addressees, and "other friends of the Afro-American Council, who have been somewhat indifferent, of late, to the work of this organization," to hear him out. Recent racial unrest in New York and lynchings in Georgia were the tip of a dangerous iceberg of long-term discrimination and violence. "The 'Jim Crowing' of the street cars of the leading cities of the South, and the peculiar political condition of helplessness into which the race has fallen" were a wake-up call to both "the derelict members of the Afro-American Council and the friends of fair play." Critics who claimed the Council had never been effective were simply mistaken. "I know of no civic organization in our history that, through annual addresses sent to the public, has done so much to create favorable public sentiment as the Afro-American Council," Walters wrote. "What other organization of Afro-Americans has had the hardihood to . . . criticize openly and above board the President (Mr. McKinley) for refusing to make some utterance against the massacre at Wilmington, N.C."[14]

Only the Council had dared to call McKinley's hand in 1898 and persuade him to speak out against lynching: "He said he had been advised by some prominent Negroes to keep quiet on the subject, but promised in his next message to Congress that he would advise against lynchers. He kept his word," Walters recalled. The Council had then become the first race group to institute test cases against disfranchisement in southern states and had even managed to convince President Roosevelt to denounce "the Lily-Whiteism of the South. Indeed, representatives of this body were present at the White House when his manifesto breaking the back-bone of this heresy was issued."

Those were the glory days of the Council's greatest strength, when it owned "the respect of the President, and of the leading men of the Nation. The leading daily papers gave adequate space to the addresses issued by the Council, with proper editorial discussion." Yet from the start, not every Afro-American leader had favored the Council, and self-doubt had plagued its leaders, who had finally relinquished control to a "certain coterie of would-be-leaders" claiming, erroneously, that the Council "did not meet the needs of the hour." While Walters did not name these "wise-acres," as he called them, the implication was not reassuring to the Tuskegee Machine, which had handpicked most of the officers from 1902 on. The new leaders, in any event, had failed to form a better organization, as promised, Walters charged.

"Up to this writing all their efforts have proved abortive. They tried utterly to destroy what had been accomplished and have not been able to organize anything to take its place." Now it was time for "the men who gave the Council such unselfish support [to] take hold again," starting in Detroit.[15] What Walters was attempting to do was reboot the original Council, bringing almost all viewpoints together in an active forum, without restrictions imposed by Tuskegee and, perhaps, without the original nonpartisan blinders of 1898. His vision of the past was oddly selective, since the Council's top-heavy leadership had bickered repeatedly, its hired lawyers had won no major court cases, and no one had ever managed to organize the hundreds of local councils Fortune had thought necessary.

Only Booker T. Washington's 1902 intervention had kept the Council from disintegrating, but at the cost of its independence and vitality. Could the Council be resurrected as a bridge between the splintering factions of the race, or was it too late? Could it somehow ward off the challenge of a well-organized opposition—the nascent Niagarites—or would it perish trying? Was the Council a new creature, or a nineteenth-century dinosaur in a twentieth-century world?

The Niagara Movement had sprung into action in Canada's Fort Erie a fortnight earlier, after weeks of planning by Du Bois and Trotter. More than two dozen carefully chosen men had shown up in response to Du Bois's call for "organized determination and aggressive action on the part of men who believe in Negro freedom and growth" and who shared his opposition to "present methods of strangling honest criticism"—that is, Tuskegee's attempts at generalized mind control. According to David Levering Lewis, the call's signers had represented "the vanguard of the Talented Tenth—educators, lawyers, publishers, physicians, ministers, and several businessmen secure enough in their professions and principles to risk Booker T. Washington's retribution."[16]

If Du Bois could no longer be brought back into the fold, there were still other Niagara sympathizers who might yet be weaned away. McGhee turned up at the first meeting, along with Harry Smith; Waller and Clifford would be among those attending the second conference a year later. Walters could lure none of them to Detroit, as it turned out, but he hoped to prevent the outward trickle from turning into a flood. And despite McGhee's deepening estrangement from the Council, Walters seemed to be holding the line. In mid-August, McGhee's angry open letter to Walters dredged up the whole sorry story of Louisville's supposedly stolen election, fairly leaping off the *Bee*'s pages: "How unmixed was the bad faith practiced with this faithful and trustful people and when treachery had run its full course, faithfully did I point out to you and begged even then for an honorable chance to save it, to no avail."[17]

McGhee still believed that Walters had betrayed him by not allowing entry of the full forces of the Suffrage League, when McGhee's naïve but honorable intent was "to save the whole from its ruin"—by hijacking the Council in 1903, in concert with Trotter. As he hinted so bitterly, how could anyone expect him to return to the scene of his humiliation? If McGhee's heartfelt letter came off, instead, as dark comedy—almost farce—replayed to a national audience, only the cynical Calvin Chase would have agreed to print it, two years later. The official call for the Detroit session, set for late August, contained much of the language of Walters's July appeal to the old guard. Signed by Steward, Cyrus Adams, and Walters, the longer letter—published in the *Age* on August 3 and the *Bee* two days later—also included both traditional membership information and a provocative call to arms, to friends and strangers alike:

> The hostility upon the part of the enemies of the race has been so persistent that many of our friends have become timid and indifferent in our defence. It is with the view of combating this opposition of our enemies, strengthening the hands of our friends, and working for the absolute undoing of all discriminations against the race, that this meeting is to be held, and we ask the hearty cooperation of every Afro-American who is interested in the welfare of the race.[18]

"It is our earnest desire that every church, college, benevolent society and other organizations send representatives," the leaders asserted. Disfranchisement was expected to be "the paramount question" of the convention, which planners hoped to be the largest ever held. And for those who had never visited Detroit, special rail fares were available, and the local citizens "are preparing to entertain the Council in first class style."[19]

A slightly different version, in Chase's *Bee*, contained an additional caveat—a reminder to all speakers and a warning to the long-winded: "By the action of the Afro-American Council, each speaker is limited to twenty minutes, and in view of the fact that a portion of the Caucasian press of the country is ever ready to misrepresent the words of Afro-Americans, all speeches must be in manuscript, in order that there may be absolute proof of just what each speaker said."[20]

By 1910, Detroit would become the nation's ninth-largest city, with just under half a million residents. The sprawling industrial and commercial center, founded as a French fort two centuries earlier, was now the largest U.S. city on the Canadian border, and home to the infant automobile industry beginning to beckon black emigrants from the South. Its Afro-American population accounted for just over 1 percent of the city's population, yet that small portion had succeeded in achieving significant political power, regularly electing a black member of the Michigan legislature. The Afro-American community was served by one local newspaper, the *Informer*, edited by F. H. Warren, and a number of local attorneys, the best-known of whom was David Augustus Straker, former president of the National Federation of Colored Men.[21]

Just before the Council opened on August 30, the nation's black editors gathered in Detroit for their now biennial meeting, reelecting Cyrus Adams as president while enlarging the AAPA's governing structure. Without a vice president since Pledger's death eighteen month earlier, the press association now emulated the Council by choosing five to succeed him, among them Council president Steward and Washington's aide, Emmett Scott (representing the *Tuskegee Student*). Its executive committee was expanded from six to thirty-five members, representing two dozen jurisdictions.[22]

Journalists heard speeches by Council activists and other leaders, including treasurer Thompson, Samuel Laing Williams, Wetmore, Mary Church Terrell, and Wilberforce University professor William S. Scarborough. The Council's address to the nation scored "a thoroughly organized movement . . . working with malignant energy to utterly destroy the civil and political rights of those for whom we stand in part as spokesmen" and denied that the United States was "a white man's country." The group denied that "the granting of suffrage to the race was a mistake, and we deny the charge that it has proved a failure. In a republic there can be but one kind of citizen, hence we deny the right of the government—general, state, or local—to discriminate in any way between citizens."

The editors denounced mob law ("a crime more dangerous to the well-being and perpetuity of society than the infractions of law by individuals") and deplored the "decadence of true Christianity in the United States" for failing to speak out forcefully on lynching, before concluding with a ringing endorsement of Roosevelt. "We heartily commend the brave and patriotic position taken by President Roosevelt in the enforcement of the Federal Constitution and the laws based upon it. His words and deeds stand out in bold relief in these times." But if the editors had no problem with praising Roosevelt, the Council was determined to be more circumspect—and less reminiscent of its recent past—by somehow avoiding rancorous political debates. Endorsing Roosevelt's successful diplomacy in helping end the Russo-Japanese War turned out to be the key. The Council opened its own session by congratulating him "upon the signal success which has crowned your wise efforts to promote the peace of the world in the happy conclusion of negotiations between the Russian and Japanese envoys at Portsmouth."[23]

Detroit's Republican mayor, George Pierre Codd, warmly welcomed delegates and visitors at the first evening session, along with recorder's court judge Alfred J. Murphy. Both "paid a high tribute to the colored race," reported the *Free Press*, which opened its friendly account of the day's events with the text of the Roosevelt telegram. But this was a day intended primarily for speeches, presumably within time limits, with thoughtful words offered by familiar speakers and newcomers alike. Robert C. Barnes welcomed delegates on behalf of the local committee, after which responses came from former president Fortune; Mrs. Jeffrey, vice president; and executive committee chairman Walters. Last were remarks from President Steward and rising stars James Napier and Mary Church Terrell, before the evening concluded with "an excellent musical program . . . given by local talent."[24]

It was Mollie Terrell's first appearance at a Council meeting in several years, and she recalled it in some detail in her diary (if not in her memoirs, written thirty years later). Her speech made a memorable impression on Straker, she wrote; he "referred to me as the Daniel Webster of the day," an honor she quietly asked be stricken from the minutes. Terrell herself preferred the oratory of William H. Lewis ("a masterpiece") and praised the "very eloquent" speech of Andrew Humphrey, whom she met for the first time in Michigan. A popular figure and former local officer, she now became a national leader in the Council, noting "They have put me on several councils, and placed me at the head of the antilynching bureau," overlooking her separate election as fourth vice president.[25]

The second day featured discussions of the serious topics outlined in Walters's July call, from disfranchisement and lynching to the quest for equal rights. Boston's Lewis, originally recruited to the Council by Booker T. Washington, reportedly delivered a "masterful oration" to an overflowing crowd at the city's Bethel AME Church, candidly unveiling the Walters vision of a new, activist Council. "What is the negro today?" Lewis asked rhetorically. "Nothing but a nondescript, an alien. People say, 'leave the negro problem to the south.' What is the result? Lynch law and disfranchisement," said the assistant U.S. district attorney. "In the north we cry for equal rights, and where does our plea find its response? We must have peace, and it must be the peace of right, not of injustice. . . . There can be no political inequality in this country, and it is left to the negro to work out his own salvation."[26]

Wetmore, the energetic Florida civil rights attorney and Jacksonville city council member, agreed with his Massachusetts colleague. Without the right to vote, "the negro is helpless," he indicated. "Let us have the disfranchisement laws of the south examined by constitutional lawyers, and let us fight them in the highest courts of the country." Detroit activist Walter H. Stowers expanded on the same theme, declaring that the South "has an organized bureau whose sole object is to run down the negro race" and which must be thwarted by legal action. Other speakers included Professor Scarborough, Charlotte, North Carolina; minister George Clement; veteran activist Bishop George Clinton; and a raft of local residents, including Straker, Mrs. Mary McCoy, and Mrs. Lucy Thurman.[27]

One of the few white speakers was Humphrey, a Constitution League adherent and author of the 1904 Republican platform plank on disfranchisement. While Humphrey's remarks in Detroit are not available, he very likely took a strong stance on reduction of congressional representation for disfranchising states, in light of his developing feud with Lewis over the best solution for disfranchisement. In a later address before the New England Suffrage League, Humphrey criticized Lewis's Detroit speech, sparking a brief battle on the front page of Fortune's *Age*. Like Lewis, a majority of the new Council believed that reducing southern representation in Congress would be counterproductive; Humphrey, conversely, advocated punitive reduction of representation. Lewis, who said he was not allowed to respond to Humphrey at the league meeting, found Humphrey's remarks "amusing" but unconvincing, he wrote in the *Age*.[28]

If the purpose of such orations as the Council witnessed was to stir up thirst for new leadership in a staid, stale organization, the speakers succeeded admirably. While overall attendance at the convention was down somewhat from its peak—just seventy-five paid delegates—those who attended were nonetheless enthusiastic, overwhelmingly supporting Walters's return. Steward, perhaps preoccupied by the needs of the college he served as acting head, was gently shunted aside—to the less powerful executive committee chair—in what seemed a Walters juggernaut. Walters was unanimously ratified as the new president, and just one vice president—the venerable Mrs. Jeffrey, selected for a fourth term—was returned to office, accompanied by Thompson, so far the Council's only treasurer, and Cyrus Adams, secretary.[29] Onetime national organizer Clinton and former vice president Lewis were recalled to service in those positions, while a handful of other current and former officers were recycled into new positions: Wetmore as legal bureau director, S. Joe Brown as emigration bureau director, and Fannie Williams as literary bureau director. Former chaplain Lewis Jordan became corresponding secretary. But the list of brand-new officers was long and nearly overwhelming, with a decided mix of ideologies. Some were committed followers of Tuskegee, others friendly but noncommittal to the Wizard. From Tennessee attorney Napier, onetime congressional candidate, and New York's Fred Chew—a Suffrage League leader—to former Texas legislator Robert L. Smith and Ohio's Scarborough, the list also represented a broad new geographic range for a new generation of leaders. Mrs. Terrell, best known for her earlier work at the National Association of Colored Women, joined Cassander Sellers of Des Moines and Detroit wunderkind Stowers as next-in-command to the triumphant bishop.

The new chaplain, Ohio's Edward L. Gilliam, and assistant secretary William Sinclair of Philadelphia were relative unknowns nationally. Bureau directors also featured mostly new faces, with Mrs. Terrell assigned to the antilynching bureau, Kealing the educational bureau, Richard Thompson to newspapers, and Michigander Dr. J. W. Ames to vital statistics. Madison Mason was brought back to head up ecclesiastical reform, in addition to Brown (emigration) and Mrs. Williams (literary).[30]

It was a new leadership for a new, more activist era, and nowhere was the new spirit more apparent than in the practical tone of the Council's annual address to the nation. If the Council placed its private trust in God to restore, gradually, a balance to the nation's attitudes toward "a persistent and judicious contention for equal and exact justice," the public need for legal action on certain fronts—primarily to test disfranchisement laws—remained imperative. "We feel that we are part and parcel of the American people in thought and effort and aspiration, and that what benefits them benefits us, and that what injures them injures us," the address read. "We therefore ask for justice and fair play under the laws as a legal right, and for an 'open door of opportunity' in the effort we are making for moral, social and material betterment as a common right which cannot be withheld from us without injury to the whole American people. A reunition of national sentiment which does not include the Afro-American people will prove in the end as much of a delusion and a snare as the long and acrimonious effort to keep the nation half free and half slave."[31]

Past agitation on the issue of lynching had led, in part, to "an appreciable falling off in the prevalence of this demoralizing species of lawlessness," the address continued. By banding together and helping finance anti-disfranchisement efforts, Afro-Americans could help defeat "all laws of state which deny to them the equal benefits of protection of government as guaranteed by the federal constitution." The address also urged greater support for education among Afro-Americans—"both of industrial and higher education"—and called attention to a less-noticed issue: the pressing need for prison reform in the South. A frank national debate was encouraged on the controversial issue of emigration from the South—preached by some Afro-American leaders "because of vicious laws and public opinion" in the South, but complicated by both climatic and economic obstacles to successful resettlement elsewhere.

"It is a long way from the slave pen to the creditable mental, moral and material status which the Afro-American people occupy today in all parts of the Republic," the address concluded. Yet buoyed by "the manly courage that laughs at obstacles that annoy but cannot hinder us in the upward movement of higher living" and the religious faith of their ancestors, America's black citizens could fully expect one day to "rest securely within the folds of the star-spangled banner, the greatest and proudest emblem of sovereignty that floats above a free people."[32]

Walters took great pride in the wording of the address, which he described to the *Free Press* afterward as "the appeal of the black man to his fellow American. . . . We state there the position of the two races as we understand it, and make our plea to the races concerned as to bettering the relations between them." Yet for Walters, it was also a signal to his own race of his new commitment to leadership—and of his slow but steady movement away from domination by Tuskegee. His primary goal was to keep the Niagara Movement as weak as possible by siphoning off possible support from the undecided. To help keep the new Council stable, Walters still needed Tuskegee's help and had no desire to antagonize Washington by asserting complete independence—at least, not yet. That much was obvious from ongoing correspondence and conversations with others, including Richard Thompson, now in Indiana. Thompson told Emmett Scott by letter in early August that the bishop intended to "kill off the Niagara movement" in Detroit, not oppose the Wizard.[33]

"He, the Bishop, is with you now till death," Scott then assured Washington. Based on Thompson's words, Scott believed that Walters—while "mercurial in temperament"—was trustworthy ("I feel sure he will be disposed to stick since he was crowded out of recognition by the other fellows"). Weeks later, Thompson repeated his analysis to Scott: "Walters is in line and I believe he will 'tote squar' from this on, if he has not done so in the past."[34] Part of this strategy had to do with separate issues on the bishop's agenda, such as his desire to obtain a federal appointment—in this case, as minister to Haiti—for Fortune, perhaps to help out the beleaguered journalist, or remove a possible future challenger. (Fortune did not receive the appointment, which went instead to veteran diplomat Henry Furniss.) How long the new arrangement might last was, in any case, almost entirely up to Alexander Walters.

Black newspapers around the nation were generally favorable in their coverage of both the convention and its aftermath. Despite his own past differences with

Walters, Fortune said nothing critical about the Council's new direction in the *Age*, saying, in fact, very little at all. His only significant comments after Detroit related to the "unjustifiable" criticism being leveled at James Napier for remarks made there regarding "the facts with reference to the conditions in the South." Napier, the new first vice president of the Council and a longtime supporter of Booker T. Washington, strongly advocated improved relations between the races and was a sharp critic of northern agitators like Trotter. "No man is in a better position to know the facts or to state the facts in a given case than Mr. Napier," Fortune wrote. "Our people should be very careful how they attempt to weaken the influence of men of [his] character."[35]

The Indianapolis *Freeman*, obviously pleased by Walters's return, endorsed the Council's action in its Washington-based news column as "in accord with the eternal fitness of things. No stronger man could have been chosen," wrote George Knox. "He has the confidence of all classes of people, and they will rally more enthusiastically under the Council's banner now that he is again at the helm." In its most enthusiastic comment in recent years, the *Freeman* went on to praise the Council, which "has the advantage of being a body that 'does things' and refuses to be content with issuing a rhetorical address and adjourning sine die. It will carry the questions of disfranchisement, Jim Crow cars, and other unspeakable discriminations to the court of last resort. It believes in the doctrine of self-help—and what is more to the point—it practices what it preaches."[36]

As he mulled the future of the revitalized Council, Walters also celebrated the birth of a new son. He and his third wife, Lelia, returned to their native Kentucky with the child—his sixth—in the fall of 1905, taking a triumphant tour of Louisville and Bardstown, where both the bishop and his wife had grown up. Two years had passed since the Louisville convention, when his powerful presence had been largely muffled by a petulant Fortune. This tour was covered at length by the *Age*, which noted Walters's rise "from a plough-boy to be the best-known Afro-American prelate."[37]

At every stop, Walters praised the Council's work to listeners, including well-attended lectures before the Foreign Mission Society and Louisville Ministers' Alliance, and was "received with a hospitality warm even for Kentucky," wrote an *Age* correspondent, traveling along. In Bardstown, Walters drew a large interracial audience for his address entitled "The Holy Land," inspired by a visit there in 1889. But if Walters's vision of a modern Canaan was to be realized, it would take more than compelling memories. The new Council must prove itself effective and productive, in order to win back faltering former members while stamping out Niagara brush fires on its left flank. Even as he traveled, Walters pondered the best strategy, working closely with Lewis Jordan, his energetic new corresponding secretary, and Wetmore, heading up the Council's legal bureau.

At year's end, a lengthy message went out from Secretary Jordan, publicizing the Council's recent good works and seeking financial support for future ones. Reprinted as a circular by the *Freeman*, among others, the letter offered a revealing self-portrait of the "new Council," or a group that had "purged itself," as Jordan put it. "The Council is non-partisan, nonsectarian, and stands for principles, not men, for the race and not for politicians," he declared. "Whatever may have been charged as a mistake in the past, the Council at its Detroit meeting purged itself and declared that it would forever stand on its original platform and begin anew the defense for the civil and political rights of the race."[38]

Its only handicap now was the legal bureau's "want for food"—sufficient funds—to "test cases constantly put into our hands." Nearly $300 had been raised in Detroit to help test Jim Crow laws, but far more was needed. Jordan gave three small examples of nonjudicial solutions involving illegal discrimination in which Jordan's complaints had produced written responses from those in authority: the posting of "Jim Crow" signs aboard Baltimore and Ohio railroad trains originating in Missouri, where no separate-car law existed; the embarrassment of Afro-American women by a conductor on the Chesapeake and Ohio railroad; and a third, unspecified "case of discrimination" reported in a Louisville newspaper.

Each recent instance had been satisfactorily resolved: railroad car signs were removed, the conductor was admonished, and the newspaper publisher acknowledged Jordan's complaint as valid, with responses reprinted as proof. "I give these three letters to show what the Council is doing to carry out the work for which it was organized," he wrote. Standing up for the rights of the race was a fitting memorial to the legacy of the great abolitionist William Lloyd Garrison, the centennial of whose birth was being observed that same month. "We would be unworthy of this great friend, whose sacrifices and sufferings for us are without parallel in history, if we sit down and allow ourselves to be manacled again," Jordan wrote.

But could the Council simply be more successful through local persistence? The three small cases cited here contrasted to earlier, large-scale cases that the Council had either helped finance or supported, two of which had failed—the "gallant fight contesting the Louisiana disfranchisement law" in 1902, and the "herculean" efforts to overturn the Alabama disfranchisement law, *Giles v. Harris* (1903) and *Giles v. Teasley* (1904), which had reached the U.S. Supreme Court. Little had been heard of the Louisiana test case since 1903, including its barely publicized dismissal in 1904 by the Louisiana supreme court, and the oversight still puzzled many Council members. The Giles cases, financed in large part—if secretly so—by Tuskegee, had been thrown out by the U.S. high court on technicalities, but it had at least brought valuable publicity to the cause.[39]

A more successful effort undertaken by Wetmore and Florida's state council in 1905 had nullified separate-car laws there by having the laws declared unconstitutional in the state's supreme court. Streetcar boycotts had been called off by victorious litigants in Jacksonville and Pensacola, but even there, the battle continued. "Our fight is one that must go on until we are free from every discriminating law. Now, to make this fight, it takes money," Jordan continued. "As we write you this letter, our legal adviser has a case in hand in Pensacola, Fla., [where] the city aims to enforce the 'Jim Crow' street car law, despite its unconstitutionality. The 13th Amendment to the United States Constitution, which made us free, the 14th which made us men and the 15th which made us citizens, are on trial as never before."[40]

On trial in another venue—the court of public opinion—was the future of the Council.

10

Competing with Niagara

New York City, 1906

Until 1905, the Council had faced only minor opposition from poorly organized malcontents, like Trotter. The Niagara Movement, which many believed had spurred Walters to his successful return in Detroit, was an entirely different creature: spirited, seemingly united, and unpredictable. Former Council leaders had defected in small but unprecedented numbers to the far more glamorous ranks of the Du Bois crowd, which yet had the potential to emerge as a more appealing alternative to rank-and-file Council members. How best to blunt the threat?

One way lay in improved communications, as corresponding secretary Lewis Jordan wrote in early 1906, proposing an innovative public relations strategy to Tuskegee: "a little semi-monthly paper in the interest of the Council." Such a project was "almost a necessity," Jordan told Emmett Scott, if the Council was to compete successfully against the *Moon*, brand-new "mouthpiece of the Niagara Movement." W. E. B. Du Bois's illustrated weekly venture, unveiled in late 1905, seemed destined to "become very readable," in his opinion. He had "some ideas about a journal along this line that would appeal to readers white and black, north and south" and would happily serve as editor, unless Scott and Richard Thompson wanted to share the job. Such a journal could support itself "with a little effort" and should cost very little to launch. "Could you suggest the feasibility of Mr. Washington taking any interest in such a journal?"[1]

The journal was a far cry from the national Council newspaper Pledger had once championed, and Jordan a far less likely choice for an editor. The Baptist minister had experience—a decade editing the National Baptist Convention's *Mission Herald*—but little clout, just life membership in the National Negro Business League and service on the executive committee. And despite his energy, not everyone had a high opinion of Jordan's talents; just days later, undercover Tuskegee operative Melvin Jack Chisum bluntly labeled him "a dangerous little tramp."[2]

Presumably, Walters knew of Jordan's proposal, and he encouraged it. The bishop spent much time talking up Council virtues to editors and local audiences alike and relished good publicity, even running signed articles in such places as the *Colored American Magazine*, which carried his lengthy preconvention article that fall. Yet fewer and fewer opportunities existed. One reliable outlet, Edward Cooper's *Colored American* newspaper, had folded in 1904, and the *Age*, while still helpful, was smaller and less effusive since Fortune left the Council.

No record exists of Scott's reply, or of Washington's reaction to the proposal. By mid-summer, Jordan's strongest rationale had vanished, along with the short-lived *Moon*, which failed to attract readers and stopped printing before the Council met. Washington was more concerned with a far more serious threat—the *Voice of the Negro*, edited by J. Max Barber, increasingly a Du Bois admirer. The *Voice* had existed since early 1904, with Washington's initial support, but its increasingly independent line during 1905 had provoked a fatal retaliation by the Tuskegee Machine, and by 1907 it also was gone.[3] If objectionable to the Wizard, the *Voice* posed no open threat to the Council. But the Niagara Movement was attracting far more attention—favorable or not—among the ranks of black editors, and obscuring the Council in some readers' eyes.

Still, at least one black newspaper, the *Freeman*, was saying good things about the Council in early 1906. Wetmore and Jordan had plans to fight a segregated railway car running into Washington, D.C., from the Virginia suburb of Alexandria, George Knox noted in an editorial. "It is an outrage to allow that Jim Crow weed to flourish under the very shadow of our national capital. . . . Let the fight go on and let all who are interested in the overthrow of unjust legislation join Secretary Jordan and Attorney Wetmore in their effort for our racial betterment."[4]

Jordan's optimistic suggestion came to naught; no new publication would be dedicated to the Council. If Walters and team hoped to publicize Council accomplishments and burnish its image among Afro-Americans, their path would not run through Tuskegee. Whatever "buzz" they might generate would have to be carried out through a grassroots appeal.

To reach the public, the Council needed to prove it could work well with—or outperform—competitors like John Milholland's biracial Constitution League, which held its well-publicized organizational meeting in New York City on February 1. A crowd of some three thousand persons—four-fifths black—had congregated at the Cooper Union to hear such speakers as Du Bois, ex-congressman George White, Mary Terrell, and Kelly Miller—and Archibald Grimké, whom Milholland had recruited, indirectly, via correspondence with Tuskegee.[5]

The meeting's theme was "Suffrage Conditions in the South," and the gathering lasted well into the morning, wrote the *New York Times*. The Constitution League's audience produced resolutions calling for reduction of southern representation in Congress, the militant credo of the new left wing of the civil rights movement, personified by the Niagara Movement, and many liberal white activists. Unlike the Niagara Movement, the new league boasted a genuinely biracial character, wealthy white benefactors, and supporters from across the political spectrum.[6]

Milholland, once a Washington admirer, had lately drifted away from Tuskegee's orbit, becoming increasingly vocal about the need for direct action on civil rights issues. His colleague Mary White Ovington, an early league supporter, was a fervent observer and supporter of the Niagara Movement. Other white league members included General Henry E. Tremaine, Andrew Humphrey, and former senator Warner Miller of New York; early black members included Council vice president William Sinclair. As the year progressed, the league would take action on a number of issues, including the infamous "separate but equal" amendment proposed by senators Joseph Foraker and William Warner to the nation's proposed railroad rate regulation statute, the Hepburn Act. Washington had asked Grimké and Miller to represent the Committee of Twelve in the matter; the pair soon joined forces with White, Sinclair, and Humphrey, at the league's request, to lobby Foraker, Warner, and other senators against the controversial amendment, which was deleted from the bill, but only after a long, arduous struggle.[7]

Yet the complicated battle over the Warner-Foraker amendment—and its implications for Afro-Americans—did as much long-term damage as short-term good. For reasons of their own, Trotter's *Guardian* and Chase's *Bee* attempted to discredit the black negotiators, claiming—without offering any proof—that White, Grimké, and Miller had deliberately favored the amendment's discriminatory language. The incident produced hard feelings on all sides and did little to advance the unity Walters desired. By the time Miller and Grimké offered their factual rebuttal in the *Age*, the factions had grown even farther apart.[8]

It was not without a sense of irony, then, that the Council sought a national day of prayer, in October, in preparation for the New York convention: "Ten million freemen, and yet slaves, are called to their knees on Sunday, October 7, 1906, before the God who has promised, 'I will answer while they are yet calling.' By the authority vested in us, the Afro-American Council proclaims this to be the day of prayer for all citizens of color and all others who love righteousness, and beg that in their petition, they beseech the Almighty to cause Justice . . ."[9]

Chase's *Bee* noted the call, with characteristic sarcasm, but with the date wrong:

> The Afro-American Council has issued a proclamation, designating October 6, 1906, a day for prayer among the millions of colored citizens of the United States. The Bee believes in prayer; it is a weapon that will cut the vengeance of the civilized but the sword and the shotgun are better weapons against the barbarians in the South. . . . Prayer is not so much needed in this contest as the cure for the proper use of the ballot. What the colored man should be taught is the correct use of the ballot. How shall we restore our civil and political rights? How shall we eliminate the "Jim Crow" laws? . . .
>
> Prayer will not remedy these evils. . . . The Afro-American Council is to meet in New York City next October, and for what? The sycophants, the apologists and trimmers will be there and for what? To extol the virtues of the Republican party . . .[10]

Chase's sentiments aside, at least one black church did respond as requested—in Rochester, home of treasurer John Thompson and scene of the Council's first meeting eight years earlier. There, Zion AME parishioners spent the day collecting funds to complete their new church building, praying for the Council's success, and listening to a sermon invoking "divine aid to obtain justice in the treatment of the colored people in the South."[11]

Between proclamation and occurrence, two major events sent shock waves across the Afro-American political landscape. An alleged armed clash in mid-August between black soldiers and white civilians near a Texas border town was forever known in racial lore as the "Brownsville affray"; one civilian died, but nearly two hundred soldiers were eventually discharged. A far deadlier second event, in late September, shattered the uneasy peace of the South's largest city: the Atlanta race riots, in which ten blacks died in a five-day bloodbath of white rage.[12] Both events would strongly influence the course of the Council's meeting, imparting a new urgency to its call for the New York convention and, inevitably, to its enduring sense of mission.

In an unusual break with past tradition, Walters issued in mid-August a "Special Appeal to Liberty Loving Negroes in all Parts of the United States," rather than the usual letter inviting delegates to attend. It was cheerfully printed by some newspapers, such as George Knox's *Freeman*, but ignored by others, in response, perhaps, to its strident tone. The appeal opened with a repetitive call—"Organize! Organize!

Organize!"—before quoting statements attributed to Secretary of War Taft and Associate Justice David Brewer of the U.S. Supreme Court on the unconstitutionality of disfranchisement. Taft, speaking in North Carolina, reportedly declared that the "grandfather clause" and other devices violated the Fifteenth Amendment. Brewer, an active dissenter in *Giles v. Harris*, expressed "astonishment that the Afro-American people have never effectively utilized this remedy" to have the South's new constitutions "properly brought before the Supreme Court" and overturned.[13]

"Our object is to organize, secure friends, employ able talent, white or black, and knock out the grandfather clause, at least," the appeal continued. "If we can obtain from the Supreme Court an opinion that the grandfather clause is illegal, a victory, which profoundly important as it would be, we can by standing together achieve such a manifestation [that] would thrill the North and again enlist its sympathies with us, at the same time strike dismay into those southern politicians who are fattening on the race problem."[14]

This appeal, which also referred to a "tremendous" organizational meeting held in New York in July, cited "the great tidal wave of indignation and resentment against the injustices perpetrated daily upon Afro-Americans of this country." Signed only by Bishop Walters, however, it concluded with a familiar litany of Council plans of organization, its goals, and information about the October meeting. Why no other major newspapers carried the appeal—neither the *Bee*, the *Gazette*, the *Appeal*, nor the *Age*—is not clear. That the *Appeal* chose to print a different version—one either unofficial or official, but prepared hastily and filled with errors—indicates that something in the August call, possibly the references to Taft and/or Brewer, may have been considered objectionable by some editors.

What is hard to miss is that the *Appeal* reported the incorrect number of the 1905 convention—as the eighth annual meeting, not the ninth—and also lifted nearly all of its text from the previous year's call. "In view of the legislation against us as citizens, not only against our civil rights, but against our suffrage, no one should question the necessity for an organization of this character, and every Afro-American, without regard for his views on other subjects, should be willing to unite in an organized effort to improve these condition," the call began, ending with a religious admonition: "It is well to remember that God helps those who help themselves."[15]

Amidst the text was a paragraph largely lifted from 1905 and repeated here for good measure:

> The hostility upon the part of the enemies of the race has been so persistent that many of our friends have become timid and indifferent

> in our defense. It is with the view of combating this opposition of our enemies, strengthening the hands of our friends, and working for the absolute undoing of all discrimination against the race that this meeting is to be held, and [we ask the hearty cooperation of] every Afro-American who is interested in the welfare of his race."[16]

Also worth noting was the mention of "reduced rates on railroads"—missing from the August version—offering a round-trip fare at a discount for delegates. Yet for all its flaws, the new call seemed more official, having at least been signed by Walters, Cyrus Adams, and Jordan. A third call to action, in the October issue of the *Colored American Magazine*, was the most elaborate yet, and presumably geared to a more selective readership, containing a lengthy chronicle of the Council's past role and future hopes. The high-circulation New York monthly, controlled by Booker T. Washington, had once periodically published articles on the Council, although this was the first such article in several years.[17]

In it Walters emphasized the Council's original ten goals, which included the need to fight disfranchisement in the South. The Council had been the first organization to test discriminatory laws in the courts, Walters wrote, as well as serving as an impetus to others outside. "A great deal more would have been accomplished had we been furnished sufficient means to carry out our work," he added. "Our present struggle should be in the courts of our land. We may be turned down by the local courts, where prejudice against the race is intense, but by appealing to the highest courts . . . I am of the opinion that we shall win in the end."[18]

Before the Council's emergence, "the Negroes' civil and political atmosphere was surcharged with self-effacement, non-resistance and his utter inferiority. It was the Council which clarified this oppressive atmosphere . . . the only voice heard in the wilderness as a distinct racial organization, crying aloud for equal rights for the black man and formed to fight oppressions of all kinds."[19]

Among Council efforts listed was the unsuccessful Louisiana test case, which Walters now glossed over in a broader appeal for renewed support, including financial contributions and the formation of active local and state councils. "What we need now, and have always needed, is the encouragement and substantial aid of the leaders and members of our race," he concluded.

But Walters might have done well at this point to explain the outcome of the Louisiana test case. He had, of course, been president when the court test was devised and instituted, although Fortune had succeeded him before the decision was made to forego a federal appeal of the negative state ruling. Many in the broader community were still waiting for a full accounting from someone in authority.

Harry Smith, the Niagarite editor of Cleveland's *Gazette*, blamed Fortune's poor leadership for dropping the ball after 1902. He and others had "lost interest" when the Council failed to pursue the case, "which has never been heard of since. All of us had given of our hard-earned means to help raise the retainer fees of the two lawyers"—Arthur Birney and Armand Romain—and "wanted tangible and telling results of material good to the race or at least some real effort to secure them. . . . Had the Council backed up its suit in the United States Supreme Court, there would have been a death blow to southern disfranchisement and as a result no limit to its strength and popularity with our people."[20]

Fortune recalled the situation differently and blamed the paid attorneys, not Council leadership. "[T]he failure to get it before the Supreme Court was due . . . to Mr. Romaine and Mr. J. Madison Vance . . . who failed to make up the case [properly]. Quite some money was spent upon this case, but not a penny of it came out of the pockets of the dear mass of the people; it was contributed by friends of the race." Boston attorney Albert Pillsbury, willing to argue the case before the high court for free, never got the chance to do so.[21]

But who was really at fault in the case, and how much more could the Council have done with it? Had the Tuskegee Machine, which controlled the Council from 1902 to 1905, simply dropped the case? Had a leadership vacuum during Fortune's absence in the first half of 1903—or a lack of funds, or both—doomed the case? No one seemed to know, and the issue would linger, unresolved, for the rest of the Council's existence.

With roughly four million residents, New York was by far the nation's largest city in 1906, with a briskly rising Afro-American population. By 1910, census figures would show its black citizenry numbering more than ninety thousand, having surpassed in size all but Washington, D.C., during the decade. Most were concentrated in the borough of Manhattan, representing about three percent of its residents, with Brooklyn a distant second.[22] If their political power had not yet matched their numbers—the first elected black state legislator was a decade way—the metropolitan black population was still influential, particularly known for its large, well-respected churches. The *Age*, edited by Tim Fortune, was arguably the nation's premier black newspaper, along with the widely read *Colored American Magazine*. It was hardly surprising that large, appreciative crowds—up to 2,500 at one event—were reported for the Council's sessions in early October.

Walter H. Brooks, former director of the ecclesiastical reform bureau, cordially welcomed delegates to the opening session at Saint Mark's Methodist Episcopal Church. But the mood among the city's Afro-Americans was not bright. Even ministers, rarely distinguished for violent statements, found it difficult to restrain post-Atlanta anger. The Reverend George Lee of Washington, D.C., former vice president, sounded a bitter, sorrowing note on the opening day, according to the *New York Times*:

> "I preached peace after the Atlanta riots," [Lee] said, "but don't misunderstand me. It was prudence, not my religion. If I had the power to stop that kind of thing, even by force, I'd use it. . . . In the South they are scheming all the time to keep the negro down, but I tell you he is bound to rise. Just so certain as they keep this thing up in the South something is going to happen. The trouble is all one-sided now. Trouble never stays on one side. There's going to be trouble on the other side pretty soon."[23]

John Dancy, D.C. recorder of deeds, gently reminded Lee and fifty official delegates that the Council's purpose was to "call men back up to their reason, not to go down and blow up the South." Yet even Dancy warned of the danger of imminent anarchy "unless the American people get back to their principles." News of the death in Ohio of former Council vice president Benjamin Arnett, after a long illness, cast a temporary pall over the proceedings; the convention sent resolutions of respect to his family with Dr. H. T. Johnson, who left town for the funeral.[24]

For all his desire to remain positive, even Walters seemed unable to muster much optimism, at least in excerpts offered by the *Times*. "If [disfranchisement] continues much longer," Walters said, "a terrible conflict is sure to come. It will bring business stagnation and desolation, but it will come, for the sense of justice is no more dead now than it was before the war broke out. . . . If such men as [Senator Tillman] stir up a war in which the color of the skin is a death warrant, the Nation will cease to be patient. The object of our enemies is to make us serfs," he continued. "It is nonsense to cry peace when there is no peace. We are determined to rise or die in the attempt to obtain our rights. We are determined to leave a heritage to our children which will save them from serfdom. It is silly and wicked to see our people die when action could save them."[25]

But the full text of his address, printed only in the *Age*, presented a different, fuller picture of the bishop's mood. The awful mob violence in Atlanta and elsewhere, the result of "downright race hatred," was tempered by the obvious courage of at least one southern governor—Robert Glenn of North Carolina—"who is to be highly commended for calling upon the citizens to aid in putting down mob violence, and authorizing sheriffs and the militia of the State to stop the mob, even if they have to shoot them down."[26]

The Council's antilynching bureau, once headed by "the able and courageous" Ida Wells-Barnett and now by "the brave and gifted" Mary Church Terrell, had worked successfully to publicize and stem the violence. Walters himself saw "no reason why we should not succeed in getting Congress and the legislatures of the States concerned to enact such laws as will put a stop to mob violence." And on the subject of court tests of disfranchisement, Walters claimed to be far from discouraged. "I still believe . . . that there is a lawyer or lawyers somewhere in this country that are able to prepare a test case so completely and to argue it so ably that the court will be forced to give us a decision, thus knocking out the grandfather clause, and putting the question at rest. I believe . . . we can collect sufficient funds to pay for such legal talent."[27]

Citing recent editorials in mainstream newspapers, Walters eyed a specific goal ($50,000) to be used to hire "very able lawyers" who might yet "force a direct and final decision. For thus far the court has steadily dodged the issue, and with both political parties not more or less favorable to the questioned legislation, it will doubtless continue to do so as long as it can." Walters's efforts were moderately successful, raising some $950 for the cause.[28] But the bishop's words, however appealing, were largely overshadowed in the press by the attention given to other speakers. One was the white editor of the *New York Evening Post*, Oswald Garrison Villard, encouraged to attend by his good friend Booker Washington, and who spoke at Mother Zion Church on Thursday afternoon, July 11. The other was Washington himself, who spoke at Mother Zion that night.

Grandson of the late abolitionist William Lloyd Garrison, Villard had helped raise large sums for Tuskegee's educational efforts, and his remarks reflected his deep-seated belief in the power of organization. "By all means organize," he said. "If there is anything above all else that the colored people need to-day it is solidarity, and particularly the solidarity which comes from standing together for one's rights under leaders loyally served and loyally followed."[29] Villard scorned any resort to retaliatory violence, despite anger over "the fifteen innocent dead in Atlanta," for to do so would "make their situation in the South all but hopeless." Better to "[o]rganize to agitate, organize to demand your rights under the Constitution, organize to fight back for yourselves by every legitimate means—by the strike, by the boycott if necessary, but best of all by argument and by reason. The Afro-American Council asks for a fund to carry to the Supreme Court the question of the ballot in the South. It ought to have a national defence fund reaching into the hundreds of thousands of dollars," he said. "With such a fund it would be able to institute a judicial investigation of such happenings as those at Atlanta . . . hire the best lawyers to prosecute the mob . . . [and] fight in the courts every unjust discrimination."[30]

Villard's endorsement of the Council still rang in delegates' ears when Washington took the lectern Thursday night. After working feverishly for weeks to calm the troubled Atlanta situation, he was determined not to let Northern sympathies for the victims explode in a counterproductive manner. With characteristic logic, he reminded listeners of the need for calm:

> To the members of my race who reside in the Northern States let me utter the caution that, in your enthusiastic desire to be of service to your brethren in the South, you do not make their path more thorny and difficult . . . by rash and intemperate utterances. Before giving advice to the Negro in the South, the Negro in the North should be very sure that what he advises is that which he himself would be willing to take into the heart of the South and put into practice. Be careful not to assist in lighting a fire which you will have no ability to put out.[31]

The widely excerpted speech was "one of the most effective and feeling addresses of his life," according to Fortune, writing in the *Age*. At its conclusion, he added, "the great audience sprang to its feet with spontaneous shouts and chorus of admiration." But in a departure from past practice, almost as many white speakers as black appeared at official Council sessions, among them Andrew B. Humphrey, secretary of the Constitution League, who "urged it as the religious duty of all Afro-Americans in the North to take an active part in politics"; Democratic congressional candidate John J. Halligan, who declared his opposition to the reduction of southern representation in Congress; Alabama postmaster and editor Joseph Manning, who said votes were being suppressed in his state among poor voters of both races; and Joseph Smith of Massachusetts, an Irish American citizen who offered to help restart the Civil War, if necessary, to restore political and civil rights to black citizens in the South.[32]

Most influential among the white speakers, perhaps, was John Elmer Milholland, moving force behind the new Constitution League, who spoke October 10 at Cooper Union. As Milholland saw it, the question was not one of the black man's sufferings or suffrage, but "whether the white man's government is as complete a failure in the Nation as it is in the South. President Roosevelt is the first President in forty years who has not found it necessary to carry to Congress some recommendations in reference to the negroes in the South," he declared. Roosevelt "is rapidly approaching a point where his action or lack of action will place him in history, bracketed with Andrew Jackson or with James Buchanan," due to "unfortunate" advisors, but "we are going to give him some advice to-night whereby he can bring about an end to the infamous condition that now exists."[33]

Mary Church Terrell, vice president and director of the antilynching bureau, also spoke during a symposium on lynching. She was applauded warmly at every appearance, but years later, she recalled only being nervous. "I went to that meeting with my heart in my mouth," she wrote in her memoirs, fearful at the thought of appearing on the same podium with such luminaries as Milholland, former governor Pinchback, and Napier. But perhaps the "sanest" address by any speaker, at least to Fortune's ears, was given by the black New York attorney who had worked so diligently on Alabama disfranchisement cases in 1903 and 1904, Wilford Smith. Not surprisingly, Smith confirmed Fortune's belief, often expressed, that it was up to Congress to end discriminatory disfranchisement practices that so heavily penalized black voters in the South. But this should not occur through reduction of representation, Smith warned in his presentation at Mt. Olivet Baptist Church.[34]

Smith dealt engagingly with dry, pragmatic legal issues not yet decided by the Supreme Court. The framers of Alabama's new constitution had openly defied the provisions of the federal Constitution's Fifteenth Amendment, Smith explained, while shrewdly shielding their actions, as political, from federal judicial scrutiny. "[T]he real kernel of this whole question is how to find a way to compel the South to respect and observe the provisions of the Fifteenth Amendment . . . . It is quite apparent to any school boy that the recent Southern constitutions are in conflict." Obtaining a specific ruling on constitutionality was almost beside the point; instead, it was "infinitely more important . . . to have the courts give an adequate and effectual remedy."[35]

Smith then recounted his own role: "It became my duty, in 1903, on behalf of the Negroes of Alabama, to prepare and present the case of Giles against Harris to the Supreme Court of the United States . . . to compel the registrars in Alabama to accord equal treatment to all citizens of the United States in the matter of registration, and to enjoin and prevent the violation of the Fifteenth Amendment by the registrars, in allowing white men to qualify as electors and refusing the same right to colored men on account of race and color." Only about one percent of Alabama's two hundred thousand black voters had since registered, while virtually all white men were now allowed to do so, he stated.[36]

"This case was brought long prior to any election, and had no connection with the matter of voting, except to call the attention of the court to the discrimination on the part of the registration officers . . . The Court, as you will know, refused to grant any relief, on the grounds that it was political; and went out of their way to say that even if registration was compelled, if there was a conspiracy to prevent Negroes from voting, they would have to go further and superintend the elections, to see that the votes were counted. It was no business of the Supreme Court whether Negroes ever voted or got their votes counted after being registered."

Smith no longer believed that judicial action would bring an end to disfranchisement, even with the right attorney pleading the case—even the right white attorney, he had been told. "I have since learned, however, that a member of this Court told a certain Bishop of the AME Church that had this case been presented by a white man of National reputation a different decision would have been handed down," he said. "According to this, it is possible for the Court to reverse itself when the next case is presented by some distinguished white attorney." Such an outcome was possible, but improbable. Smith believed instead that only congressional action was likely to end disfranchisement, and he termed it the "bounden duty" of the national government to do just that.

"The only effectual remedy for discrimination for disfranchisement is the enactment of a National Registration Law so that the Federal Government will take charge of the registration of electors for Federal offices in all the States. The Federal Government has enacted a national bankruptcy law for the protection of the creditor class," he concluded. "With how much greater propriety and right, and with how much greater reason, can it enact a National Registration Law, for the protection of citizenship, in view of the conditions obtaining in the South?"[37]

To no one's surprise, Walters was reelected president of the Council. Officers of the Council elected with him included both old and new faces. Napier and Mrs. Terrell were reelected as vice presidents, as were treasurer Thompson, secretary Cyrus Adams, and corresponding secretary Jordan, also named national organizer. Former vice presidents Elias Morris and Bishop Grant were brought back to that office, while Fannie Williams was once again selected as assistant secretary and Bishop Clinton shifted from organizer to chaplain.[38]

But in line with Walters's hopes of attracting new blood into the Council, five new vice presidents were chosen, including one Niagara Movement sympathizer, Brooklyn's Reverend Owen M. Waller; a suspected Trotterite, the Reverend Henry J. Callis of Boston; Richard Le Roy Stokes, a former Tuskegee stenographer now working for Fortune at the *Age*; Constitution League member Dr. William Sinclair of Philadelphia; and CME bishop Robert S. Williams of Georgia. Executive committee chairman William Steward was returned to office, with a new secretary, Kelly Miller. All bureau directors from Detroit were also returned, with one exception; Dr. John R. Francis of Washington, D.C., now headed the bureau of vital statistics.[39]

The election was one of just three major actions taken by the Council in New York. Another was the adoption of a resolution "requesting President Roosevelt to appoint a commission to visit the South, and obtain information upon which Federal action may be taken to put an end to the present conditions there." The last was the Council's address to the nation, high-minded, but strangely muted, making few specific demands or requests. Drafted largely by Kelly Miller, new secretary of the executive committee, it lacked the urgency and directness of early addresses. Its tone was instead conciliatory, but almost artificially so.[40]

The address opened with a recitation of continuing injustices and recent violence against Afro-Americans, ranging from "the recent Atlanta barbarities" to the "demonstrated fallacy of the vociferously proclaimed doctrine that denial of civil and political rights would promote order and racial peace." The South's "sinister designs against the Negro's political rights" and the civil discrimination of "Jim Crow" car laws should be tested in the nation's courts, it declared. Lynching and mob violence should be dealt with by the government, which was duty bound to "punish the guilty and protect the innocent."[41]

The Council also called for national aid to education in the rural South and asked the government to employ Afro-Americans "rather than foreign labor in the prosecution of the work of the Panama Canal." Such demands were deemed "reasonable and just, and they are set forth soberly and without vindictive vehemence," the address continued. "We appreciate the support and sympathy of our friends in the North and appreciate the manly and courageous attitude of a growing number of fair-minded Southern white men, who are taking a liberal and humane attitude in the issues involved in the relation of the races."

In a gesture aimed clearly at Niagarites, the Council invited "all kindred organizations and agencies to unite or cooperate with it in its efforts to attain the desired end. The President of this Council is hereby authorized to invite a conference of the officers of all such National organizations looking toward the formation of a permanent standing committee of safety." But its ending lacked a clear focus, sounding less like a call to action than a Sunday sermon: "We ask the cooperation of all true Americans, North and South, on the patriotic task of promoting peace and harmony between the races. . . . But the peace which we advocate is the peace of righteousness and honor. The effect of righteousness shall be peace, and the fruits of righteousness, quietness and assurance forever."[42]

In the weeks that followed, black newspapers generally spoke well of the New York gathering. From friends old and new alike, the consensus seemed to be that the Council was once again a vital, inclusive forum for almost all viewpoints among the various Afro-American camps. Even with its relatively weak address, the Council seemed destined for action.

Calvin Chase, once a bitter critic of the Council's Tuskegee ties, had recently been "converted"—some would say bribed—to a more favorable position. His *Bee* described the meeting as "one of the largest that has ever been held by that organization," attended by "a representative body of men who seem to be in earnest in explaining the position of the colored people to the American people. The speeches of the delegates were mild but pointed." Chase even endorsed Walters: "the man to lead, and if the Council will follow his leadership, the Bee is of the opinion that victory will ultimately come to the colored race."[43]

It was a welcome change from his past verbal brickbats, although some might still question his sincerity—or at least, his internal consistency. Almost like clockwork, the *Bee* reverted to its unpredictable course. A week later, it carried three editorials with dissonant themes on the meeting, each unsigned, yet obviously reflecting Chase's inner conflicts. He had been treated well, he said—"as well as anyone"—but others had not ("there were many who came a great distance and to some extent, were not placed on the official program"). Yet an unnamed "clique" still wanted to control the Council, and Chase questioned whether all viewpoints had been given equal time ("that is the complaint that was made by certain delegates") before ridiculing the national address ("reads as if it had been prepared by men who were muzzled and afraid to speak"). To gain a "substantial membership," the Council must discard its "exclusivity."[44]

In a second editorial, Chase swallowed old resentments against Tuskegee and called Washington "a friend to his people," his latest speech "manly and timely." The *Bee* "has now thrown away any personal feelings it may have had against him, and is willing to give him credit for whatever good he may do." Charges that Washington had anything to do with causing the riot at Atlanta were unbelievable; "he had no more to do with it than the editor of The Bee." And last but not least, the address to the country—which Chase had already termed "childish and weak"—could not be blamed on either Washington or his friends on the committee, as Sylvester Corrothers charged, since Washington arrived after the address was prepared ("The Bee will admit that the address of the Council is weak, but whose fault is it?").[45]

Outside Washington, views of the meeting were generally more positive. The *Freeman* disagreed firmly with Chase's equivocations, praising the address in its news coverage as "one of the strongest ever given out by a Negro assembly." On its editorial page, the *Freeman* endorsed the Council's performance: "It did its work nobly, and a spirit of harmony pervaded the entire proceedings that awakens new hope," Knox wrote. "There is every reason to believe that effective work will be done for the race by this splendid organization. . . . The people of this country have faith in the Council. They have forced the 'kickers' to the rear."[46]

Yet even in New York, the postmortem was tinged with doubt. Both during and after the convention, the *Age* displayed conflicting opinions, first calling the meeting "the most successful session in the history of the Afro-American Council," at least by several criteria: amount of money raised ("over $1,000"), "increased membership, enthusiasm and amount of practical work accomplished," along with an apparent "desire for harmony and action that must win friends to our cause." The Council had "voted to employ a paid secretary and organizer," Jordan, "who would devote his entire time to the work of the Council with headquarters in Washington, D.C."[47]

But subtler editorial opinion emerged in a later article, which recounted the Council's convention activities after an opening section citing its "uneven existence and history. At first it was composed largely of the prominent men and women from all walks of life, but it has been somewhat torn by internal dissensions and politics." As now organized, however, the Council was "full of promise to effect far-reaching results. Its program and purposes are in the hands of men who have had wide experience in national movements. The Council does not stand for force, but law. . . . The Afro-Americans are more united in purpose than at any time since 1865. There is more intelligence, more money and more experience in the subtleties of organization in the Council to-day than ever before . . ."[48]

Fortune may not have written either news article, although little was published in the *Age* without his attentive eye and approval. Speaking on his editorial page, however, Fortune's perversely melancholy streak asserted itself. "The meeting . . . brings very sad reflections to the mind of the writer of this article, who has given sixteen years of his life and his means to the effort to organize the Afro-American people for their own protection," Fortune wrote. "We speak but the sad and solemn truth when we declare that while the National Afro-American Council exists, and will continue to exist, it has no organization in the literal sense, it has not the people behind it, because the people do not appreciate the need of organization."[49]

Speaking from his perch in Cleveland, Harry Smith would have agreed, if for quite different reasons. His *Gazette* roundly criticized the Council for its past failures, dismissing any chance of future success. Smith had even withdrawn from the Council over the failure of the Louisiana test case, he said, "when the organization discontinued its only good excuse for existence. When Bishop Alexander Walters succeeded to the presidency a year ago we hoped—but in vain.

We hoped because it was during his incumbency of office prior to Fortune's election, that the suit referred to was started." Smith claimed to have asked Walters repeatedly for answers about the Louisiana case, "only to receive answers to every other question except those relative to it. The real reason the league died and the national council has been dying for several years is apparent and was again made plain at its annual meeting in New York last week—it is nothing but a 'windjamming' affair."[50]

The Niagara Movement had spoken. For all its efforts, nothing had changed for the Council except the calendar—and soon enough, the Niagara Movement would seek to have the last word.

11

Farewell to the Wizard

Baltimore, 1907

Reverberations from Brownsville continued to dominate the civil rights agenda across the United States as leaders from the Council and the Niagara Movement gathered in Washington in mid-January, joined by interested observers. There they all hoped to hear a report from Council legal bureau director J. Douglas Wetmore, investigating the case on instructions of Bishop Walters. The Brownsville incident had by now become a national cause célèbre to defenders of the Afro-American soldiers dismissed—in all, 167 men—who were seen as innocent victims of racial hatred. Even the facts of the case were hotly disputed: one white civilian had been killed and another wounded during an early morning altercation in August 1906 between Brownsville residents and other armed men, identified by some observers—some, but not all—as soldiers from the military installation nearby. No soldier ever confessed, nor was any individual soldier ever identified, and a Texas grand jury refused to indict any of a dozen soldiers who were detained and later released.[1]

An official army investigation, however, concluded that unidentified black soldiers were involved in the shooting and concluded that their identities were known to other soldiers, among whom a "conspiracy of silence" prevailed. In November, President Roosevelt ordered the War Department to dismiss, dishonorably, all 167 black soldiers from three companies in the 25th Infantry, some of whom had served capably for more than a decade and had been awarded medals of valor. Secretary of War William Howard Taft carried out the order, reluctantly but dutifully, despite Mollie Terrell's personal plea.[2]

Mrs. Terrell had approached Taft at the behest of John Milholland, whose Constitution League would report on its investigation of the case in December to a U.S. Senate inquiry spearheaded by Ohio's Joseph B. Foraker. The league report, compiled by Andrew Humphrey and George White and based on field reports from attorney Gilchrist Stewart and journalist Richard Stokes (a Council vice president), exonerated the soldiers of any wrongdoing. It sharply criticized the federal government's haste and assumption of guilt without any documented proof. In the end, it was Roosevelt's own belief—sincere, unyielding—in the soldiers' guilt that led to the dismissals. A few black leaders, Booker T. Washington apparently among them, agreed, at least privately. Washington, however, had begged Roosevelt not to take the action, calling the blanket dismissal "in my opinion, a great blunder." Rebuffed and rebuked, he suffered in silence, unwilling to repudiate the president despite damage to his own credibility.[3]

Liberal whites and militant blacks, furious with Roosevelt, attacked the White House in print. New York newspapers took the lead, with Milholland's *World* calling the president's order "an executive lynching," and the *Times* calling it "in flat contravention . . . of the Constitution." Roosevelt's provocative annual message in December virtually painted Afro-Americans as "a criminal race," while subliminally condoning white supremacy and proposing to end lynching by first ending black criminality. Whatever his intentions, Roosevelt came off as appallingly insensitive on the subject of race, and his small coterie of black advisers—Booker T. Washington, really—as ineffective, at best.[4]

By January, the situation had become wildly polarized, with Tuskegee spying on the meeting with Wetmore and operative Charles Anderson now accusing Stokes of "double-dealing" and "play[ing] false with both [Stewart] and the Constitution League" and Stewart of lying in his own report ("It proves . . . that the soldiers actually did the shooting"). Stewart, or so Anderson claimed, was also boasting that the Foraker inquiry would derail Roosevelt's political aspirations and "knock out 'The Booker T. Washington Cabinet.'"[5]

Washington was resigned to the situation. He still admired Roosevelt and Taft, even if he disagreed with them over Brownsville; to the Wizard it was a closed issue, however unfortunate. But Washington could not persuade others of the correctness of his strategy, at least not without exposing his own failure to influence Roosevelt. Unable to stop the agitation, he grew increasingly frustrated by his handicap, blaming Milholland and the Constitution League for fomenting public agitation, and proving so angry with his onetime ally that he sought to hurt him financially, by sabotaging Milholland's pneumatic-tube contract with the Post Office Department. This plan was thwarted, when Postmaster General George Cortelyou informed the Wizard that Milholland had no current dealings with the department and was no longer associated with the firm in question.[6]

It was as if the ground underneath Tuskegee had begun to give way, slowly. This was the opening tremor in a seismic shift—the ideological earthquake that

Washington had once discounted but long dreaded, and could no longer forestall. His control of the Council had begun to slip, visibly, in New York, as even those still friendly to him now asserted a careful new independence from Tuskegee on critical issues. While his attempts to squelch the Niagara Movement were having the desired gradual effects, the Council annoyingly insisted on offering Niagarites an additional forum.[7]

When the Council's steering committee on Brownsville convened in Washington on January 10, its hope was to raise both public awareness and much-needed funds for the soldiers' defense. Committee members included vice presidents Grant and Mrs. Terrell, also director of the antilynching bureau; national organizer Jordan; executive committee secretary Miller; Wetmore; and the local Council president, the Reverend Sylvester Corrothers. Others in attendance were journalists Fortune and Chase, Bishop J. W. Smith, Dr. John Francis, the Reverend H. T. Johnson, the Reverend George Lee, and the Reverend E. W. Lampton. Washington's last-minute informant at the meeting was James A. Cobb, a young Louisiana lawyer whose loyalty to Roosevelt and Washington soon brought him appointment as special assistant U.S. attorney for the District of Columbia. (According to Anderson, Wetmore's report to the Council forum was his second major report in as many weeks; Wetmore and Mrs. Terrell had earlier "put some so-called information in the hands of Senator Foraker.")[8]

Although only a fragmentary record exists of Wetmore's remarks, including one reference to the "keen injustice inflicted upon the colored soldiers by the President; the Atlanta riot; and other indignities" (prompting two New York newspapers "who do not love the negro" to take up the cause), what the group heard from Wetmore seemed gratifying and informative. His report on the Brownsville situation prompted the Council to adopt a resolution favorable to Senator Foraker, and to send a delegation—Walters, Wetmore, and Jordan—to meet with him at the Capitol. But an equally important agenda item was money. The Council's treasury balance was just over $200, according to Walters, after expenditures of more than $1,000 during the past year. So at a well-attended public meeting at the same church that evening, the bishop introduced the Council's fund-raising speakers.

Cobb wrote Emmett Scott days later about the meeting, providing an admirably balanced account. Having assured Bishop Grant there would be "no abuse" of the president—or anyone else—Walters was apparently unable to stifle the outspoken Corrothers, who issued "a few slurs" against Roosevelt and Washington. The rest of the meeting was dignified, Cobb wrote, even if all the speakers—Fortune, Wetmore, Jordan, and Walters—pointedly "protested against the action of the president in re the soldiers." (Grant did not attend.)[9]

Ever the proselytizer, Fortune made a spirited appeal for contributions to continue the fight. So far, he said, he had raised through his newspaper "just $12" from the "ten millions of our people who feel outraged over the affair. The difficulty with our race is, it won't support its leaders." The Brownsville affair had apparently energized and revitalized him. On this evening, he was his old self, by turns "caustic" and "thoughtful," and his remarks were applauded from beginning to end. ("His friends said it was the best speech they had ever heard him make," wrote J. W. Smith in the *Age*.)

Even if the president had "outraged a fundamental principle of citizenship" by dismissing the Brownsville soldiers, Fortune ventured, the race had a duty "not to make this a race issue. Let us not abuse the President, but differ with him, [with] dignity, with positiveness, with firmness in the right." For Fortune, the key was to act with responsibility—an unusually conciliatory position for the old firebrand and fierce critic of Roosevelt. "We have come upon some very serious times, and it requires all of us to be very thoughtful, conservative and positive. No need to fly off the handle and get hot in the collar," he said. "This is not a question of policy, but one of principle, which involves all the people of the United States."[10]

"We have plenty of leaders and no followers," he reminded his listeners. "Talk has moved the world. Agitate! Agitate! Since the dismissal of the colored soldiers, we have had orators to burn. Let us now stop talking and do something." Yet through it all, Fortune's evident desire to please his mentor, Washington, mirrored his own desperate need for Tuskegee's quiet financial assistance, as well as the Council's continuing need for that friendship and support.[11]

In the end, the Washington, D.C., conference caused no disruptions or new hostility between Council participants and Tuskegee. Walters's exasperating unpredictability led to no such break as with Milholland; Washington and Walters continued to correspond cordially for some time, even as the prelate flirted with Niagara and drifted recklessly toward the Democratic Party. Nor did the Wizard ever lose his patience with the gifted Mrs. Terrell, whose perceptiveness and influence remained valuable assets. In both cases, their occasional usefulness insulated them from any vindictiveness. But Wetmore, once a valuable informant, now became an object of surveillance by vigilant lieutenant Charles Anderson, who reported a month later that "I have a way of finding out what goes on in the office of the apartment" of the New York attorney, including his friendliness with the opposition—Du Bois and Owen Waller, or even, on occasion, Judge Terrell, who "had better take a stitch in his tongue."[12]

And while Washington remained personally fond of Fortune, the erratic idealist had grown far less useful since leaving the Council. Weary of complaints, increasingly disturbed by Fortune's instability and resurgent alcoholism, Washington had already turned to Anderson as his primary source of inside information; he now began laying final plans to take over the *Age*, and to set his former protégé free.[13]

As the spring wore on, plans took shape for the upcoming annual session of the Council in Baltimore in June. The city was now the nation's seventh largest, with half a million residents in 1906, including about eighty thousand Afro-Americans. Baltimore's black population, second only to that of Washington, D.C., in the 1900 census, had slowed its growth in recent years and was about to be surpassed in size by New York and New Orleans.[14]

Yet the Maryland city was distinctive in other ways. A stronghold of radical sentiment, according to August Meier, Baltimore had never had a particularly strong attachment to the Council. Former resident Ernest Lyon, now U.S. minister to Liberia, had been its only national officer so far. Other local Council leaders included Harry S. Cummings, the first black member of the Baltimore city council and a strong Roosevelt supporter; Mrs. Ella Smith, Charles Stewart, Dr. William Bishop—all of whom had served on the national executive committee; and the Reverend Abraham L. Gaines, who chaired the local planning committee. Gaines had attended the New York convention, offering a "dignified and able address" there entitled "American Prejudice and Suppression of American Institutions."[15]

The city boasted a respected Afro-American college (Morgan College) and a flourishing black business community. Baltimore's widely read independent black newspaper, edited by John Henry Murphy, avidly supported Booker T. Washington. Yet the *Afro-American Ledger* was also deferential in its treatment of his opposition—for good reason, since the city's elite circle of college-educated professionals included many known for anti-Tuskegee sympathies. Notable were educator Mason Hawkins; the Reverend George F. Bragg, an Episcopal priest; and attorney William Ashbie Hawkins, architect of the antidisfranchisement effort in Maryland in 1905, and a participant in Walters's experimental conference in Washington that same year.[16]

New York had opened the Council's floodgates to dissent and paved the road to Baltimore. The decision to hold the next annual session there had been a clear signal of the Council's new tolerance—indeed, its welcoming attitude—for radical dissenters. The Council's call now amplified and reinforced that message, indicating that this meeting would be different from most previous ones, both in attitude and in the makeup of its attendance. "The situation is grave and demands the exercise of wisdom, prudence, patience and intelligent effort to overcome the dangers menacing what political and civil rights we have left," warned Walters in early June.[17]

He deemed the meeting urgent for many reasons, including the "unceasing energy of those bent upon the creation of a public sentiment" against black citizens. In addition,

> The open advocacy by Senator Tillman, Governor Vardaman, John Temple Graves and others of the repeal of the Fourteenth and Fifteenth Amendments . . . thus reducing the Afro-Americans of the South to serfdom; the timid and uncertain stand of those who essay to befriend us, even by President Roosevelt, who has said so much about "fair play" and the "Door of Hope" but who has dealt us a severe blow in the dismissal of the colored soldiers of the 25th Infantry without an adequate trial; the bold and defiant assaults of those satisfied with nothing short of our absolute undoing, certainly necessitates the meeting of the leaders of the race in an advisory way.[18]

All "similar organizations"—the Niagara Movement, by implication—were invited to send representatives. "In this crisis we all should be willing to lay aside all jealousies, bickerings and strife to meet and confer together on vital questions which concern us all. At all hazard, let all the factions get together and make a united attack upon the enemy," the call continued. The past good work of the Council—helping create a "favorable sentiment against lynching and the humiliating 'jim crow' laws," as well as battling against "all forms of injustice and discriminations"—made it the strongest possible forum for uniting the race.[19]

But others, notably Council members from Louisville, were heading to Baltimore with a strictly political agenda in mind: arousing popular sentiment against William H. Taft as the 1908 Republican presidential nominee. Only weeks before the convention opened, Kentucky members issued a sharply worded public statement denouncing the nomination of Taft "or any other man who brands us as a race of criminals and traitors. . . . We are prepared with the aid of our white friends to defeat any candidate the Republican party may nominate in 1908."[20]

The Louisville delegation could not expect to sway the convention on its own, and Baltimore's proximity to Washington, D.C., provided a convenient opportunity for the capital city's moderates and conservatives to participate. But the call's criticism of Roosevelt, along with the militant tone of 1906 speeches in New York, unnerved most Republican appointees, who were hesitant to risk their reputations by associating publicly with the radical Niagara Movement, or even its new host. Before the convention opened, at least two veteran members with strong political connections resigned from the Council: Cyrus Adams, longtime secretary, and its only life member; and Richard Thompson, head of the newspaper bureau.[21]

Only John Dancy, in fact, made the trip from the capital to Baltimore's Bethel AME Church. Dancy—"special champion of the Administration," in Chase's unflattering depiction—delivered the Council's response to the address of welcome by Dr. W. E. Cherry, president of the First Branch City Council, in the absence of Mayor Barry Mahool. Cherry complimented the Council's work and commended the delegates' energy; Dancy, adept at reading the crowd, was more circumspect, yet clearly apprehensive. "I have been with you since your inception, and stand with the Council for the restoration of every right now denied us," Dancy declared on Thursday, "but I do not believe in censuring those who have been our friends in a thousand instances because of one mistake on their part; neither do I believe in condemning President Roosevelt for his position in the Brownsville matter, because he has been the negro's friend in any number of instances."[22]

Dancy had every right to worry. As the *Bee* soon put it, "Mr. Dancy seemed to be walking around with a chip on his shoulder, but before the committee on address to the country could knock it off he took the ankle express for Washington, declaring that he could remain no longer." Dancy had warned "that the committee on address should not adopt or pass anything condemning or criticizing the President." Delegates openly jeered, suggesting that the District's recorder of deeds "board the train and return to Washington."[23]

Roughly two hundred delegates attended opening day sessions, cheering speakers who lashed out at President Roosevelt and his official decisions, including the host, the Reverend Gaines, who had razor-sharp words for both the chief executive and the nation. "Ten millions of American citizens are denied by American prejudice complete enjoyment of their natural rights," Gaines said. "American prejudice has grown to the extent that for 10,000,000 negro-American citizens, the constitutional guarantee of the jury trial, evidence and punishment mean absolutely nothing." Next, Corrothers "pitched into the President, Secretary Taft and Booker Washington, whom he characterized as the political agent of the President," according to the *Sun*. The nation's seven hundred thousand black voters could easily vote the Democratic ticket, said Corrothers, if Roosevelt did not "do the right thing by them." No one who stood in the way should be spared, he exclaimed: "even the black men who stood in the way of the race getting its rights should be struck out of the way."[24]

The thick anti-Roosevelt atmosphere had not dissipated when Walters made his annual address that evening. If the race was facing an improved situation, in some respects, he declared, the playing field was still far from level. Only the most oblivious observer could miss the distinct recent improvement in public sentiment towards lynching, he asserted: "[S]entiment, in the South, as well as in the North, is against it. Ten years ago the entire press of the South openly advocated lynch law; to-day you cannot find but a few of the prominent Southern papers that would do such a thing." Yet real dangers from lynching persisted, and only concerted action—a combination of agitation and developing "better Negro citizens"—would finish the job and "rid the land of the lynch demon," he said. "It will never be done if we fold our arms and sit idly by . . . The strong arm of the National Government is needed to deal a knock-out blow to lynch law."[25]

On other fronts, news was less favorable. Jim Crow segregation laws, taking hold across the South, "must be fought to the death. . . . It is a disgrace to our civilization and we must ever fight it. There must not be any let up until the last Jim Crow car has passed into oblivion," Walters declared. On the question of suffrage, the ballot remained the "insignia of full citizenship, and the obtaining of it should be the ambition of every man, whether he be black or white." But to battle disfranchisement in the South required educating "the masses to an appreciation of the ballot" and "flooding the country with literature on the subject."

Still, some progress was being made, even if some race leaders were discouraged by the slow pace, among them the absent Tim Fortune, who "has announced his intention to sever his connection with all negro organizations because the masses are slow to take hold and support them." Fortune had simply "forgotten how enthusiastically they support their churches and benevolent institutions," said Walters. "The truth is, that they have not been sufficiently educated along these particular lines. It requires years and years of patient toil to educate a people up to an appreciation of their rights."

The Brownsville incident was disturbing, but the dismissed soldiers had found at least one hero who would fight for them: "All honor to Senator Foraker of Ohio, the noblest Roman of them all. But for his manly and courageous stand our brave black boys might have gone down in shame and disgrace," Walters continued. "In history he will go down as one of our nation's greatest benefactors . . . side by side with Thaddeus Stevens and Charles Sumner." Foraker was clearly "the favorite of the crowd, and every mention of his name was received with vociferous applause," wrote the *Sun*. Not so President Roosevelt and his administration, who were "handled without gloves by some of the speakers," including Walters. Roosevelt had compounded his unfair treatment of "these defenseless men without money or political pull" by insulting the entire race in his last message to Congress, Walters fumed, scorning black leaders who "are decrying our agitation. They say we complain too much; that we must not be on the defensive; that we must wait and murmur not." This strategy, Walters said, "is contrary to the nature of things. The worm is on the defensive and will turn when your tread upon it; the hen will protect her brood; the bear and the lioness their cubs. It is only the craven and the cowardly who refuse to make some kind of defense for ourselves when we are imposed upon."[26]

And on a subject he rarely broached in public—social equality, including interracial marriage—the prelate's prose waxed almost purple. "Whatever social equality may signify to the white, to the ignorant negro, and, apparently, to many who are not ignorant, it means one thing—the right to stand on the same footing with a white woman as that on which a white man stands with her," Walters opined, with surprising—even shocking—candor. For the twice-widowed clergyman, now married to his childhood sweetheart and recently a new father, such pursuits were a fool's game for black men. "Why should we be breaking our necks to marry white women when we have all shades of color in our own race, from the blue-eyed blond to the black beauty in ebony," he asked the crowd. But for once, Walters would have to clarify his remarks. The statement on social equality had not originated with him, he soon admitted, sheepishly; he had been quoting "a recent magazine article by Thomas Nelson Page," with which he strongly disagreed. This "new propaganda, that every negro wants to marry a white woman," was nothing more than a "lie," he said.[27]

National organizer Lewis Jordan took verbal aim at Mississippi's Governor Vardaman, U.S. Senator Ben Tillman of South Carolina, and *Clansman* author Thomas Dixon, who would "risk their political fortunes by attacking any people as they do us. A dead animal and the negro race are the only two things which the enemy will proceed to discuss without asking any questions as to the results. The Afro-American Council is seeking no office, and boosting no man, but contending for fair play for the oppressed," declared Jordan, who envisioned a Brownsville defense fund of $1 million—"one dollar each from a million" black Americans—enabling the Council "to employ the best legal talent from our own race and from our white friends."[28]

There were other tirades from other speakers, including, for the first time, Archibald Grimké, lured to the convention by a desire to assert newfound independence from Booker T. Washington and the *New York Age*—for which he had now stopped writing—and to vocalize his increasingly sharp criticisms of Theodore Roosevelt's Brownsville actions, and the Republican Party in general. Yet his new distance from Tuskegee was not driven by personal disenchantment, for Grimké and Washington remained on cordial terms for years. Grimké was more interested in championing Joseph Foraker than in opposing Washington, and Washington, wisely, allowed him to drift away without interference. If the fact that Grimké was also gravitating toward the Niagara Movement was galling, the Wizard waved that off as well.[29]

As Dancy had discovered, the Niagara mindset predominated in Baltimore, to the near exclusion of all other viewpoints. Other speakers with similarly militant speeches—and sympathies attuned to or favoring Niagara—included Joseph McGirt, the Reverend George Bragg, William Sinclair, and Lafayette Hershaw. Joining them in anger, if not in outright Niagara fervor, was Calvin Chase.

By Friday morning, the Council's feverish oratory seemed to have subsided, as delegates prepared to elect officers for the coming year, hear the address to the country, and adjourn. But what should have been a routine endorsement of a prepared slate instead sparked an unusual battle—and a two-hour outburst of angry feelings and increasingly nasty insults—over a position traditionally overlooked: that of legal advisor. Wetmore was stepping down as legal bureau director, and Howard University law professor William Henry Harrison Hart was the chosen nominee. As the hero of the fight against Jim Crow segregation for his 1905 legal victory over the state of Maryland, Hart, a committed Niagarite, should have faced little opposition. But no one counted on Calvin Chase, attending his second convention in as many years after a lengthy absence, to lead the sudden attack.[30]

The gadfly of Washington journalism appeared in full battle dress, objecting vigorously to Hart and turning the Sharp Street Memorial Church auditorium "from a lamblike gathering [into] a place of hot debate," which Bishop Walters tried in vain to appease. Charges and countercharges filled the room with language (and personal insults) more appropriate to a barroom brawl than a gathering of educated professionals. The "red-hot debates and oratory . . . would have made Daniel Webster hide his face," wrote the *Sun*.[31]

Chase's opposition seemed more personal than professional, as did his preference for his own candidate, Washington attorney Thomas L. Jones. Chase snarled that Hart had refused to employ a black attorney in his own (successful) lawsuit, whereupon an onlooker teased Chase—and brought an appreciative laugh from the tense audience—by suggesting Hart was unaware of Chase's legal prowess. Another substitute candidate, James A. Cobb, was put forward by Miller, Corrothers, and Dr. John R. Francis but was soon rejected for being absent. Jones was present but refused to run. Walters halted the wrangling by simply announcing Hart's election, leaving Chase to fume over the "gag rule" and recount the whole affair in detail in his *Bee*.[32]

As expected, Walters was reelected president, along with a handful of officers: vice presidents Napier, Sinclair, Bishops Grant, and Bishop Williams; secretaries Jordan and Fannie Williams; and treasurer Thompson. Steward was reelected as chairman of the executive committee, along with secretary Kelly Miller and several bureau directors: Mary Church Terrell (antilynching), S. Joe Brown (emigration), and Dr. Francis (vital statistics). Chaplain George Clinton, a perennial officer, was reassigned to the ecclesiastical reform bureau. But new faces were in the majority, shifting the old geographic balance in a distinctly mid-Atlantic direction and upsetting the ideological balance with outspoken reformers. New vice presidents included three Marylanders—the Reverend William Alexander, the Reverend George Bragg, and J. C. Fernanders—plus Sylvester Corrothers of Washington, replacing Mrs. Terrell. The Reverend Abraham Gaines of Baltimore became recording secretary, while the new chaplain was the Reverend J. F. Robinson, also of Maryland. New bureau directors, in addition to Hart, included Grimké (literary) and Hershaw (newspapers), both of Washington, and H. W. Barrett of Baltimore (business), plus Joseph McGirt of Pennsylvania (education).[33]

Yet even the end of the election did little to staunch the rhetoric. High feelings persisted, with a number of delegates loudly denouncing Booker T. Washington as "a Judas to his race" and criticizing his devotion to the "almighty dollar," according to the *Sun*. Following remarks by Washington attorney Joseph R. Stewart on the political success of Irish immigrants—which he attributed to "their skill in using the power of the ballot"—other delegates called for dividing Afro-American votes into both parties, helping to end "the tyranny of the White House."[34]

The address to the nation, which the Council heard for the first time on Friday night, June 28, bore Grimké's unmistakable imprint, both in the flow of its text and the general thrust of its demands. Grimké's fluid prose and subtle nuances proclaimed his tangible pro-Foraker stance on Brownsville—and a softened version of his strongly anti-Roosevelt sentiments of recent months in the *Age*. The address opened with a refreshingly global view, congratulating "the nations of the world in their effort to promote universal peace through their representatives now assembled at The Hague," and applauding "aroused humane sentiment in behalf of the natives of the Congo Free State, who have been so cruelly treated by the Belgian government." After acknowledging "the general progress of the American people" and a recent philanthropic gift aimed at improving education of rural black children, however, the address turned to the meat of its subject: injustice to the nation's Afro-American citizens, as follows:

> The story for the year for the colored people in America has been but a repetition of the old story of their struggles and wrongs. Unexampled

> has been their oppressions and unexampled has been their successes also. Denied nearly everywhere in the South the rights of American citizens, equality at the ballot box . . . in the courts . . . on the railroads, equality of opportunity and equality of protection from mob violence, the race has gone on doing the labor of the South and . . . lifting the level of its own life in many lines at one and the same time. . . .
>
> . . . At the North the race has been knocking at the door of opportunity open to all other races in the Republic, but closed to it alone—closed to it alone not because it is bad, worse than other races, but solely because it is black, darker than other races. . . .[35]

Even in the North, white America was placing obstacles in the path of black advancement. "When the colored seek as they are doing, along industrial, educational and political lines to strengthen themselves where they are weak, the white people of the Nation, in spite of their boasted freedom, Christianity and civilization, put themselves in the way of the race's progress from its weakness," the text continued.

"Injustice toward us as a race is everywhere increasing, race prejudice is growing in the Republic, North and South alike" despite "our love, our best blood and our most devoted services in peace and in many wars. Gratitude to us seems to be dying in the heart of the Nation, and a bitter and relentless race hatred and contempt are growing to monstrous strength in the souls of the American people."

Politically, the Council held a mixed view of the nation's president, partly positive—"We approve the stand of President Roosevelt, in behalf of fair play and a square deal for all American citizens, as exemplified in the appointment of Dr. Crum and the Indianola post office affair"—but on balance, mostly negative:

> We deplore his discharge of 167 soldiers of the 25th United States Infantry without any competent legal evidence of guilt as subversive of fundamental right. We trust that he will yet see the injustice done these patriotic soldiers who have devoted their best years to make the Nation glorious, and will exercise his characteristic courage in correcting this great wrong. We also regret that President Roosevelt, in his annual message, by implication at least, holds the whole Negro race responsible for crime committed by the few, a pernicious principle which is applied to no other.[36]

To Ohio's Senator Foraker, in contrast, the race owed a singular debt. "At great peril—at the peril of his political life—Senator Foraker has championed the cause of the black battalion against the enormous and unexampled injustice and wanton abuse of executive authority. To the great Senator of Ohio, the colored people owe undying love and gratitude," the drafters asserted. "Let them repay a part of this debt by standing as bravely by him in his fight for political life as he stood by the black battalion on the floor of the Senate, in the Senate committee on military affairs and on the platform and in the press."

The Council also expressed its "sense of deep gratitude . . . for its brave and effective defense of the black battalion" to the Constitution League and to unnamed assisting organizations, as well as to three Georgians (former governor William J. Northen, former representative William Fleming, and the Reverend Q. A. Ewing) who had all acted courageously to restore racial harmony after the Atlanta riots.

Education was deemed a key weapon in the race's advancement, but the Council adamantly opposed "any special educational brand as a badge to racial inferiority," as well as continued silence in the face of "great wrongs at the hands of the South [and] the nation," as suggested by many white leaders, and by some black leaders. "As colored men we declare now and here that we will not be silent or patient at the bidding of such unworthy counsellors, regardless of their high official position or their race or color." Instead, the Council called on its members to "cry aloud against injustice and oppression," and to

> spare neither those who wrong us nor those who abet our enemies. We will cry aloud on the platform, from the pulpit, in the press against our enemies and oppressors, and . . . indicate our position at the polls—smite them in municipal elections, State elections and next year at the National elections. Let us show no quarter to our foes . . . who in obedience to American colorphobia preach to the colored people patience and submission to intolerable conditions and wrongs.[37]

For Afro-Americans to achieve political success, however, required them to "learn to love our friends and serve them, at whatever cost of personal or party sacrifice and loss and at the same time to punish our enemies and seek their destruction at the polls, regardless of any ill consequences to party or self." Only such concerted action would "advance . . . the interests and the rights of the race North and South alike."

Unified political efforts would even make it possible for the voices of black voters to be heard at the highest national level, as vengeance for the unfair treatment of the black soldiers at Brownsville: "We can make this vote a terror even to as powerful and autocratic a ruler as the present occupant of the White House, and to Secretary Taft, and to Senator [Henry Cabot] Lodge of Massachusetts and Senator [William] Warner of Missouri, who have vied with each other to do the bidding of President Roosevelt in relation to the black battalion."[38]

The Council called on Afro-American voters to "unite, organize, concentrate everywhere in the North to defeat at the polls the enemies of the race, and in the South to defeat those same enemies." Above all else, the race desired "Justice, liberty, equality before the law . . . and with nothing less, God helping us, will we be content as free men and American citizens."

It was a remarkably pointed challenge for both Council members and the race and would go down in history as the strongest—and most negative, by far—challenge ever issued by such a national group. Its elegant but radical language would give all appearances of a virtual merger of the Niagara Movement, whose members now stood at the highest ranks of the group, and the Council, entering its tenth year of existence.

The address of 1907 was arguably the best written and most compelling ever offered by the Council. But this address would have one other distinction, surpassing all others—it would be the last such address ever issued by the Council.

Despite its controversial speeches and political threats, the Council's session received little coverage by mainstream newspapers beyond the Baltimore-Washington area. Major newspapers in New York, Philadelphia, and other large U.S. cities never mentioned the convention, which was overlooked by the wire services, as well. Local coverage, however, was diligent, if sensational. The *Baltimore Sun* reported on the first and last days of the convention, headlining its final article "Booker T. Named 'Judas,'" despite the relative insignificance of that statement in the story and its vague attribution to "many of the delegates." And both the *Washington Post* and the *Evening Star* gave significant coverage to all three days of the convention, concentrating on prominent city residents.

The *Post* gave front-page play to its short articles on the first and last days' sessions, emphasizing the "vigorous" criticism by speakers of Roosevelt "and his official family beneath its combative headlines: "Attacked the President," "Again Attack President," and finally, "War on the President, Afro-Americans Publish a Political Blacklist." The *Evening Star* carried longer, more measured stories, with more neutral headlines on inside pages. "Colored Bishop Praises Foraker" blared the first day's account, followed successively by "Defense of the President" and "Race Prejudice Talk." The latter article contained a virtually complete text of the annual address—a major public relations boost for the Council—tempered by a detailed account of the Chase-Hart battle.[39]

Among the nation's black newspapers, reaction to the Council's new assertiveness and anti-Roosevelt fervor was generally favorable, as in Washington's *Bee*—if not in Baltimore's own *Afro-American Ledger*, which suggested the Council look elsewhere in the future. "We are not so sure that we are pleased with what was accomplished by the Afro-American Council," the newspaper observed, archly. "We cannot say that we are in hearty accord with many of the speeches made nor with the utility of them. Several of them could have been left out and a better impression made." Baltimore's Afro-American community had worked too hard to build up racial harmony to let outsiders unravel accomplishments with "injudicious speeches and bombastic talk . . . [w]ind, nothing but wind," editor Murphy wrote. "If there are any more such conventions to be held, we will gladly contribute our mite for their sustenance elsewhere."[40]

In New York, the *Age* reprinted the *Ledger*'s editorial without comment, saying elsewhere that it believed the Council should consider "adopt[ing] different tactics and a different policy," since speeches and "time-worn" resolutions had done little to decrease prejudice against blacks for the past twenty-five years. A lack of coverage by major newspapers (in New York, at least) was just one indication "that the public is tired of this kind of thing and is looking to the race for something else." More important, in the *Age*'s opinion, was the meeting's geographical imbalance. "Outside of Baltimore and Washington there were scarcely a dozen individuals present. Strong and useful men of the race do not attend such gatherings anymore; they have seen their weakness, and, we fear, harmfulness. If the race was convinced that such gatherings . . . [were] accomplishing any good in allaying racial prejudice, such gatherings would be attended by hundreds and thousands of our best people."[41]

Fortune had avoided Baltimore because he was "tired of spending his time and money on the railroad train traveling to conventions which the race does not want and does not appreciate." Organization had lately become "more necessary than ever it was before," but having "already spent a lifetime in that sort of thing," he was prepared to spend no more of his time on it. Better that he "attend to his own business after long years of effort to get the people to organize for the protection and defense of their civil and political rights."[42]

Two weeks later, Fortune bared his exasperation with Walters, who had publicly tweaked Fortune for his poor example. "Bishop Alexander Walters, the president of the National Afro-American Council, is a real good man with a great big heart, but he is also as full of impulses as an egg is of meat. If he does not have a care he will allow his impulses to run away with him in the matter of Mr. Fortune's position toward the council."[43]

He had no desire to "break up the council"—that was "all nonsense"—nor was he "in cahoot with Dr. Booker T. Washington, as has been insinuated, or with anybody else, and he has no reason to believe that Dr. Washington has any other feelings than friendship toward the council, such as he has manifested for years. . . . Mr. Fortune does his own thinking and will always do it." Those who knew Fortune well heard far more than frustrated whimpers. As close friends were already aware, he was headed for a complete breakdown. By October, he had been bought out of the *Age*—victim of the combined pressures of mental deterioration, a broken marriage, financial woes, and Tuskegee's desire for a more consistent hand at the helm, in the person of Fred R. Moore. His biographer describes the next four years of Fortune's life as the "years of degradation" for the once-proud journalist, whose bout with mental illness was alarming but not permanent; he would eventually recover—and would have, ironically, the last laugh on his former Council associates, by outliving them all.[44]

Washington's *Bee* spoke highly of the Council's Baltimore gathering in almost every detail—except for the election of Hart—and characterized it as "the most successful history of the organization" in its headline. Chase gave special praise to national organizer Jordan, "one of the most busy men present," and to Walters, whose opening address was described as "forcible and eloquent" and whose large photograph graced the *Bee*'s next front page. The bishop's speech "electrified the large audience present and enthused the delegates present," wrote Chase.[45]

Equally as important as this meeting, he noted, would be that in Columbus in 1908. This same detail appealed to Richard Thompson, writing in his weekly news column in the *Freeman*: "Not a little significance is attached to the selection of Ohio's capital, as 1908 is a presidential year, and a meeting of the council in this political hotbed, on the eve of the National Convention of the Republican party, with the Taft-Foraker fight approaching a climax, cannot fail to fill a large place in the public eye."[46]

Thompson noted that the Baltimore session had "created a stir, and has been the talk of [Washington, D.C.], especially among the leaders and their lieutenants." His resignation from the Council had obviously not affected his news judgment, or his sense of what readers wanted to hear; he warmly described Walters, whose "outspoken address made a good impression, and from his standpoint, the issues were very exhaustively and courageously presented."[47]

In a separate reflection on the meeting, editor George Knox called the annual address "wisely cautious"—oddly inappropriate, given its threats of political sabotage—and in keeping with the organization's reputation as America's annual "Negro Congress." It came off almost as parody, instead—for with each new sentence, the former Council stalwart seemed more and more to be poking fun, rather broadly, at a target he found almost pompously self-important. With tongue firmly in cheek, perhaps, Knox continued:

> The council meets from year to year to "pass" on the more important happenings of the Negroes, to discuss the ways and means to greater liberty, and to wage a continuous war against "chronic" wrongs. Age and decorum have given the body respectability and today its utterances are viewed as the sentiments of the Negroes generally. The quality of men composing the council is in keeping with its high purposes. Consequently an air of importance attaches to its deliberations, and most especially is the annual address considered, since it embodies the best thought of a thoughtful gathering of individuals.[48]

Was Knox serious or chuckling when he described "the very distinguished" Walters, "who by the way is responsible for the existence of the Council," as a "wise and sagacious leader in the deliberations of the organization"? One can only surmise. The annual address showed "caution and reserve, commendable qualities that were strictly in accord with the gravity of the situation."[49]

Two weeks later, the *Freeman* assumed a bantering tone, suggesting it would "like to know" if the Council had "practically absorbed the Niagara Movement and carried off the shining lance of the Constitutional League"; if the planners of next year's convention were professional checker players; and if Washington's absence had "turn[ed] the hose on several tons of ammunition carefully stored up in the editorial sanctum of the Boston Guardian."[50]

And in late August, the newspaper posed a more pointed question, one that had lingered for months in the minds of other observers after Baltimore: "Will the Afro-American Council absorb the Niagara Movement, or be absorbed by it?" Just how effective could the new Council be without its core of veteran members, all but expelled by the onrush of Niagarites? Moderates and conservatives who had supported the Council since 1898, like Dancy, were powerless to reclaim the Council from the "sterile coup," in Stephen Fox's phrase. Without an anchor, or perhaps even a pilot, the Council now began to drift, driven by ideological winds on uncharted seas toward a distant horizon.[51]

In September, Thompson recounted his conversation with legal counselor Hart, and Hart's optimistic assessment of recent developments in the battle against "Jim Crow" railroad cars, including a federal order mandating precisely equal accommodations on trains which chose to segregate the races. "Assuming that this is a true statement of the situation, it looks as if the Afro-American

Council is justifying its existence," Thompson wrote.[52] But by November, the pace had slowed considerably, to the point where a bemused *New York Age* wondered aloud what was going on. "We are not hearing a great deal now of the work of the Afro-American Council," wrote Fred Moore, but

> We trust under the leadership of Bishop Walters that this organization will not lose its opportunity to influence the race for good. . . . We hope that the Bishop will not permit the organization to rest on its oars until just before the annual meeting and then make a spurt in the way of activity. The Afro-American Council should be at work all the year, and we earnestly exhort the members of the race everywhere to stand by the Bishop and hold up his hands in his important work.[53]

Others might have pondered the same questions. Plans to move the Council's working offices to Washington, D.C., had fallen through. National organizer Jordan remained instead in Louisville, where his energies were gradually redirected into other pursuits. Walters, planning a personal move from Jersey City into the metropolis of New York, was perhaps preoccupied by other matters, including a December meeting with Trotter and other militants in Boston. When the end came for the Council, as it seems to have done during the winter of 1907 to 1908, there was little warning—and almost inexplicably, no public notice afterward. It was as if the great ship, out of fuel and nearly unoccupied, capsized at sea, and was not heard of again.

By the spring of 1908, the Council, for all practical purposes, had simply ceased to exist.

Epilogue

Slouching toward Columbus

In his seminal biography of William Monroe Trotter, author Stephen Fox pays only limited attention to the National Afro-American Council and its longtime leader, Alexander Walters. Fox's oversight is understandable, since neither the group nor the man played a significant role in Trotter's life, except, perhaps, for that brief period in the winter of 1907 to 1908, when both Walters and Trotter were searching for paths out of the wilderness. The Niagara Movement had cut both men adrift, if in different ways; Trotter had left the movement in disgust, while Walters had lost the rudder of his Council to Niagarites.

So it was that Walters traveled to Boston in late December 1907 to address the Boston Literary and Historical Association, and then remained for an extraordinary conversation with Trotter and the Reverend William Scott, president of Boston's Suffrage League. According to Fox, the three men "sent out a call for a race conference in Philadelphia in April," one open only to trusted colleagues. "Race traitors, spies, and stool-pigeons are not wanted nor will such as are known to be of that class be admitted," the *Guardian* warned its readers in March.[1]

In a stunning bit of organizational choreography, Walters promptly joined the Niagara Movement's Washington, D.C., branch and began charting a quixotic course toward leadership of the new group still gestating in Philadelphia. If W. E. B. Du Bois was not exactly the kind of participant Trotter might have envisioned, Du Bois's brilliant mind and exceptional credentials made him desirable to Walters, who offered, over objections from a dumbfounded Trotter and Scott, to pay Du Bois's travel expenses from Atlanta.[2]

Walters soon discovered the difficulties of working with Trotter, he told Du Bois in early April—something the Atlantan already knew well, from their stormy

Niagara days—but he may still have underestimated Trotter's shrewdness. When Du Bois decided not to attend the conference, Walters was disappointed. With the last-minute appearance of Archibald Grimké, another brilliant thinker and potential ally, the bishop's hopes probably soared again. But in mid-March, with the conference weeks away, Walters took time to attend the joint meeting in Washington of the Board of Bishops of the "three great bodies of Negro Methodism"—his own African Methodist Episcopal Zion, plus the African Methodist Episcopal and Colored Methodist Episcopal denominations. There he was appointed secretary of a new committee, on "The Civic and Political Condition of the Negroes of America," and helped prepare an address to the nation, one adopted unanimously by the group.[3]

That address, and his role in helping draft it, caught the eye of the *New York Age*, which editorially portrayed Walters on March 19 as orchestrator of a political hijacking attempt, designed to seduce the bishops away from Republican presidential candidate Taft and toward his Democratic opponent. Walters's angry response occupied nearly two full columns in the *Age* a week later. He remained a Republican, Walters implied, but neither a Taft nor Roosevelt Republican. "There are thousands of Negroes who will never vote for Secretary Taft, for they know that a vote for Taft is a vote for President Roosevelt, and rather than do this, they will remain away from the polls," Walters wrote.[4]

"With us, it is not a question of policy but one of principle. As Republicans, are we to say nothing of the broken pledges of the party to the race in its last National platform? We are tired of the negative position of our own party; we want it to take a positive and aggressive position in our favor." The *Age* had unfairly depicted the Bishops as under the influence of "three or four colored preachers, one a Bishop and a few Democratic politicians who attempted to make it appear that the bishops . . . were bitterly opposed to President Roosevelt and . . . Taft." His colleagues were "a respectable body of Black Republicans, protesting against unjust treatment on the part of the President and Secretary of War of their fellow citizens who had been summarily dismissed from the Army."[5]

Walters vented his spleen but deceived no one as to his real intention—to defeat Taft, and even the Republican Party itself, if he had to. Like Grimké and the bishops, he preferred Foraker—but unlike Grimké, did not necessarily believe Foraker would be nominated. Grimké's intense lobbying on Foraker's behalf helped swing the bishops away from Tuskegee and Roosevelt, according to Dickson Bruce. Yet the *Age* was not convinced, describing Walters on April 2as "lean and hungry of look, leaning far away into the audience from the place where he howled" at a New York public meeting in late March. He and Du Bois had sworn to defeat Taft or Roosevelt—by supporting Democrat William Jennings Bryan, if necessary, said the *Age*. "What madness is this that has come upon these wise men?" pondered Fred Moore.[6]

Grimké had taken the same oath, but Trotter's professional jealousy blinded him to Grimké's strategic usefulness. By the time the Philadelphia conference opened, Trotter had determined not to let Grimké take part; only a concerted effort by George White and others changed his mind. The price of admission to the conference was later described as a pledge to "declare their allegiance to Bryan or the Democratic party in the event of Mr. Taft's nomination."[7]

But resolution was short-lived. White also demanded admission for Calvin Chase, and when this was refused, White and many others left the meeting. Grimké and Walters remained to the end, with Walters "greatly annoyed" when the Reverend J. Milton Waldron of Washington, D.C., was selected instead as president. Trotter had outwitted his colleague and ensured his own control of the National Negro American Political League by his election as corresponding secretary.[8]

Still, there might be too much of a good thing, as Du Bois pointed out in June. His interesting solution to the problem, as he saw it, of overcrowding in the world of civil rights organizations, was one of streamlining. Writing in the *Horizon*, Du Bois called for "Union" of the "four organizations standing for essentially the same things."

> Each organization once had its raison d'etre: the Niagara Movement crystallized a faint dissatisfaction into an organized and articulate protest. The [Afro-American] Council is the first and oldest of these organizations. The [National Negro American] Political League is a union of men in these two organizations to effect one great interest. The [Negro] Academy is a step toward Science and Art.[9]

The difficulty with having so many organizations, Du Bois said, was money. "The combined annual dues of all of them . . . [are] a prohibitive fee for the mass of colored men. . . . members are wasted by duplication of energy." Would the three other leaders—Walters, Waldron, and Grimké—consider meeting with Niagarites in Oberlin that summer to consolidate?[10]

There was no public response, for good reason: Du Bois's proposal satisfied no one else, and Trotter did not trust Du Bois. Grimké rejected the merger because he felt his academy's scholarly pursuits might be compromised by affiliation with a political movement. Walters reluctantly agreed to ask his executive committee to shift the Columbus meeting to Chicago, if Du Bois would agree to meet in

Chicago, but Du Bois declined. None of it mattered in the end, for the Negro American Political League was all but stillborn, the Niagara Movement was on life support, and the Council, for all practical purposes, was already dead.

Despite the new league's efforts, Taft was nominated by the Republicans and went on to defeat Bryan in the fall. In the spring of 1909, the league renamed itself in Columbus and finally selected Walters—not even present—as its president, Trotter as secretary, and Grimké as treasurer. But lagging attendance "and a woeful lack of harmony" dogged the new National Independent Political League for months to come. It bore little resemblance to the once-proud Afro-American Council, now vanished from the scene.[11]

The old Afro-American Council never reached Columbus, as planned, nor did Alexander Walters. That the league, the group he now led, had finally reached the Ohio capital, however bedraggled, was a tribute to Walters's sheer staying power. In 1909, the Council was dead, and the Niagara Movement dying, but Walters persisted, easily the most resilient of the nation's early civil rights leaders, first of the old group to join the new NAACP, and one of the few to join the new National Urban League as well. In many ways, he became the Council's living, enigmatic epitaph, a vibrant memory of the organization he had founded, relinquished, reclaimed, revived, and then discarded.[12]

By 1919, Walters and all but one of the other Council giants had passed into history, leaving Fortune behind to tell their stories. Washington was the first to die, at fifty-eight, in November 1915. Among his many obituaries was a lengthy one by Fortune, published the following spring as "The Quick and the Dead." Thornbrough describes it as "a kind of apology for his own life," but the most telling portion focused on Fortune's relationship with his now-departed mentor.[13]

Having recovered his vigor and intellectual focus, Fortune's memories of his relationship with Washington remained vivid, if not necessarily objective. Their partnership, as he now described it, was one of equals ("I helped make him leader") until Fortune's health had begun to fail and he resigned as president of the Council. Since Fortune had sold the *Age* in 1907, they had seen each other just five times. "We did not fall out and quarrel," Fortune recalled. "We were on speaking terms to the last, but he had no further use for me in his business."

Washington was a "very great man" who had done a "very great work," but Fortune believed his own work for the race—between 1890 and 1904, at least—was greater, and more like that of the true race giant, Frederick Douglass. "I had everything in common with Mr. Douglass and his methods, and nothing in common with the policies of Dr. Washington, especially his personal and political ones. . . . I helped rather than hindered him in the doing of it."[14]

A year later, in February 1917, Alexander Walters, fifty-nine, followed the Wizard into the next world, and Fortune, now writing for the *Age* as Washington bureau chief, expressed his deep personal sadness: "I knew him for thirty years, and we labored side by side for many years for what we considered the best interests of the race . . . There will not be another to do things in the way he did them, in the place where he was."[15] Yet nowhere did he mention the Council, or Walters's long involvement with it.

Nearly two years later, in December 1918, George White died in his sleep in Philadelphia, a fortnight after turning sixty-six. A lengthy unsigned obituary appeared in the *Philadelphia Tribune*, where Fortune occasionally worked, which recounted White's early career in detail, concentrating on his two terms in Congress and his close relationship with President McKinley. The obituary, almost certainly penned by Fortune, was laudatory, mentioning many high points of White's life, if not his service to the long-forgotten Council. Yet there was, nonetheless, a hint of it: "To have known Mr. White didn't necessarily mean that you would share all his views, but it is safe to say that . . . you were compelled to respect him. He has played the part assigned to him by the hand of fate, and this done, he has sheathed his sword."[16]

Having had the last word for three colleagues, Fortune struggled on for another decade, actively writing for such publications as Marcus Garvey's *Negro World* until his own death at seventy-two. A detailed obituary in the *New York Amsterdam News* recalled, in one paragraph, that Fortune had "entered the final stage of his active career" at the time of the "rise of Booker T. Washington." His Afro-American Council "might be called the parent of the Niagara Movement, the National Association for the Advancement of Colored People, and all similar organizations since."[17]

In penning a tribute to his old colleague a week later, Kelly Miller summed up Fortune's life in typically elegant fashion. "For a season, bridging the decline of Douglass and the rise of Booker T. Washington, [Fortune] was the most influential Negro in the nation. A record of his life would be an adequate history of the Negro race for the past fifty years." Ideologically, Fortune had traveled a long, winding path, having "witnessed the exploitation and failure of every theory propounded for the solution of the race's problems," including amalgamation ("how can the Negro be amalgamated when the white race is unwilling to amalgamate with him?"). Miller shrewdly reduced the three basic theories to two-word epigrams:

> Frederick Douglass said "Get white." Marcus Garvey said "Get out." Booker T. Washington said "Get along." In his declining days, For-

> tune's despairing soul . . . inclined to the theory of Marcus Garvey. But here again he found that it is as hard for the Negro to get out as it is to get white. And so, in final analysis, there remains only the expediency of getting along, which Fortune's dying soul witnessed, and quaked.[18]

The four titans of a vanished era—Fortune, Washington, Walters, and White—were now gone, their once-proud National Afro-American Council now only a vague memory in the minds of an ever-dwindling few. Its flaws had been many, its accomplishments few. Yet at the time of its creation, it had represented the best hope the race had to offer itself; if its members could not sustain the momentum during the decade of their gatherings, the dream was nonetheless nourished, the flame guarded.

Its best legacy, perhaps, would be the very number of its former members who went on to meet, in New York, in 1909 and afterward, this time to found a more lasting organization. One by one, they would move on: Walters, Du Bois, Mrs. Wells-Barnett, Mrs. Terrell, Miller, McGhee, Grimké, even White, to continue the twin battles against racial injustice and for racial progress. The civil rights movement, which the Council had spawned and nurtured, would now thrive—and in its shadow the Council lived on, however invisibly, for generations to come.

Appendix

Notes

Bibliography

Index

Appendix

National Afro-American Council Constitution

ARTICLE I.

This organization shall be known as the NATIONAL AFRO-AMERICAN COUNCIL[1]

ARTICLE II.

The objects of this Organization shall be:

(1) To investigate and make an impartial report of all lynchings and other outrages perpetrated upon American citizens.

(2) To assist in testing the constitutionality of laws which are made for the express purpose of oppressing the Afro-American.

(3) To promote the work of securing legislation which in the individual States shall secure to all citizens the rights guaranteed them by the 13th, 14th, and 15th Amendments to the Constitution of the United States.

(4) To aid in the work of prison reform.

(5) To recommend a healthy migration from terror-ridden sections of our land to States where law is respected and maintained.

(6) To encourage both industrial and higher education.

(7) To promote business enterprises among the people.

(8) To educate sentiment on all lines that specially affect our race.

(9) To inaugurate and promote plans for the moral elevation of the Afro-American people.

(10) To urge the appropriation for school funds by the Federal Government to provide education for citizens who are denied school privileges by discriminating State laws.

ARTICLE III.

Membership.

Section 1. The Afro-American Council shall be composed of members as follows:

1st. All persons who hold life membership.

2d. Council Delegates, representing duly accredited Local Councils.

3d. Affiliated Delegates, representing organizations of similar plans and purposes co-operating with the Afro-American Council.

Sec. 2. Every local Afro-American Council shall be entitled to representation in the National Council by delegates elected on a basis of one delegate to every fifty (50) members, said delegates to qualify upon presentation of credentials and payment of 10 cents for each member so represented. Provided, however, that any Local Council having less than fifty (50) members shall be entitled to one vote, upon presentation of credentials and payment of the annual tax of Five Dollars.

Sec. 4. Religious and secular organizations which have for their aim and work the mental and moral elevation of the race, and which desire to co-operate with the National Council may be represented by affiliated delegates, not more than two delegates to each organization. Said delegates shall have the right to vote upon payment of Five Dollars for each delegate.

Sec 4. Editors of Afro-American newspapers, and Principals of Academic Schools and Colleges, may be admitted to membership in the National Council and be entitled to a vote upon presentation of credentials and payment of the annual tax of $5.00.

ARTICLE IV.

Officers:

Sec. 1. The officers of the National Council shall be: A President; Nine Vice-Presidents; A Recording Secretary; An Assistant Secretary; A Financial Secretary; A Treasurer; A Chaplain; A Sergeant-at-Arms; An Executive Committee.

Sec. 2. The Officers shall serve one year, or until their successors are appointed or elected, and are members of the Executive Committee.

Duties of Officers:

Sec. 1. The President shall preside at all meetings of the Council. He shall appoint the members of the committees whose appointment is not otherwise provided for, shall fill all vacancies pending action of the Council or Executive Committee, and perform such other duties as are usually incumbent upon the presiding officer of legislative bodies.

Sec. 2. The Vice-President shall preside in the absence of the President, and perform such other duties as are usually incumbent upon his office.

Sec 3. The Recording Secretary shall keep a faithful record of all proceedings of the Council; record the names and residences of the members in a Roll Book kept for that purpose; shall notify the members of the time and place of the annual meetings; and perform such other duties as may be required by the Council.

Sec. 4. The Assistant Secretary shall assist the Recording Secretary at the annual sessions of the Council, and act in the absence of said Secretary.

Sec. 5. The Financial Secretary shall receive and keep a record of all moneys belonging to the Council, and make such disbursements as may be ordered by the Council upon drafts signed by the Chairman of the Executive Committee and countersigned by the President of the Council. At the end of six months the Financial Secretary shall turn over to the Treasurer all moneys collected and unexpended, with a full report of receipts and disbursements for that term. A semi-annual report shall be made to the Executive Committee and an annual report to the Council. A good and sufficient safety bond shall be given by the Financial Secretary, in the sum of One Thousand Dollars, for the faithful performance of the duty of said secretary.

Sec. 6. It shall be the duty of the Treasurer to keep an accurate account of all moneys received from the Financial Secretary. He shall pay out of moneys so received all orders drawn by the Financial Secretary and countersigned by the President. He shall give a safety bond in the sum of One Thousand Dollars for the faithful performance of his duties, make an annual report to the National Council and a semi-annual report to the Executive Committee.

Sec. 7. The Chaplain shall open meetings of the Council with prayer, and perform other such duties as usually pertain to his office.

Sec. 8. The Sergeant-at-Arms shall keep order and preserve the decorum of the Council.

ARTICLE VI.

Fees.

Sec. 1. The Annual Tax shall be Five Dollars ($5.00) for each voting delegate to the National Council.

Sec. 2. Life Membership shall be granted by a majority vote of the Executive Committee. The fee for such membership shall be Fifty Dollars ($50.00), payable Ten Dollars ($10.00) upon filing application and the remaining Forty Dollars ($40.00) within one year from date of application.

ARTICLE VII.

Salaries.

Sec. 1. No officer shall receive pay for service rendered to the National Council except the Financial Secretary.

Sec. 2. The Executive Committee shall determine the amount that shall be paid to officers for traveling expenses and stationery, also the salary of the Financial Secretary.

ARTICLE VIII.

Elections.

Sec. 1. The officers of the National Council shall be nominated by a special committee appointed by the Executive Committee at its annual session.

Sec. 2. Should a vacancy occur in the offices of the Council by death, resignation or otherwise, the Executive Committee shall have power to fill such office made vacant for the remainder of the term.

Sec. 3. The election of all officers shall be determined by a majority vote of the National Council.

ARTICLE IX.

Local Councils.

Whenever ten or more persons who are in sympathy with the objects set forth in this Constitution shall desire to organize a Local Council, they shall have power to do so.

When any State or Territory shall have as many as ten local councils said councils shall have power to organize a State Council; their representation in the National Council shall be as provided for in Article III in this Constitution.

ARTICLE X.

Amendments to the Constitution.

Sec.1. To amend the Constitution the proposed amendment shall be submitted to the Executive Committee and receive its approval: 1st, by a vote of two-thirds of the members present, and 2d, by the ratification of the National Council.

ARTICLE XI.

Politics.

The Afro-American Council shall be non-partisan.

ARTICLE XII.

Executive Committee.

Sec. 1. The Executive Committee shall be composed of members of the National Afro-American Council. Each State and Territory shall be entitled to three members, one woman and two men, on said Committee.

Sec. 2. Members of the Executive Committee shall be elected at the annual session of the State Council in the several States and Territories; where there are no State Councils the members of the Executive Committee may be nominated by the accredited representatives of the State, present at the annual session of the Council, and elected by the National Council.

Sec. 3. If any State or Territory is without delegates at the annual session of the National Council, and therefore without representation on the Executive Committee, the Executive Committee may nominate members to be elected by the National Council, to represent said States and Territories on the Executive Committee.

Sec. 4. The Officers of the Executive Committee shall be a Chairman and Secretary, to be chosen by the Committee.

Sec. 5. Fifteen members of the Executive Committee shall form a quorum for business.

Sec. 6. It shall be the duty of the members of the Executive Committee to form local organizations in the States and Territories which they represent.

Sec. 7. The Executive Committee shall have the general management of the affairs of the National Council when said body is not in session, subject to the direction of the National Council.

Notes

Introduction: The Four Titans

1. Excellent biographical sketches of the four men are found in the *Dictionary of American Negro Biography*, Rayford W. Logan and Michael R. Winston, ed. (New York: W. W. Norton, 1982). In addition to these sketches, I have drawn details from full-length biographies, cited elsewhere, of Washington (Louis R. Harlan, *The Making of a Black Leader* and *The Wizard of Tuskegee*); Fortune (Emma Lou Thornbrough, *T. Thomas Fortune: Militant Journalist*); White (Benjamin R. Justesen, *George Henry White: An Even Chance in the Race of Life*); and for Walters, both his memoir, *My Life and Work*, and George Mason Miller, "'A This Worldly Mission': The Life and Career of Alexander Walters (1858–1917)," Ph.D. diss., State Univ. of New York at Stony Brook, 1984.

2. Miller, "'A This Worldly Mission," 19–21. Walters's father, Henry, was born in Larue County, Kentucky, as the son of his master; Walters was told "on good authority" of his grandfather's kinship to Lincoln.

3. See Timothy T. Fortune to Booker T. Washington, January 21, 1887, in Louis R. Harlan and Raymond W. Smock, ed., *The Booker T. Washington Papers* (Urbana: Univ. of Illinois Press, 1973–1989), 2:327 . Fortune generally preferred to use his first initial and middle name; his biographer, Emma Lou Thornbrough, chooses "Tim."

4. Washington wrote fairly regularly to McKinley, according to the index of the William McKinley Papers (LOC); five letters from 1897 to 1901 appear in Harlan's *BTW Papers*. According to Mary Fisher, Bishop Benjamin W. Arnett of Ohio was considered "the most powerful individual Negro at the [McKinley] White House" (see "Benjamin William Arnett," *DANB*, 18).

5. Walters, *My Life and Work*, 191–92.

6. *Southern Workman and Hampton School Record*, June 15, 1899.

7. "Aims to Help Negro, Opening Sessions of the Afro-American Council," *WP*, December 30, 1898.

8. Walters's letter to the *New York Age* in March 1898 was reprinted in *My Life and Work*, 98.

9. Walters, *My Life and Work*, 98–102. North Carolina signers included Dancy, Bishops George W. Clinton and James W. Hood, the Reverend J. W. Smith, and H. C. Denney. Nine Virginians signed the same call.

1. Resurrecting the League: Rochester, 1898

1. *Negro Population, 1790–1915* (Department of Commerce, U.S. Bureau of the Census. Washington: Government Printing Office, 1918), 93.

2. "Afro-American Conference," Rochester *Union and Advertiser*, September 15, 1898.

3. Ibid.; "Ceremonies but No Statue," *New York Sun*, September 15, 1898.

4. Walters, *My Life and Work*, 98–99; "Afro-American Conference." Frazier B. Baker, of Lake City, South Carolina, had been shot and killed in February; Isaac H. Loftin, of Hogansville, Georgia, survived a shooting incident in September 1897. Walters lists 112 names as signers, 32 of them from New York. Fortune claimed a larger figure of 150 signers.

5. Walters, *My Life and Work*, 102–4.

6. "The Afro-American Council," *Appeal*, September 24, 1898; Thornbrough, *T. Thomas Fortune*, 179. None of these four signers was listed by Walters in *My Life and Work*. John Adams and his brother Cyrus published the *Appeal*, a regional weekly based in Saint Paul, which served six U.S. cities.

7. "Afro-American Conference"; *Negro Population, 1790–1915*, 93. Philadelphia had 62,813 black residents in the 1900 U.S. census, behind Baltimore, Washington, D.C., and New Orleans. New York had 60,666 residents, fifth largest.

8. Thornbrough, *T. Thomas Fortune*, 179–80; "Afro-American Conference."

9. "Afro-American Conference." Since copies of the *Age* for 1898 are not available, the lower Walters figure is relied on elsewhere.

10. "The Afro-American Council," *Appeal*; "Afro-American Conference."

11. Emma Lou Thornbrough, "The National Afro-American League, 1887–1908," in *Journal of Southern History* 27 (4) (November 1961), 496, 499–500.

12. Rayford W. Logan, "Joseph Charles Price," in *DANB*, 503.

13. Thornbrough, "Afro-American League," 500–501.

14. John E. Fleming, "Alexander Walters," in *DANB*, 98–102; Miller, "'A This Worldly Mission,"160. At least eleven active ministers signed the Walters call, according to Fleming.

15. *New York Freeman*, June 4, 1887; *WCA*, December 24, 1898, January 21, 1899. Journalist Calvin Chase told the *Evening Star* that Fortune's remarks had been "political only," never advocating "physical assassination." The *Colored American* chided Fortune for impetuous behavior, while John E. Bruce agreed that Fortune did not mean what he said.

16. *WCA*, December 24, 1898, January 21, 1899.

17. Ida B. Wells-Barnett, "First Convention of the National Afro-American Council," in Cyrus Field Adams, *The National Afro-American Council, Organized 1898: A History, etc.* (Washington, D.C.: Cyrus F. Adams, 1902), 6. Wells-Barnett's sequence of events confirmed the newspaper's version of the proceedings.

18. "Leaders Clash on Race Theories," Rochester *Union and Advertiser*, September 16, 1898; *WCA*, September 24, 1898; Wells-Barnett, "First Convention"; Thornbrough, *T. Thomas Fortune*, 180. Others members were W. E. Bowen and Mrs. R. Jerome Jeffrey, head of the Rochester Colored Women's League. The minutes show that Fortune "declined the position but was afterward prevailed upon to accept." Wells-Barnett claimed Fortune would have accepted the presidency had she not intervened. *Crusade for Justice: The Autobiography of Ida B. Wells*, Alfreda Duster, ed. (Chicago: Univ. of Chicago Press, 1970), 256.

19. "Leaders Clash." Members of the committee on address included Wells-Barnett, Dancy, Chris Perry, F. S. Cunningham, and Douglass's daughter, Rosetta Douglass Sprague.

20. Ibid.

21. Walters, *My Life and Work*, 106.

22. John E. Bruce, "Introduction," in Walters, *My Life and Work*, 10; Louis R. Harlan, *Booker T. Washington: The Wizard of Tuskegee, 1901–1915* (New York: Oxford Univ. Press, 1983), viii. According to Harlan, many of Booker T. Washington's friends—and many of his enemies—referred to him regularly, if only privately, as "the Wizard." To detractors, the

term evoked a somewhat unflattering image of the "Wizard of Oz," villain of the popular 1900 fantasy book by L. Frank Baum, but was just as often intended by admirers as a frank tribute to the Tuskegeean's astonishing effectiveness.

2. The Black Judases: Washington, D.C., 1898

1. *Negro Population, 1790–1915*, 43, 93. Washington, D.C., had 86,702 black residents in 1900, roughly 31 percent of the city's total population (278,718).

2. Walters, *My Life and Work*, 110–12.

3. Ibid.

4. Cheatham was appointed recorder of deeds for the District of Columbia in May 1897. Lyons succeeded Blanche K. Bruce as U.S. Treasury register in 1898.

5. "Negroism Exalted," Raleigh *News and Observer*, July 21, 1898; "The Convention Very Harmonious," Raleigh *Morning Post*, July 21, 1898. The *N&O's* journalistic drumbeat after White's July 20 speech reprinted selected quotations from White's stump speech; the fuller version in the *Morning Post* was far less inflammatory.

6. For a comprehensive account of the violence, see H. Leon Prather's *We Have Taken a City: Wilmington Racial Massacre and Coup of 1898* (Cranbury, N.J.: Associated Univ. Presses, 1984). Prather and other historians contributed centennial essays to *Democracy Betrayed: The Wilmington Race Riot of 1898 and Its Legacy* (Chapel Hill: Univ. of North Carolina Press, 1998), ed. David S. Cecelski and Timothy B. Tyson.

7. "To Stop Violence," *WES*, November 11, 1898; "The Wilmington Refugees," *WES*, November 14, 1898; "Manly Speaks," *Newark* (N.J.) *Dispatch*, as reported in the *News and Observer*, November 25, 1898; "To Suppress Race Wars," *NYT*, November 18, 1898.

8. Jeffrey J. Crow and Robert F. Durden, *Maverick Republican in the Old North State: A Political Biography of Daniel L. Russell* (Baton Rouge: Louisiana State Univ. Press, 1977), 135–36; "Simple Justice," *Boston Globe*, December 2, 1898; Congressman White Lectures," *WCA*, December 17, 1898; "Answers Senator McLaurin," *WB*, December 10, 1898; George H. White to William McKinley, December 12, 1898, William McKinley Papers (LOC). White's letter, dated the day of McKinley's departure, proposed a brief side trip to the state's only public college for blacks in Greensboro, where the president's train stopped briefly. It was never answered.

9. Jesse Lawson to John P. Green, December 23, 1898, John P. Green Collection, Western Reserve Historical Society.

10. *Official Programme: First Annual Meeting of the Afro-American Council at the Metropolitan Baptist Church, Washington , D.C., Thursday and Friday, December 29 and 30, 1898, Bishop Alexander Walters, president*. Daniel A. P. Murray Pamphlet Collection (LOC).

11. Ibid.

12. Lawson to Green, December 23, 1898.

13. "Low Rates for Delegates" and "What Must We Do To Be Saved?" *WB*, December 24, 1898; "Racial Troubles, Discussion under Auspices of National Protective Association. President McKinley Criticized—Appeal to Congress and Resolutions Adopted," *WB*, December 24, 1898, reprinted from *WES*, December 20, 1898.

14. *WCA*, December 24, 1898, January 21, 1899.

15. "The President is a thoroughly despicable character and I despise him, but I am glad he went to Tuskegee," Fortune wrote Washington on December 14 and 16, 1898 (*BTW-P*, 4:532, 4:535). Fortune's public rhetoric would grow steadily more purple by May 1899, when

he described McKinley memorably as "a man of jelly who would turn us loose to the mob and not say a word."

16. "Racial Troubles," *WES*, December 20, 1898.

17. Thornbrough, *T. Thomas Fortune*, 182–83; "Mr. Fortune Undertakes to Explain," *WES*, December 21, 1898. Fortune accused the *Star* of "twist[ing]" his "extemporaneous remarks."

18. Editorial, *WB*, December 24, 1898; "Only Political Assassination," *WES*, December 21, 1898.

19. J. M. Holland to Booker T. Washington, December 21, 1898, *BTW-P*, 4:543–44. Mrs. Holland, a reporter in the women's department of the *New York Tribune*, wrote Washington soon after the speech.

20. Holland to Washington, December 21, 1898; Timothy T. Fortune to Booker T. Washington, December 27, 1898, *BTW-P*, 4:549–50.

21. Wilmington, North Carolina, *Morning Star*, September 4, 1898.

22. White to McKinley, December 12, 1898; "Aims to Help Negro," *WP*, December 30, 1898.

23. "The Negro in Politics," *AME Church Review* 15 (October 1898), 594–603.

24. "Afro-American Council Will Begin Its Sessions To-day at Metropolitan Baptist Church," *WP*, December 29, 1898; "The Council's One Mistake," *WCA*, January 14, 1899. The *Colored American* expressed a fervent preference for "a man—the best that can be found" as financial secretary. Wells-Barnett succeeded J. Frank Blagburn in this post and was herself succeeded by John Bruce in August 1899.

25. "Not Born To Conquer, Remarkable Paper Read before Negro Academy," *WP*, December 29, 1898.

26. Ibid.

27. "Afro-American Council," *WES*, December 29, 1898.

28. "Report of the Treasurer," June 2, 1902, in Adams, *The National Afro-American Council*, 12–14.

29. Ibid., 12. No source was listed for the funds used to pay these first bills.

30. Ibid.

31. "To Solve Our Own Problem," *WCA*, January 14, 1899.

32. Ibid.

33. "Aims to Help Negro," *WP*, December 30, 1898.

34. "Aims to Help Negro"; official minutes, "Special Session of the National Afro-American Council, December 29–30, 1898," in Adams, *The National Afro-American Council*, 6.

35. "Aims to Help Negro"; "Special Session."

36. "Aims to Help Negro." Wells-Barnett's objection to U.S. rule of its recently acquired overseas territories—Cuba, Puerto Rico, and the Philippines—already signaled a new flash point among black intellectuals and journalists.

37. Ibid.

38. Ibid.

39. "Memorial to President. Colored Men from Pittsburg Present a Protest against Lynching," *WP*, December 30, 1898; "Colored Men in Session. A Large Meeting in Washington to Protest against Southern Outrages," *NYT*, December 30, 1898.

40. "Memorial to President."

41. "A Great Uproar, Pandemonium Reigned at the Afro-American Council," *WES*, December 30, 1898.

42. Ibid.; "A Noisy Gathering," *Baltimore Sun*, December 31, 1898.

43. "A Case in Point," editorial, *WP*, January 2, 1899.

44. "Mendacity of the Local Press," editorial, *WCA*, January 14, 1899.

45. "Two Noisy Sessions, Plenty of Excitement at the Afro-American Council," *WP*, December 31, 1898.

46. "Mendacity of the Local Press."

47. Ibid.

48. "Clamor for Hearing. Afro-American Delegates Anxious to Go on Record," *WES*, December 31, 1898.

49. Ibid.

50. "Two Noisy Sessions."

51. "The Negroes Appeal, A Committee Calls at the White House," Raleigh *News and Observer*, January 1, 1899; "An Influential Delegation," *WCA*, January 7, 1899. The *Colored American* described the group as "the finest aggregation of colored men ever brought together for a visit of this company."

52. "The Negroes Appeal"; "Memorial on Race Troubles," Raleigh *News and Observer*, January 1, 1899.

53. The *News and Observer* listed twenty-four names, the *Colored American* twenty-five. Both listed Walters, Arnett, Clinton, and nineteen others: Lyons, Cheatham, White, Pinchback, Dancy, Lawson, Robert Pelham, John Mitchell Jr., George Murray, C. S. Morris, J. Frank Blagburn, James Lewis, Richard Thompson, E. J. Sanford, Daniel Murray, Alfred B. Cosey, W. H. Ferris, L. A. Bray, and I. T. Bradley. The *N&O* added Fortune, Théophile Allain, and Cyrus Adams, while the *CA* added only Edward E. Cooper and William A. Pledger.

54. "Will Not Be Suppressed," *WP*, January 3, 1899.

55. "An Influential Delegation."

56. Jere A. Brown to John P. Green, January 21, 1899, John P. Green Collection, Western Reserve Historical Society (LOC). Brown, who served two terms in the Ohio House in the late 1880s, was a staunch Republican; he had also served as a U.S. customs inspector, internal revenue clerk, and immigration inspector in Cleveland.

57. "Negro Daily Under Way. A Committee Appointed to Secure Subscriptions to this Commendable Enterprise," *WCA*, January 14, 1899.

58. "Two Noisy Sessions"; "As to An Afro-American Daily," *WCA*, January 14, 1899; "Negro Daily Under Way." Non-journalists included bishops Arnett, Grant, Turner, and Walters, ministers R. R. Carter, Elias C. Morris , and H. T. Johnson; Lyons, White, Dancy, J. P. Peaker, James C. Napier, Henry Demas, Henry A. Rucker, J. W. Anderson, Dr. William D. Crum, L. Wilder, Mrs. A. D. Carey, and Daniel Murray. The editor envisioned an alternative fund of $10,000.

59. "At the Nation's Capital," *NYA*, April 27, 1899; Armistead S. Pride and Clint C. Wilson II, *A History of the Black Press* (Washington, D.C.: Howard Univ. Press, 1997), 213; "Simple Justice," *Boston Globe*, December 2, 1898. Terrell's column for the *Age* boomed Pledger's proposal: "I take it for granted that he has his 'daily newspaper scheme' with him, for Col. Pledger is a man of wonderfully tenacious purpose." The *Record* appeared as a daily until 1904, then as a weekly until 1910.

60. Richard W. Thompson to Booker T. Washington, September 14, 1899, BTW-C (LOC); "Council's Plan of Work, Congressman George H. White Places the Issue of the Order before the People," *WCA*, May 13, 1899. Thompson was corresponding secretary of the local council, whose president was now Pinchback. Jesse Lawson chaired the local committee, whose members also included Cheatham, Lyons, Murray, Miller, Cooper, local physician Dr. Lucy E. Moten, and Henry Arnett, secretary.

61. "White Places the Issue."

3. All Eyes on McKinley: Chicago, 1899

1. "A Mistrial Was Ordered," Charleston, South Carolina, *Sunday News*, April 23, 1899.

2. Willard B. Gatewood Jr., *Black Americans and the White Man's Burden: 1898–1903* (Urbana: Univ. of Illinois Press, 1975), 198. Gatewood cites reports of Rev. Elijah Strickland's lynching in the *Richmond Planet, Indianapolis Freeman*, and *Indianapolis Recorder.* Sam Hose had sought payment from his employer, who attacked him, and Hose had fled after killing the employer. The rape charge was concocted to incite the lynch mob.

3. *Congressional Record*, 56th Cong., 1st sess., 33, 1–2151. White provided these figures while preparing to introduce his antilynching bill, on February 23, 1900.

4. "At the Nation's Capital," *NYA*, April 27, 1899. Terrell noted Fortune's presence in Washington for the executive committee meeting, as well as a brief vacation, but said he "found little time for rest or newspaper work." Terrell served as second vice president of the District of Columbia chapter of the Council in 1898; by the fall of 1899, Mary Church Terrell had been elected third vice president, according to Council letterheads; see Lawson to Green, December 23, 1898, and Richard W. Thompson to Booker T. Washington, September 14, 1899, BTW-C(LOC).

5. "Attack on the President," *NYT*, May 11, 1899.

6. Ibid.

7. Thornbrough, *T. Thomas Fortune*, 189–90; *NYA* quoted in *Boston Transcript*, July 24, 1899; *WB*, August 5, 1899.

8. "A Law to Stop Lynching. Afro-American Council Wants to Make It a Crime against the United States Government," *NYT*, August 18, 1899.

9. *Negro Population, 1790–1915*, 93; Henry L. Suggs, ed., *The Black Press in the Middle West, 1865–1985* (Westport, Conn.: Greenwood Press, 1996), 48–49.

10. "Colored Men in Session. Second Annual Meeting of Afro-American Body Opens," *Chicago Tribune*, August 18, 1899.

11. "List of Delegates," *Appeal*, August 26, 1899. The local councils named as represented included those in Cambridge, Massachusetts; Washington, D.C.; Evanston, Illinois; Clarksville and Mound Bayou, Mississippi; Kansas City, Kansas; and Rochester, Saint Paul, Chicago, Philadelphia, Nashville, Des Moines, Milwaukee, and San Francisco.

12. Thornbrough, *T. Thomas Fortune*, 191, 212; "Benjamin William Arnett," 17–18; "Spirit of the Press," *Recorder*, July 22, 1899. The *Recorder* noted that "the efforts of certain colored men to array the colored race against the administration on account of the Philippine policy was mentioned, and Mr. Lyons assured the President that, in his own opinion, it would amount to little."

13. "Negro Leader Is Upheld. Afro-American Conference Indorses Booker T. Washington," *CT*, August 20, 1899; Mary M. Fisher, "Reverdy Cassius Ransom," in *DANB*, 512–14; "Chicago Suffers from Heat," *CT*, August 20, 1899.

14. Letter to the editor, *Daily Inter-Ocean*, August 25, 1899; Reverdy C. Ransom to Booker T. Washington, August 31, 1899, *BTW-P*, 5:194.

15. W. E. B. Du Bois, "Two Negro Conventions," *Independent*, September 7, 1899.

16. "Colored Men in Session."

17. Ibid.

18. "To Aid Negro Race," *Daily Inter-Ocean*, August 18, 1899.

19. Ibid.; "Negro Leader Is Upheld."

20. "Negro Leader Is Upheld."

21. "Executive Committee," *Appeal*, August 26, 1899. The Committee's membership listed women members from Alabama, Arkansas, Colorado, Florida, Georgia, Illinois, Indiana, Iowa, Kansas, Kentucky, Louisiana, Massachusetts, Michigan, Minnesota, Mississippi, Missouri, New Jersey, New York, North Carolina, Pennsylvania, Rhode Island, South Carolina, Tennessee, the District of Columbia, and Oklahoma Territory. California and Delaware added female members to their delegations by year's end.

22. "Quarrel over Office," *Daily Inter-Ocean*, August 17, 1899; *Crusade for Justice*, 60; Evelyn Brooks Barnett, "Mary Church Terrell," *DANB*, 583–85. Wells-Barnett claimed that the NACW planners deliberately excluded her from the list of local participants.

23. "Women Have a Peaceful Session," *CT*, August 18, 1899; Mary Church Terrell, *A Colored Woman in a White World* (reprint, Amherst, N.Y.: Humanity Books, 2005), 189.

24. "Second Annual Convention of the National Afro-American Council," minutes, in Adams, *The National Afro-American Council*, 7; "Try Political Move," *Daily Inter-Ocean*, August 19, 1899. Other speakers were Mrs. C. H. Phillips of Tennessee, Mrs. T. H. Lyles of Minnesota, Mrs. Williams of Louisiana, Miss Imogene Howard of New York, and Mrs. J. Silone Yates of Missouri.

25. "Banquet at Sherman House," *CT*, August 20, 1899.

26. Ibid.; Duster, *Crusade for Justice*, 262.

27. "The National Council, A Meeting of Earnest Representative Afro-Americans," *Appeal*, August 26, 1899.

28. "Text of the Resolution," *CT*, August 20, 1899; "Officers Are Elected," *CT*, August 20, 1899. Théophile T. Allain to Booker T. Washington, August 20, 1899, *BTW-P*, 5:176.

29. "Officers Are Elected."

30. "Want Negro Vote Used."

31. Ibid.

32. "A Meeting of Earnest Representative Afro-Americans"; Thornbrough, *T. Thomas Fortune*, 212; "Second Annual Convention of the National Afro-American Council," 7. Fortune spent the late summer of 1899 in Saratoga receiving medical treatment for an undisclosed ailment.

33. "The Afro-American Quarrel," *NYT*, August 21, 1899.

34. "Officers Are Elected"; "Officers of the National Afro-American Council," *Freeman*, September 2, 1899. The *Tribune* said Allain and Buckner of Chicago made a "bitter fight" against Walters's reelection. A separate list in the *Appeal* edition of August 26 lists Reverdy Ransom as both chaplain and vice president, instead of Grant.

35. "Report of the Treasurer," 12.

36. "Bureaus," *Freeman*, September 2, 1899. Professor B. A. Johnson of Salisbury, North Carolina, headed the educational bureau, the Reverend Archibald J. Carey of Chicago the ecclesiastical reform bureau.

37. Thornbrough, "The National Afro-American League," 503–4; Emmett Scott to Booker T. Washington, August 23, 1899, *BTW-P*, 5:181; "Closes in a Tumult," *Sunday Inter-Ocean*, August 20, 1899; David Levering Lewis, *W. E. B. Du Bois: Biography of a Race, 1868–1919* (New York: Henry Holt , 1993), 230. Lewis says that Du Bois was being sincere, if also opportunistic.

38. "Convention Opens Today," *Daily Inter-Ocean*, August 17, 1899; "Closes in a Tumult." White was listed both as "George H. White, M.D., of Tarboro, N.C." and "Bishop George H. White, North Carolina."

39. "The Annual Address." Other members included attorneys James Napier, Jesse Lawson, and Ferdinand Barnett; Bishop Lucius Holsey; educator B. A. Johnson; and businessmen I. T. Montgomery, I. F. Bradley, and Buckner. Active journalists Bruce and Adams had little visible influence on the final product.

40. Ibid.

41. Ibid.

42. "The Afro-American Council," editorial, *CT*, August 21, 1899.

43. "The National Council," *Appeal*, August 26, 1899; "Aftermath of the Council," *WCA*, August 26, 1899; "Two Negro Conventions."

44. Thornbrough, *T. Thomas Fortune*, 192.

45. Timothy T. Fortune to Booker T. Washington, December 31, 1899, *BTW-P*, 5:295.

46. "The Council at Work," *WCA*, January 6, 1900.

47. "The Political Horoscope," *WCA*, January 13, 1900; "Gentlemen of the Pulpit, Press and Bar Participate in a Feast, Intellectual and Gastronomic," *WCA*, January 13, 1900. White, Brown, and Murray also consulted U.S. attorney general John W. Griggs and Albert E. Pillsbury, former Massachusetts attorney general. Council members at the meal were Walters, Fortune, Bruce, McGhee, Brown, Lawson, Cicero Harris, Murray, Pinchback, and Cooper.

48. "Gentlemen of the Pulpit"; Timothy T. Fortune to Booker T. Washington, December 31, 1899, *BTW-P*, 5:295; Timothy T. Fortune to Booker T. Washington, December 30, 1899, *BTW-P*, 5:294–95; Richard W. Thompson to Booker T. Washington, February 3, 1900, BTW-C (LOC).

49. Fortune to Washington, December 30, 1899. Thompson wrote Washington at least three more letters in 1900 and corresponded regularly with Emmett Scott. (See, for instance, *BTW- P*, 5: 461–63, 473–74, 631–32; 7:33–35. 358–59, 8:140–43, and 9:594–97.) Washington vigorously raised funds for the project, as demonstrated by his 1900 correspondence with Francis Garrison, Giles Jackson, Richard Hallowell, Jesse Lawson, and Emmett Scott. (See, among others, *BTW-P*, 5:450–51, 458, 553–55, 566–67, 647–48, and 651.

50. Booker T. Washington to Emmett J. Scott, March 11, 1900, *BTW-P*, 5:457. Others attending were Edward Cooper, Calvin Chase, and Daniel Murray.

4. Playing at Presidential Politics: Indianapolis, 1900

1. Editorial, *Gazette*, May 5, 1900. Thompson later contributed $20.50 collected during the May 9 "John Brown concert" in Rochester.

2. "The Test Case of the Louisiana Constitution, Document No. 1," in Adams, *The National Afro-American Council*, 26–29. The case's full name was *State ex rel. David J. Ryanes vs. Jerry M. Gleason, Registrar.* George White estimated the cost. Republican Edmunds served as one of Vermont's senators from 1866 to 1891.

3. Editorial, *WCA*, May 12, 1900; Booker T. Washington to Emmett J. Scott, March 11, 1900, *BTW-P*, 5:457.

4. Editorial, *Gazette*, May 26, 1900; Kenneth L. Kusmer, "Harry C[lay] Smith," in *DANB*, 564–65; "Friction between Delegates," *INSE*, August 31, 1900.

5. "Two Lively Sessions, Nothing Dull about the Afro-American Council," *INJO*, August 31, 1900.

6. "Benjamin William Arnett." Arnett died in 1906 of uremic poisoning at age sixty-eight. The other bishops were: Clinton and Harris of North Carolina (AME Zion), Grant of Pennsylvania (AME), and Holsey of Georgia (CME).

7. "Report of the Treasurer," June 1902.

8. Donald B. Johnson, comp., *National Party Platforms, Volume I, 1840–1956* (Urbana: Univ. of Illinois Press, 1978), 109.

9. "Is Lynch to Blame?" editorial, *Gazette*, June 30, 1900.

10. Ibid.; Johnson, *National Party Platforms*, 109, 123–24.

11. Benjamin R. Justesen, "George Henry White, Josephus Daniels, and the Showdown over Disfranchisement, 1900," in *North Carolina Historical Review* 77 (January 2000), 1–33.

12. Johnson, *National Party Platforms*, 118.

13. "Southern Negro's Plaint," *NYT*, 26 August 1900.

14. Ibid.

15. Benjamin R. Justesen, "Black Tip, White Iceberg: Black Postmasters and the Rise of White Supremacy in North Carolina, 1897–1901," *North Carolina Historical Review* 82 (April 2005), 224. In the 1885 general assembly, White had served in the state senate and Pritchard in the house. The "lily-whites" essentially sought to remove black officials from party ranks in the South and render disfranchisement a dead issue.

16. "Noted Negroes Here, Two National Gatherings in the City This Week," *INSE*, August 27, 1900; "Distinguished Colored Men. Party Headed by Representative White Arrives," *INJO*, August 28, 1900; "Senator Pritchard Denounced," *INSE*, August 30, 1900.

17. Alexander Walters to Booker T. Washington, August 14, 1900, *BTW-P*, 5:595; Duster, *Crusade for Justice*, 264–65.

18. "Senator Pritchard Denounced."

19. "Bitter Republican Speech," *INJO*, August 30, 1900; "Afro-American Press," *Recorder*, September 1, 1900. MacCorkle, governor of West Virginia from 1893–1897, was a rare voice of moderation on the disfranchisement issue among leading Democrats.

20. "Colored Editors Meet"; "Indorsed McKinley, Afro-American Editors Issue the Following Statement," *Recorder*, September 1, 1900.

21. "Indorsed McKinley." Perhaps out of convenience, not every member newspaper sent an editor. Mrs. Fox, of Indiana, represented a Mississippi newspaper; Green, Washington's *Bee;* and White, the *True Reformer* of Littleton, North Carolina.

22. "Are Playing with Fire, Democrats Who Hope to Divert the Afro-American League," *INJO*, August 27, 1900; "Secret Meeting Held. Colored Men Gather in a Cellar on Indiana Avenue," *INJO*, August 28, 1900.

23. "Secret Meeting Held"; "Tried to Silence Hill," *INSE*, August 30, 1900; "Roosevelt's Insult, What He said about San Juan Colored Troops," *INSE*, August 30, 1900.

24. "Distinguished Colored Men."

25. Ferdinand L. Barnett to John P. Green, August 9, 1900, John P. Green Collection, Western Reserve Historical Society (LOC).

26. Ibid.; Duster, *Crusade for Justice*, 263–65. Wells-Barnett was a controversial traveling speaker, mostly in Missouri, for the national committee during the 1900 campaign.

27. *Negro Population, 1790–1915*, 93; Suggs, *The Black Press in the Middle West*, 53–58.

28. "Roosevelt's Insult."

29. "Colored Men Loyal," *INJO*, August 29, 1900. Gov. James A. Mount, as yet "out of the city," appeared later in the week.

30. Ibid.; "Kerens Wired Council Delegates," *Gazette*, September 8, 1900; "Prominent Colored Men Here," *INJO*, August 29, 1900. Other Missouri delegates were J. Silas Harris, J. H. Pelham, A. R. Chinn, O. M. Wood, Nelson Crews, C. H. Tandy, and John Wheeler. National committeeman R. C Kerens had instructed them to meet in Saint Louis, promising to "furnish transportation to Indianapolis and return."

31. "Will Not Indorse, Afro-American Council Issues Public Address," *INSE*, August 30, 1900; "Colored Men Loyal"; Suggs, *The Black Press in the Middle West*, 54. The popular Taggart was national chairman until 1908 and on the DNC until 1916, when he was appointed, briefly, to the U.S. Senate.

32. "Mayor Taggart Speaks," *INJO*, August 29, 1900.

33. "The Afternoon Session, Bishop Alexander Walters Delivers the Principal Address," *INJO*, August 29, 1900.

34. Ibid.

35. Ibid.

36. Ibid.

37. "Committee on Resolutions," *INJO*, August 29, 1900. Other members: Lyons, Pledger, Lewis, Knox, Crossland, Pelham, Steward, Lyon, White, F. L. Barnett, Cyrus Adams, Hightower Kealing, George Jackson, James Howard, Peter J. Smith Jr., J. J. Blackshear, Gurley Brewer, Lillian Fox, and V. Allison Sweeney. Allain's materials included a J. W. Lyons speech on service by black officials under McKinley, and a speech by South Carolina's white supremacist senator, "Pitchfork Ben" Tillman.

38. "Self Help Is Needed," *INJO*, August 30, 1900.

39. Booker T. Washington to Francis J. Garrison, March 11, 1900, *BTW-P*, 5:458; Giles B. Jackson to Booker T. Washington, June 1, 1900, *BTW-P*, 5:553; Emmett J. Scott to Booker T. Washington, June 21, 1900, *BTW-P*, 5:565. According to Scott, attorney Anthony Leopold Gussman had "named the price of $7,000 for his services."

40. Louis R. Harlan, "The Secret Life of Booker T. Washington," *Journal of Southern History* 37(3) (August 1971), 397; Louis R. Harlan, *Booker T. Washington: The Making of a Black Leader, 1856–1901* (New York: Oxford Univ. Press, 1972), 297–99.

41. "Third Annual Convention," minutes, in Adams, *The National Afro-American Council*, 9.

42. "Closes in a Tumult," *Sunday Inter-Ocean*, August 20, 1899; "Negro Leader Is Upheld," *CT*, August 20, 1899. Both newspapers listed Carey as the elected chaplain, and Ransom as a vice president.

43. "The Evening Session," *INJO*, August 30, 1900; James G. Spady, "Richard Robert Wright Sr.," in *DANB*, 674.

44. "Ejected from the Hall," *INSE*, August 30, 1900.

45. Ibid.; "Politics Left Out," *INJO*, August 30, 1900.

46. "Afro-American Council," *Recorder*, September 1, 1900; "Afro-American Council Notes," *Freeman*, September 1, 1900; "Fired Out! John P. Green's Fate at the National Afro-American Council Meet of Last Week," *Gazette*, September 8, 1900.

47. "Fired Out!"; "Sentinel Is Praised for Its Fair Reports by Delegates to the Council," *INSE*, August 31, 1900.

48. "Politics Left Out," *INJO*, August 30, 1900. Serving with White were Fortune, McGhee, Lyons, and Wright.

49. "Friction between Delegates. Congressman White Had Been Offered Presidency of Council," *INSE*, August 31, 1900; "Senator Pritchard Denounced," *INSE*, August 30, 1900.

50. "Senator Pritchard Denounced."

51. Ibid.; "Politics Left Out"; "An Enemy of the Negro," *INSE*, August 30, 1900.

52. "Two Lively Sessions," *INJO*, August 31, 1900; "Friction between Delegates."

53. "Two Lively Sessions."

54. Ibid.; "Friction between Delegates."

55. "Two Lively Sessions."

56. "Friction between Delegates."

57. "Afro-American Convention," *Freeman*, September 1, 1900.

58. "Fired Out!"; "The Afternoon Session," *INJO*, August 31, 1900.

59. "The Afternoon Session."

60. "Two Lively Sessions"; "Bitter Republican Speech," *INSE*, August 31, 1900.

61. "Bitter Republican Speech."

62. "The Afternoon Session"; "Afro-American Council Notes."

63. "Afro-American Council Notes."

64. "Afro-American Convention," *Freeman*, September 1, 1900.

65. "Third Annual Convention," minutes, 8–9; Duster, *Crusade for Justice*, 253–54; "Afro-American Council Notes."

66. Duster, *Crusade for Justice*, 265.

67. Alexander Walters to Booker T. Washington, August 14, 1900, *BTW-P*, 5:595.

68. "The Afro-Americans. Council Closes with Speech by Booker T. Washington," *INSE*, September 1, 1900; "The Council Closes," *INJO*, September 1, 1900; *BTW-P*, footnote, 5:630. In the audience were poet James Whitcomb Riley and the U.S. minister to Austria. Washington purposefully arrived as late as he could, according to Harlan's footnote.

69. "Governor Spoke Plainly," *INJO*, September 1, 1900.

70. Ibid.

71. Ibid.

72. Ibid.; *BTW-P*, footnote, 5:630.

73. "Subject of Comment. Why Booker T. Washington Did Not Touch on Politics," *INJO*, September 1, 1900.

74. "Subject of Comment"; Jesse Lawson to Booker T. Washington, October 3, 1900, *BTW-P*, 5:648; John Coburn to Booker T. Washington, September 3, 1900, *BTW-P*, 5:629; Richard W. Thompson to Booker T. Washington, September 3, 1900, *BTW-P*, 5:631; Duster, *Crusade for Justice*, 265. Thompson had resigned as associate editor of the *Colored American* and desired a position at the U.S. Census Bureau.

75. "Resolutions Adopted," *INSE*, August 31, 1900.

76. Ibid.

77. "Address to the Country," *Freeman*, September 1, 1900.

78. "Will Be No Race War," *INJO*, September 1, 1900; Richard W. Thompson to Booker T. Washington, February 3, 1900, BTW-C (LOC). The previous subcommittee, as listed in the letterhead, averaged forty-six years in age, due primarily to the presence of Pinchback, aged sixty-two; Judson Lyons, forty-one, was the youngest member at the time.

79. "Will Be No Race War"; "Afro-American Council Notes"; Emmett J. Scott to Booker T. Washington, July 17, 1902, *BTW-P*, 6:494–97.

80. "Report of the Treasurer," June 1902; Jesse Lawson to Booker T. Washington, October 3, 1900, *BTW-P*, 5:648.

81. Giles B. Jackson to Booker T. Washington, October 5, 1900, *BTW-P*, 5:649; "To Test Disfranchisement Law," *INJO*, August 29, 1900; "Afro-American Council Notes."

82. "To Test Disfranchisement Law"; Giles B. Jackson to Booker T. Washington, October 5, 1900, *BTW-P*, 5:649–50.

83. Jesse Lawson to Booker T. Washington, October 8, 1900, *BTW-P*, 5:651–52.

84. Lawson to Washington, October 8, 1900; "Report of the Treasurer," June 1902.

85. "Afro-American Council. Members Endorse McKinley Administration," *Appeal*, October 13, 1900.

86. "Afro-American Council, Sub-Executive Committee to meet in Washington, Dec. 28," *Recorder*, December 1, 1900.

87. "The President's Message."

88. Editorial, *Gazette*, January 12, 1901; editorial, *WCA*, January 19, 1901; editorial, *CG*, January 19, 1901.

89. *Congressional Record*, 56th Cong., 2d sess., 34, 1:737 (January 8, 1901).

90. Editorial, *Gazette*, January 19, 1901; *Congressional Record*, 56th Cong., 2d sess., 34, 1:1634–38.

91. *Congressional Record*, 56th Cong., 2d sess., 34, 1:1634–38.

92. "Valedictory of the Negro," *Freeman*, February 16, 1901.

93. Benjamin R. Justesen, "George Henry White and the End of an Era," in *Washington History* 15(2), Fall/Winter 2003–2004, 34–51.

5. Nowhere Else to Turn: Philadelphia, 1901

1. "At the White House," *WES*, March 6, 1901.

2. "Washington: The Capital City and Its Happenings," *Appeal*, March 9, 1901.

3. "At the White House"; "The Capital City and Its Happenings."

4. White's refusals from George B. Cortelyou, McKinley's private secretary, dated June 1and June 4, 1901, are found in the William McKinley Papers (LOC).

5. "Protest against a Negro Postmaster," *WES*, March 6, 1901; Justesen, "Black Tip, White Iceberg." Martin was appointed Athens postmaster in 1897, when white opposition had been less than unanimous. Howard said he now "believed the President would recognize their [current] wishes." White had successfully nominated at least three dozen black postmasters during his first term, but only a handful after his 1898 reelection.

6. "The Capital City and Its Happenings"; Miller, "A This Worldly Mission," 251; Jesse Lawson to Booker T. Washington, March 5, 1901, *BTW-P*, 6:48. Miller asserts that Pinchback and others opposed Romain, but "no one else would take the case." Lawson assured Washington that "I am very glad that we will not be compelled to draw on you for that amount."

7. "Report of the Treasurer," June 1902.

8. "A Dull Season in Summer, But Our Correspondent Finds Plenty of News Items," *Freeman*, July 27, 1901.

9. Ibid.

10. "Mr. White's Dilemma," *WP*, April 18, 1901.

11. "May Transfer Mr. Youngblood," *WP*, April 20, 1901.

12. "Ex-Representative White. Why He Is Entitled to Consideration at the Hands of the President," letter, *WP*, April 25, 1901.

13. Letters, George B. Cortelyou to George H. White, June 1 and June 4, 1901, William McKinley Papers (LOC); "Question of Common Sense," letter, *WP*, May 7, 1901; "Up the Palisades," *WCA*, May 11, 1901. Cortelyou, McKinley's private secretary, was responding to separate letters from White of May 31 and June 3, 1901.

14. Alexander Walters to Booker T. Washington, June 27, 1901, *BTW-P*, 6:160.

15. Walters to Washington, June 27, 1901; Albert E. Pillsbury to Booker T. Washington, July 30, 1901, *BTW-P*, 6:183.

16. Pillsbury to Washington, July 30, 1901.

17. Booker T. Washington to Hollis B. Frissell, June 7, 1901, *BTW-P*, 6:151.

18. "A Press Release," dated June 17, 1901, *BTW-P*, 6:155; Harlan, *The Wizard of Tuskegee*, 245; Michael Perman, *Struggle for Mastery: Disfranchisement in the South, 1888–1908* (Chapel Hill: Univ. of North Carolina Press, 2001), 190–91.

19. Dickson D. Bruce Jr., *Archibald Grimké: Portrait of a Black Independent* (Baton Rouge: Louisiana State Univ. Press, 1993), 94. Bruce thinks Grimké engineered the correspondence, which had begun in early 1900.

20. Ibid.; Willard B. Gatewood Jr., *Black Americans and the White Man's Burden, 1898–1903* (Urbana: Univ. of Illinois Press, 1975), 209. Trotter's journalistic career is explored at length by Stephen Fox in *The Guardian of Boston: William Monroe Trotter* (New York: Atheneum, 1970).

21. "The Test Case of the Louisiana Constitution, Document No. 1," in Adams, *The National Afro-American Council*, 26–28.

22. Ibid.

23. Ibid.

24. Ibid.; Alcée Fortier, ed., *Louisiana: Comprising Sketches of Parishes, Towns, Events, Institutions, and Persons, Arranged in Cyclopedic Form*. Vol. 3 (Century Historical Association, 1914), 383–84.

25. "A Dull Season."

26. *Negro Population, 1790–1915*, 93; John A. Saunders, *One Hundred Years after Emancipation: History of the Philadelphia Negro, 1787 to 1963* (Philadelphia: F. R. S. Publishing Co., 1963), 111; Roger Lane, *William Dorsey's Philadelphia and Ours: On the Past and Future of the Black City in America* (New York: Oxford Univ. Press, 1991), 101–2, 197–228. Between 1900 and 1910, New York's black population increased by more than 51 percent, followed by Philadelphia at 34.9 percent.

27. Lane, *William Dorsey's Philadelphia*, 219–20; "The Philadelphia Branch of the Afro-American Council," *Colored American Magazine*, August 1901.

28. "Bad Nigger with a Winchester. Colored Editors Declare for Armed Resistance to Lynch Law," *WP*, August 7, 1901.

29. Ibid.

30. "Bad for the Negroes, Recorder Cheatham Condemns Incendiary Advice," *WP*, August 8, 1901.

31. Ibid.

32. "Afro-Americans Meet, Fourth Annual Session of National Council Opened," *Philadelphia Record*, August 8, 1901.

33. Ibid. According to Michigan historical records, three black state legislators had served so far: William W. Ferguson, 1893–1896; Joseph H. Dickinson, 1897–1900; and Dr. James W. Ames, 1901–1902, all of Wayne County. Illinois, Indiana, Minnesota, and Ohio had also elected black state legislators.

34. "Delegates to Hayti," *Philadelphia Item*, August 8, 1901; "Fourth Annual Convention," 10. Wibecan soon became financial secretary of the Council, while Lawson became corresponding secretary.

35. "Delegates to Hayti."

36. "Colored Men Denounce Pro-Lynching Sentiment," *Philadelphia Inquirer*, August 9, 1901; "Lynchings Denounced, Afro-American Council to Appeal for Federal Aid," *Philadelphia Record*, August 9, 1901; "Fourth Annual Convention," minutes, 10.

37. "Want a Trial by Jury," *Philadelphia Record*, August 9, 1901.

38. "Education of the Negro," *Philadelphia Record*, August 9; "Negroes Want Women of their Race Protected in the South," *Philadelphia Item*, August 11, 1901; "Report of the Treasurer," June 1902.

39. "Fourth Annual Convention," minutes, 10–11.

40. "At Philadelphia," editorial, *Freeman*, August 17, 1901.

41. "Ex-Congressman White Indignant," *WB*, August 17, 1901; "Great Bodies Convene," *WCA*, August 10, 1901. The *Colored American* said White was "conspicuous among those present" at meetings of the AME Zion Women's Home and Foreign Missionary Society and its Bishops' Council in Atlantic City.

42. "Afro-American Council, The Meeting a Farce," *WB*, August 17, 1901; "Ex-Congressman White Indignant."

43. "Race Problem His Issue," *Philadelphia Record*, August 10, 1901; "White Quits in a Huff," *Baltimore Sun*, August 10, 1901.

44. "At Philadelphia"; "Echoes of the Afro-American Council," *WCA*, August 31, 1901.

45. "Echoes of the Afro-American Council"; Emmett J. Scott to Booker T. Washington, August 13, 1901, *BTW-P*, 6:186.

46. "The Second Baptist Lyceum," *WCA*, October 19, 1901.

47. "Negroes Want Women Protected."

48. Ibid.

49. Ibid.; "Race Problem His Issue."

50. "Negroes Want Women Protected."

51. Emmett J. Scott and Lyman Beecher Stowe, *Booker T. Washington, Builder of a Civilization* (New York: Doubleday, Page, 1917), ix. Roosevelt wrote a lengthy preface to the memorial volume, which also contains his September 14, 1901, letter to Washington (49). For a useful discussion of the controversial meal, see Harlan, *The Wizard of Tuskegee*, 3–5.

52. Justesen, "Black Tip, White Iceberg," 198–202.

53. Jesse Lawson to Booker T. Washington, October 20, 1901, *BTW-P*, 6:257; Booker T. Washington to Philander C. Knox, October 24, 1901, *BTW-P*, 6:266; Aubrey Robinson Jr., "Robert Herberton Terrell," in *DANB*, 585–86.

54. Edward E. Cooper to Booker T. Washington, December 12, 1901, *BTW-P*, 6:345; Whitefield McKinlay to Booker T. Washington, December 14, 1901, *BTW-P*, 6:347–48.

55. McKinlay to Washington, December 14, 1901; Booker T. Washington to Whitefield McKinlay, December 16, 1901, *BTW-P*, 6:348–49. McKinlay, a prominent black businessman in Washington, D.C., was one of Booker T. Washington's closest friends and strongest supporters.

56. Whitefield McKinlay to Booker T. Washington, November 13, 1901, *BTW-P*, 6:318; Booker T. Washington to Theodore Roosevelt, November 6, 1901, *BTW-P*, 6:289. Chase had been convicted of criminal libel, and Roosevelt said he could not appoint "anyone with a jail record." While noting that Chase was "treated unjustly in that criminal libel matter," Washington said he "does not bear a good reputation among the colored people."

57. Thornbrough, *T. Thomas Fortune*, 222–23.

6. Fortune at the Helm: Saint Paul, 1902

1. The other two posts—U.S. Treasury register and U.S. minister to Haiti—were currently held by Judson W. Lyons and William F. Powell, respectively. Both remained in office until the second Roosevelt administration.

2. "Cheatham Must Vacate," *WP*, December 18, 1901; Booker T. Washington to Theodore Roosevelt, November 6, 1901, *BTW-P*, 6:289; "Recorder Cheatham," editorial, *WB*, November 16, 1901. Cheatham's first wife, Louisa, had died in 1899; in November 1901, he married Laura Joyner.

3. "Cheatham Must Vacate"; Whitefield McKinlay to Booker T. Washington, December 14, 1901, *BTW-P*, 6:348.

4. "Cheatham Must Vacate"; Emmett J. Scott to Booker T. Washington, July 17, 1902, *BTW-P*, 6:495.

5. Alexander Walters to Emmett J. Scott, April 2, 1902, BTW-C (LOC); Fredrick L. McGhee to Emmett J. Scott, March 25, 1902, *BTW-P*, 6:424–26

6. McGhee to Scott, March 25, 1902; *Negro Population, 1790–1915*, 93; "Be Sure to Attend," *Appeal*, July 5, 1902; "Call for Meeting," *Appeal*, July 5, 1902. Dr. William T. Francis was chairman of the program committee for the convention.

7. Fredrick L. McGhee to John P. Green, June 21, 1902, John P. Green Collection , Western Reserve Historical Society (LOC).

8. Wheaton, a transplanted Marylander, had gone to law school in Minneapolis before entering Republican politics in the mid-1890s.

9. "Call for Meeting."

10. Ibid.

11. "Programme," *Appeal*, July 5, 1902.

12. Fredrick L. McGhee to Booker T. Washington, April 5, 1902, *BTW-P*, 6:435–36.

13. "Mr. White on Our Children," *WCA*, February 1, 1902; "Afro Americans Meet, Listen to an Address by Ex-Congressman White," *Brooklyn Daily Eagle*, February 13, 1902.

14. Benjamin R. Justesen, ed., *In His Own Words: The Writings, Speeches, and Letters of George Henry White* (Lincoln, Nebr.: iUniverse, 2004), 236; "Hon. George H. White Talks of the Future," *WCA*, May 3, 1902.

15. George Henry White, "What Should Be the Negro's Attitude in Politics?" in Daniel Culp, ed., *Twentieth Century Negro Literature, or a Cyclopedia of Thought on Vital Topics Relating to the American Negro* (Napierville, Ill.: J. L. Nichols, 1902).

16. "N.A.A.P.A.," *Appeal*, July 19, 1902.

17. Ibid.

18. Ibid.

19. Ibid.

20. "Are Coming for Council," *SPPP*, July 9, 1902; "Threaten to Bolt Council," *SPPP*, July 10, 1902.

21. "N.A.A.C.," *Appeal*, July 12, 1902; "Threaten to Bolt Council."

22. "N.A.A.C."

23. Ibid. Other members included William Steward, Bishop Clinton, Peter Smith, J. E. Mason, J. Madison Vance, Mrs. J. E. Porter, Nelson Crews, and William Vernon.

24. Ibid.

25. Ibid.

26. Peter J. Smith Jr., to Booker T. Washington, July 3, 1902, *BTW-P*, 6:492.

27. "Booker T. Washington," *Appeal*, July 12, 1902.

28. Ibid.

29. Ibid. Kennan (1845–1924), a well-known journalist and world traveler, had written a two-volume book called *Siberia and the Exile System*, published in 1891.

30. "Booker T. Washington."

31. Scott to Washington, July 17, 1902; "Harmony Seemingly Reigns."

32. Duster, *Crusade for Justice*, 322–23; editorial, *Guardian*, July 19, 1902, reprinted as "Afro-American Council's Mistake," *Broadax*, July 26, 1902. In February 1909, "the feeling prevailed at our conference that an effort would be made to tie us to the chariot wheels of the industrial education program" by Oswald Villard, Wells-Barnett recalled.

33. "Chips," "Afro-American Council's Mistake," *Broadax*, July 26, 1902; editorials, *Chicago Conservator*, August 23 and October 10, 1903, cited in Thornbrough, *T. Thomas Fortune*, 246–47.

34. Editorial, *Guardian*, July 19, 1902.

35. Exhibit K, in letter, William E. B. Du Bois to Oswald G. Villard, March 24, 1905, *BTW-P*, 8:238.

36. "Threaten to Bolt Council, Revolt in Afro-American organization," *SPPP*, July 11, 1902; "Election Causes a Row in the Afro-American Council," *SPPP*, July 11, 1902; Exhibit K, in Du Bois to Villard, March 24, 1905.

37. "Harmony Seemingly Reigns, The Afro-American Council Adjourns," *SPPP*, July 12, 1902; editorial, *WCA*, July 19, 1902; Miller, "'A This Worldly Mission," 196.

38. Scott to Washington, July 17, 1902.

39. "Afro-American Council's Mistake"; "Address to the Country," *Appeal*, July 19, 1902. Washington's name was the only one missing from the list of resolutions committee members, appointed earlier in the convention.

40. "Address to the Country."

41. Ibid.

42. Ibid.

43. *Appeal*, July 26, 1902.

44. "Legal Bureau," and "Friday, July 11th," *Appeal*, July 19, 1902; "Election Causes a Row"; "Harmony Seemingly Reigns."

45. Alexander Walters to Booker T. Washington, October 24, 1902, *BTW-P*, 6:558.

46. George H. White to Booker T. Washington, January 22, 1902, BTW-C (LOC). The letter responded to Washington's previous letter to Mrs. White, who had begged Washington for help earlier that month, without her husband's knowledge (Cora L. White to Booker T. Washington, January 3, 1902, BTW-C).

47. George H. White to Booker T. Washington, December 30, 1902, BTW-C (LOC); Emmett J. Scott to Richard W. Thompson, December 11, 1902, *BTW-P*, 6:611; "Richard W. Thompson" in Frank L. Mather, ed., *Who's Who of the Colored Race* (Chicago: F. L. Mather,

1915), 263; "Pritchard Arraigned," *WB*, December 13, 1902; "The Dream of Whitesboro," in Justesen, *George Henry White*, 356–76.

48. Harlan, "The Secret Life of Booker T. Washington," 397. Washington reportedly "swore he would never work with a committee of lawyers again."

49. "The President Snubs 'White' Republicans," *NYT*, October 8, 1902.

50. Ibid.; Walters to Washington, October 24, 1902.

51. James S. Clarkson to Booker T. Washington, November 20, 2002, *BTW-P*, 6:588–89.

52. Timothy T. Fortune to Booker T. Washington, November 3, 1902, *BTW-P*, 6:572; Timothy T. Fortune to Booker T. Washington, December 10, 1902, *BTW-P*, 6:610.

53. "Plan of Council Organization, President Fortune Formulates It on the Eve of Leaving the Country," in Adams, *The National Afro-American Council*, 1.

54. Ibid.

55. This list is based on references in the official minutes, 1898–1902, and dues payments recorded by the treasurer's report, both in Adams, *The National Afro-American* Council, and various newspaper lists of delegates.

7. Dueling Portraits: Louisville, 1903

1. William A. Pledger to Booker T. Washington, April 13, 1903, *BTW-P*, 7:112–13.

2. Booker T. Washington to Timothy T. Fortune, February 17, 1903, *BTW-P*, 7:80–81.

3. Cyrus F. Adams, "The Afro-American Council, the Story of Its Organization—What It Stands For—Its Personnel," *Colored American Magazine*, March 1903.

4. "Future of the Negro," *WES*, January 27, 1903.

5. Ibid.

6. "The Story of Its Organization."

7. Ibid.

8. "Negroes in Federal Office," *NYT*, April 16, 1903. The posts of U.S. minister to Haiti and Liberia, D.C. recorder of deeds, and U.S. Treasury register had been held almost exclusively by black men since the Grant administration.

9. Roosevelt appointed John R. A. Crossland in 1902, followed by Ernest Lyon in 1903.

10. Charles M. Christian, *Black Saga* (New York: Houghton Mifflin, 1995), 292; "North Carolina Speaks for Vick," *WB*, March 14, 1903; "Judge J. C. Pritchard," *WB*, June 13, 1903. Mrs. Cox, Indianola postmistress, was forced by death threats to flee; unable to remedy the situation otherwise, Roosevelt closed the post office. In North Carolina, Vick was replaced for political reasons at the apparent insistence of Senator Pritchard.

11. Alexander Walters to Booker T. Washington, February 7, 1903, *BTW-P*, 7:39.

12. Ibid.

13. Pledger to Washington, April 13, 1903.

14. Richard W. Thompson to Emmett J. Scott, February 4, 1903, *BTW-P*, 7:33–34.

15. Ibid.

16. Booker T. Washington to Alexander Walters, February 13, 1903, *BTW-P*, 7:73–74.

17. Alexander Walters to Booker T. Washington, February 21, 1903, *BTW-P*, 7:84–85; Booker T. Washington to Alexander Walters, February 26, 1903, *BTW-P*, 7:98.

18. Booker T. Washington to Emmett J. Scott, April 6, 1903, *BTW-P*, 7:112.

19. James H. Hayes to Booker T. Washington, February 3, 1903, *BTW-P*, 7:70.

20. Charles W. Anderson to Booker T. Washington, May 13, 1903, *BTW-P*, 7:138; "Future of the Negro."

21. Anderson to Washington, May 13, 1903.

22. "A Statement in the Philadelphia North American," June 7, 1903, *BTW-P*, 7:171–73; Archibald H. Grimké to Booker T. Washington, June 6, 1903, Archibald Grimké Papers, Moorland-Spingarn Research Center.

23. Thornbrough, *T. Thomas Fortune*, 240–41.

24. "Next Meeting in Louisville, Ky.," *Appeal*, July 12, 1902.

25. *Negro Population, 1790–1915*, 43, 93; G. F. Richings, *Evidences of Progress among Colored People*, 8th ed. (Philadelphia: Geo. S. Ferguson Co., 1902), 55–57. The Louisville institution closed in 1930 but reopened and is now known as Simmons College of Kentucky.

26. Christian, *Black Saga*, 302.

27. "Booker Washington and His Race," *NYT*, July 1, 1903.

28. Ibid.

29. Peter J. Smith to Booker T. Washington, February 11, 1903, BTW-C (LOC), cited in Harlan, *Wizard of Tuskegee*, 41; James S. Clarkson to Booker T. Washington, June 30, 1903, and telegram, Washington to Fortune, June 29, 1903, *BTW-P*, 7:186. Harlan also cites communications to Pledger, Napier, Emmett Scott, George Knox, and other trusted allies.

30. "They Split on the Picture of Booker Washington," *LCJ*, July 3, 1903; "Almost a Riot over a Picture," *Louisville Herald*, July 3, 1903, reprinted in *WB*, July 11, 1903.

31. "Afro-American Council. Meet at Louisville," *WCA*, July 11, 1903; letter to the editor, *WCA*, July 18, 1903. Others included Council treasurer Thompson, Hayes, Charles S. Morris, Alfred Cosey, and Hayes.

32. "The Afro-American Press Association," *WCA*, July 11, 1903; "Meet at Louisville."

33. "The Afro-American Press Association," *WCA*, July 11, 1903; "Meet at Louisville"; "Negroes Hostile to B. T. Washington," *NYT*, July 3, 1903. A. B. "Corey" is presumably Alfred B. Cosey of Jersey.

34. "Negroes Hostile"; "They Split on the Picture."

35. Exhibit K, in William E. B. Du Bois to Oswald G. Villard, March 24, 1905, *BTW-P*, 8:238–39. Scott had been named a missionary bishop by the Methodist Episcopal Church in 1904.

36. Paul D. Nelson, *Fredrick L. McGhee: A Life on the Color Line, 1861–1912* (Saint Paul: Minnesota Historical Society Press, 2002), 110–11; *Saint Paul Daily Globe*, June 28, 1903; Fredrick L. McGhee to William M. Trotter, June 15, 1903, both cited in Nelson, *Fredrick L. McGhee*, at 108–11.

37. "They Split on the Picture"; Timothy T. Fortune to Booker T. Washington, July 7, 1903, *BTW-P*, 7:200. Other new board members were Emmett Scott, Cyrus Adams, Napier, Madison Mason, H. T. Johnson, William T. Francis, Bishop Hood, and newcomers Mary Dethridge, Alexander Manning, Walter Cohen, Mary McCoy, Cecile Rodney, Charles Stewart, and Matthew Lewey.

38. "Sat upon, New England Negroes Again Vanquished," *LCJ*, July 4, 1903.

39. "Negroes on Lynching," *NYT*, July 4, 1903; "Asks Congress to Help," *LCJ*, July 4, 1903.

40. "Asks Congress to Help."

41. "Sat upon."

42. Ibid.

43. Ibid.

44. "Booker T. Washington Talks to 3,000," *LCJ*, July 3, 1903.

45. Ibid.

46. Ibid.

47. Ibid.

48. "The Afro-American Council," editorial, *WES*, July 6, 1903.

49. "Negroes Hostile to B. T. Washington." The italicized portion appeared only in the *Times;* neither the *Times* nor the *Courier-Journal* printed the portions not italicized.

50. "An Address before the Afro-American Council," *BTW-P*, 7:189–190. The full speech was included in Ernest Davidson Washington's *Selected Speeches of Booker T. Washington* (Garden City, N.Y.: Doubleday, Doran, 1932), 92–100.

51. *Congressional Record*, 56th Cong., 1st sess., 33, 1:1365. See also Benjamin R. Justesen, "George Henry White, Josephus Daniels, and the Showdown over Disfranchisement, 1900," *North Carolina Historical Review* 78 (January 2000), 1–33.

52. "A National Fraud," editorial, *WB*, July 11, 1903.

53. Ibid.; "Afro-American Council," *WCA*, July 11, 1903.

54. "It was Hot! Not the Weather but the Louisville Meeting of the National Council," *CG*, July 11, 1903.

55. "Afro-American Council," editorial, *CG*, August 1, 1903.

56. Editorial, *Recorder*, July 11, 1903; "Grand Sessions of the NAAPA and the National Afro-American Council Held in Louisville, Ky.," *Freeman*, July 18, 1903.

57. Harlan, *Wizard of Tuskegee*, 44–50.

58. Ibid., 49–55; Bruce, *Archibald Grimké*, 102–3; press release, *BTW-P*, 7:258. The list began with Trotter, Archibald Grimké, George Forbes, and Clement G. Morgan but gradually added Judson Lyons, the Reverend Francis Grimké, Lafayette Hershaw, Napoleon Marshall, and Calvin Chase.

59. Harlan, *Wizard of Tuskegee*, 49–50

60. Harlan, *The Making of a Black Leader*, 246–47, 298; *State of Louisiana Ex. Rel. David J. Ryanes vs. Jeremiah M. Gleason, Supervisor*, Case No. 67606, filed April 30, 1902, from Records of the Louisiana Supreme Court, University of New Orleans Library. Romain had formally discontinued the original suit in April 1902, filing an amended petition on the same date.

61. "The Joy of Giving," *Freeman*, December 26, 1903.

62. Ibid. All but Pledger visited the White House. The convention's dates were later moved back to September 6–8, 1904.

63. Ibid.; "At the White House," *WES*, December 12, 1903.

64. "Pandemonium at Suffrage Meeting," *WES*, December 14, 1903; "At the White House," *WES*, December 11, 1903.

65. "Money Needed," *Appeal*, December 5, 1903. Bureau director Vance lived in New Orleans, vice director McGhee in Saint Paul, and finance committee chairman Lawson in Washington, D.C.

8. Enduring the Interregnum: Saint Louis, 1904

1. Booker T. Washington to Theodore Roosevelt, December 28, 1903, *BTW-P*, 7:381.

2. Harlan, *Wizard of Tuskegee*, 63–75; Bruce, *Archibald Grimké*, 106–9; Lewis, *W. E. B. Du Bois*, 304–8; typewritten list of invitees to Carnegie Hall, Archibald Grimké Papers, Manuscript Division, Moorland-Spingarn Research Center. At least seventeen had held national office, served on the national executive committee, or headed a Council bureau,

such as Emmett Scott. Others active at Council meetings included S. Laing Williams, Kelly Miller, and R. L. Smith.

3. Booker T. Washington to William H. Baldwin Jr., January 19, 1904, *BTW-P*, 7:400.

4. Booker T. Washington to Timothy T. Fortune, January 19, 1904, *BTW-P*, 7:400–401. "One thing you should keep constantly in mind, and that is to organize local Afro-American Councils as far as possible," Washington wrote. "There are very few of these Councils at present."

5. Timothy T. Fortune to Emmett Scott, January 28, 1904, BTW-C (LOC); Thornbrough, *T. Thomas Fortune*, 258; Timothy T. Fortune to Emmett J. Scott, March 28, 1904, BTW-C (LOC). One informant was Florida attorney J. Douglas Wetmore.

6. Booker T. Washington to William H. Steward, April 7, 1904, BTW-C (LOC), cited in Thornbrough, *T. Thomas Fortune*, 259. Fortune reprinted his own letter to Steward in a 1916 retrospective on Washington, "The Quick and the Dead."

7. Booker T. Washington to William H. Steward, April 21, 1904, *BTW-P*, 7:484.

8. *Negro Population, 1790–1915*, 43, 93.

9. Emmett J. Scott, "The Louisiana Purchase Exposition," and W. S. Scarborough, "The Negro and the Louisiana Purchase Exposition," *Voice of the Negro*. Vol. 1 (8), 300–315.

10. "A Dead Corpse," *WB*, August 27, 1904. Parker was the Democratic nominee for president in 1904.

11. "The Afro-American Council," *Appeal*, September 17, 1904. An identical account was carried in that same day's edition of the *Bee*, without comment.

12. "Negroes to Debate the Race Question, Disfranchisement in South to be Discussed during Convention," *Saint Louis Daily Globe-Democrat*, September 7, 1904;

13. "Resolution, Offered by S. Joe Brown of Iowa and Adopted by the National Afro-American Council," *Freeman*, September 17, 1904

14. Booker T. Washington to George L. Knox, October 17, 1904, *BTW-P*, 8:97–98.

15. "Appeal to Country, Afro-Americans State Grievances and Ask for Justice. Crimes in the South," *Saint Louis Daily Globe-Democrat*, Friday, September 9, 1904; "At Last He Came Out," *Palladium*, September 10, 1904.

16. "At Last He Came Out."

17. Emmett J. Scott to Charles W. Anderson, July 5, 1904, *BTW-P*, 8:8.

18. "National Council," *Appeal*, September 17, 1904.

19. Ibid.

20. Kansas City, Missouri, *Rising Son*, September 9, 1904.

21. Lewis, *W. E. B. Du Bois*, 315–16; Fredrick L. McGhee to Booker T. Washington, September 14, 1904, *BTW-P*, 8:66–69; Nelson, *Fredrick L. McGhee*, 111.

22. *State of Louisiana Ex. Rel. David J. Ryanes vs. Jeremiah M. Gleason, Supervisor*, Case No. 14,651, Louisiana Supreme Court. The Louisiana constitution afforded no jurisdiction to its supreme court in the case of a "person who is denied the right to register as a voter." *Giles vs. Harris* (1903) had held that "deprivation of a man's political rights may be alleged to involve damage in an amount of estimation in money." But since Ryanes had not alleged any damages exceeding $2,000—the only applicable grounds for appeal—the court lacked jurisdiction.

23. Harlan, *Wizard of Tuskegee*, 247; Harlan, "The Secret Life of Booker T. Washington," 397; Shawn Leigh Alexander, "'We Know Our Rights and Have the Courage to Defend Them': The Spirit of Agitation in the Age of Accommodation, 1883–1909," Ph.D. diss., Univ.

of Massachusetts, 2004, 377; "Address to the Country." Other signers included secretary Cyrus Adams, vice presidents Adams, Farmer, and Settle; chaplain D. P. Roberts; national organizer Guy; and legal bureau director Vance.

24. "Address to the Country."

25. Ibid.

26. Carolyn Wedin, *Inheritors of the Spirit: Mary White Ovington and the Founding of the NAACP* (New York: John Wiley, 1998), 66–71. Ovington and Milholland were close associates.

27. "Avoid Race Problem, Negro Leaders Ignore Topic in Call on President," *WP*, November 12, 1903. White introduced Bishop Arnett, Lyons, John Green, and other members to Roosevelt.

28. Letters, James H. Hayes to Booker T. Washington, December 27, 1904, and Booker T. Washington to James H. Hayes, December 31, 1904, *BTW-P*, 8:168–71.

29. Hugh M. Browne to Booker T. Washington, July 18, 1904, *BTW-P*, 8:22; Harlan, *Wizard of Tuskegee*, 82.

30. Browne to Washington, July 18, 1904. Browne and Washington's crony, Charles W. Anderson, were also included.

9. Walters Redux: Detroit, 1905

1. "Bishop Wa[1]ters," *WB*, December 10, 1904.

2. Perman, *Struggle for Mastery*, 116–17.

3. Ibid.

4. "Do We Want Reduction of Southern Representation?" Letter dated January 12, 1905, *NYA*, January 26, 1905.

5. Ibid.

6. "The Age Vindicated, Committee Will Ask President to Act on 15th, Not 14th, Amendment," *NYA*, March 9, 1905.

7. Ibid.

8. Ibid.; Emmett J. Scott to Charles W. Anderson, February 20, 1905, *BTW-P*, 8:195; Whitefield McKinlay to Booker T. Washington, February 22, 1905, *BTW-P*, 8:198.

9. "The Age Vindicated"; Fox, *The Guardian of Boston*, 77.

10. McKinlay to Washington, February 22, 1905. Others included the Reverend Henry H. Proctor, the Reverend Richard H. Boyd, William Hawkins, and John A. Hagan.

11. "The Age Vindicated."

12. Lewis, *W. E. B. Du Bois*, 314–15.

13. "The Afro American Council, Bishop Walters Calls upon the Old Guard to Rally," letter dated July 21, 1905, *Appeal*, July 27, 1905. Other addressees were bishops J. W. Alstork, James W. Hood, Thomas H. Lomax, C. H. Phillips, C. T. Shaffer, J. W. Smith, Benjamin T. Tanner, Evans Tyree, and Robert S. Williams; clergymen George Bragg, Henry J. Callis, George C. Clement, James H. McMullen, George W. Moore, Charles S. Morris, C. H. Parrish, and Charles T. Walker; and Herschel V. Cashin, Harry Cummings, Dr. Edward W. Lampton, John Mitchell Jr., James Napier, Richard Thompson, J. H. Wallace, Phil Waters, and Martha V. Webster.

14. "Bishop Walters Calls upon the Old Guard to Rally."

15. Ibid.

16. Lewis, *W. E. B. Du Bois*, 316.

17. *WB*, August 12, 1905; Nelson, *Fredrick L. McGhee*, 110–11.

18. "Call to Meet at Detroit, Eighth Annual Session of Afro-American Council," *NYA*, August 3, 1905.

19. Ibid.

20. "Call to Meet at Detroit," *WB*, August 5, 1905.

21. *Negro Population, 1790–1915*, 43, 93; Dorothy Drinkard-Hawkshawe, "David Augustus Straker," in *DANB*, 574–76; Dorothy Drinkard Hawkshawe, "David Augustus Straker, Black Lawyer and Reconstruction Politician, 1842–1908"(Ph.D. diss., Catholic Univ. of America, 1974), 139. The short-lived federation, founded in Detroit in 1895, had goals similar to those of the Council.

22. "National Afro-American Press Association," *Appeal*, September 9, 1905.

23. Ibid.; "Praised Roosevelt, Afro-American Council Sent President a Telegram," *Detroit Free Press*, August 31, 1905.

24. "Praised Roosevelt."

25. Diary entries for August 30, 31, and September 1, 1905, Mary Church Terrell Papers (LOC). Mrs. Terrell refers to her appointment as antilynching bureau director in *A Colored Woman in a White World* (220–21) but gives no other details of the Detroit meeting.

26. "Demands Equality, Give the Negro White Man's Rights, Said W. H. Lewis," *Detroit Free Press*, September 1, 1905.

27. Ibid.

28. "Eighth Annual Meeting of the National Afro-American Council," *Appeal*, September 9, 1905; "Lewis Answers Humphreys," *NYA*, October 12, 1905.

29. *Detroit Informer*, September 2, 1905, cited in Alexander, "We Know Our Rights," 411. In 1905, Steward had become acting president of the State University of Louisville, now known as Simmons College of Kentucky.

30. "Eighth Annual Meeting of the National Afro-American Council, Successful Session at Detroit, Michigan," *Appeal*, September 9, 1905.

31. "Address to the People of the United States," *Appeal*, September 9, 1905.

32. Ibid.

33. Emmett J. Scott to Booker T. Washington, August 7, 1905, *BTW-P*, 8:339; Richard W. Thompson to Emmett J. Scott, October 15, 1905, *BTW-P*, 8:412–13.

34. Thompson to Scott, October 15, 1905

35. "Mr. J. C. Napier," *NYA*, September 21, 1905.

36. "Negro Doctors Confer," *Freeman*, September 16, 1905.

37. "Kentucky Honors Walters, Bishop Visits Louisville and Old Home at Bardstown," *NYA*, November 9, 1905.

38. "The Afro-American Council Is Right Down to Business," *Freeman*, December 30, 1905.

39. Harlan, *Wizard of Tuskegee*, 245–47.

40. Alexander, "We Know Our Rights," 406–7.

10. Competing with Niagara: New York City, 1906

1. Lewis G. Jordan to Emmett J. Scott, February 12, 1906, *BTW-P*, 8:520–21.

2. Melvin Jack Chisum to Booker T. Washington, February 20, 1906, *BTW-P*, 8:530.

3. Lewis, *W. E. B. Du Bois*, 324–28; Harlan, *Wizard of Tuskegee*, 104–5.

4. Editorial, *Freeman*, February 3, 1906.

5. Bruce, *Archibald Grimké*, 147–48. Milholland had written Washington asking him to encourage Grimké to attend; Washington complied, if reluctantly.

6. "Negroes Have an Inning at the Cooper Union," *NYT*, February 2, 1906; "Constitution League Meeting," *NYA*, February 8, 1906.

7. Bruce, *Archibald Grimké*, 149–51.

8. Ibid.; "How the Warner-Foraker Amendment Was Killed," *NYA*, August 2, 1906.

9. "Proclamation. Ten Million Negroes Called to Prayer," *Freeman*, August 25, September 1, 8, 15, 1906.

10. "The Day for Prayer," *WB*, August 18, 1906.

11. "Denounce Mob Violence and Demand Justice," *NYA*, October 11, 1906.

12. A detailed account of the Texas incident can be found in Ann J. Lane, *The Brownsville Affair: National Crisis and Black Reaction* (Port Washington, N.Y.: n.p., 1971). Harlan gives a succinct account of the Atlanta riot in *Wizard of Tuskegee*, 299–301.

13. "Special Appeal to Liberty Loving Negroes in All Parts of the United States," *Freeman*, August 18, 1906; Perman, *Struggle for Mastery*, 123. Brewer's *Giles* dissent reasoned that the federal government had to be able to supervise its own elections, thereby mandating jurisdiction.

14. "Special Appeal."

15. "Afro-American Council, Call for Meeting at New York City, October 9, 10, 11, 1906," *Appeal*, October 6, 1906.

16. Ibid. The words bracketed here were present in the 1905 call, but omitted in 1906.

17. August Meier, "Booker T. Washington and the Negro Press," in *Along the Color Line: Explorations in the Black Experience* (Urbana: Univ. of Illinois Press, 1976), 56–74. The magazine, founded in Boston around 1900, had nearly failed in 1904, when Washington moved it to New York and hired Fred R. Moore as editor.

18. "The Afro-American Council and Its Work," *Colored American Magazine*, October 1906.

19. Ibid.

20. "The Real Reason," editorial, *CG*, October 20, 1906.

21. "Afro-Americans Failure to Organize," editorial, *NYA*, October 25, 1906. Fortune mistakenly refers to Pillsbury as "Peabody."

22. *Negro Population, 1790–1915*, 43, 93. New York's total population in 1910 was 4.77 million, with 91,709 listed as black. In 1900, the city's black population (60,666) ranked fifth, behind New Orleans, Baltimore, Washington, and Philadelphia. In 1910, Manhattan alone held 60,534 black citizens, up from 36,246 in 1900, while Brooklyn had 22,708 black citizens.

23. "Talk of War on Whites at Negro Conference," *NYT*, October 10, 1906.

24. Ibid.; "Afro-American Council Protests against Wrongs," *NYA*, October 11, 1906.

25. "Council Protests against Wrongs."

26. "President's Annual Address," *NYA*, October 11, 1906.

27. Ibid.

28. "President's Annual Address"; *Brooklyn Daily Eagle*, October 12, 1906. Walters quoted favorable editorials from the Providence *Tribune* and Philadelphia *Press*.

29. "The Aims of the Afro-American Council, Address of Oswald Garrison Villard," *Colored American Magazine*, November 1906, 349–53.

30. Ibid.

31. "Extracts from an Address before the Afro-American Council," October 11, 1906, *BTW-P*, 9:94–96.

32. "Council Ends Best Session," *NYA*, October 18, 1906; "To Act on Race Fight," *NYT*, October 11, 1906.

33. "Council Ends Best Session."

34. "Afro-American Council," *Bee*, October 13, 1906; Terrell, *A Colored Woman in a White World*, 220–21; "Wilford Smith's Address," *NYA*, October 11, 1906. Chase described Mrs. Terrell as "the center of attraction"; just "the mention of her name by the speakers was a signal for applause."

35. "Wilford Smith's Address."

36. Ibid.

37. Ibid.

38. "Officers of the Afro-American Council," *NYA*, October 18, 1906.

39. Ibid.

40. "Council Ends Best Session."

41. Ibid.

42. Ibid.

43. Editorial, *WB*, October 13, 1906.

44. "The Afro-American Council," editorial, *WB*, October 20, 1906.

45. "Booker Washington," editorial, and "The Address to the Country," editorial, *WB*, October 20, 1906.

46. "The Afro-American Council," article, and "The Afro-American Council," editorial, *Freeman*, October 20, 1906.

47. "Council Ends Best Session."

48. "Council Protests against Wrongs."

49. "Failure of the Afro-American People to Organize," editorial, *NYA*, October 11, 1906.

50. Editorial, *CG*, October 20, 1906.

11. Farewell to the Wizard: Baltimore, 1907

1. Thornbrough, *T. Thomas Fortune*, 284–85. For extended treatments of the Brownsville incident, see Lane, *The Brownsville Affair*, and John D. Weaver, *The Brownsville Raid* (College Station: Texas A&M Univ. Press, 1992). Weaver also recounts the legacy of the incident in a second book, *The Senator and the Sharecropper's Son* (College Station: Texas A&M Univ. Press, 1997).

2. Richard B. Sherman, *The Republican Party and Black America: From McKinley to Hoover, 1896–1933* (Charlottesville: Univ. Press of Virginia, 1973), 57; Terrell, *A Colored Woman in a White World*, 310. Taft delayed the order for thirty-six hours, until ordered by Roosevelt to resume the firings. Mrs. Terrell and Gilchrist Stewart later visited the White House to plead with Roosevelt to reverse the action, but he refused to do so.

3. *Preliminary Report of Commission of the Constitution League of the United States on the Affray at Brownsville, Tex.*, 59th Cong., 2d sess., Senate Document No. 107; Harlan, *Wizard of Tuskegee*, 310–11.

4. Harlan, *Wizard of Tuskegee*, 318–20.

5. Sherman, *The Republican Party and Black America*, 58–59; *NYT*, November 8, 1906; Charles W. Anderson to Booker T. Washington, January 4 and January 21, 1907, *BTW-P*, 9:181, 197.

6. Booker T. Washington to George B. Cortelyou, January 28, 1907, BTW-C (LOC); Cortelyou to Washington, February 16, 1907, *BTW-P*, 9:129; Sherman, *Republican Party and Black America*, 62.

7. August Meier, *Racial Ideologies in the Age of Booker T. Washington* (Ann Arbor: Univ. of Michigan Press, 1963), 179–82.

8. "Agitate! Agitate! Agitate!," *NYA*, January 17, 1907; Anderson to Washington, January 4, 1907. Bishop Smith of Washington wrote the article. Others at the afternoon session included the Reverend Abraham L. Gaines and "A. Houston."

9. James A. Cobb to Emmett J. Scott, January 14, 1907, BTW-C (LOC).

10. Ibid.

11. Ibid.; Thornbrough, *T. Thomas Fortune*, 285.

12. Charles W. Anderson to Emmett J. Scott, February 25, 1907, *BTW-P*, 9:223–24.

13. Thornbrough, *T. Thomas Fortune*, 285, 296–302; Harlan, *Wizard of Tuskegee*, 320–22.

14. *Negro Population, 1790–1915*, 43, 93. Baltimore grew from 508,000 residents in 1900, with 79,258 black residents, to 568,495 in 1910, of whom 84,749 were black.

15. Meier, *Racial Ideologies*, 180; "Agitate! Agitate! Agitate!"; "Council Protests against Wrongs"; *NYA*, October 11, 1906. Local committee members included the Reverend Bragg, Cummings, William Hawkins, the Reverend S. L. Z. Johnson, John Hurst, W. R. Waller, and Dr. Howard Young.

16. Meier, *Racial Ideologies*, 180; Pride and Wilson, *A History of the Black Press*, 133–35. Morgan College, established in 1867, has since been renamed Morgan State University.

17. "Call for Meeting, The National Afro-American Council at Baltimore, Md., June 26–28, 1907," *WB*, June 8, 15, 22, 1907.

18. Ibid.

19. Ibid.

20. "To Afro-Americans," *LCJ*, June 14, 1907, clipping in Archibald Grimké Papers, Moorland-Spingarn Research Center. Signers included Lewis Jordan, J. S. Young, the Reverend J. G. Robinson, and Carey B. Lewis.

21. "Afro-American Council," *WB*, June 29, 1907.

22. "Negroes Cheer Foraker, Then They 'Roast' Mr. Roosevelt over Brownsville Affair," *Baltimore Sun*, June 27, 1907; "Defense of the President," *WES*, June 28, 1907.

23. "Afro-American Council," *WB*, June 29, 1907.

24. "Attacked the President, Speakers at Afro-American Council Also Criticized Taft," *WP*, June 27, 1907; "Negroes Cheer Foraker."

25. "The Meeting of the Council, The Faithful Gathering in Annual Session, Attitude of Masses, President Walters' Address," *NYA*, June 27, 1907.

26. "President Walters' Address"; "Negroes Cheer Foraker"; "The Bishop Says 'All Honor to Senator Foraker, the Noblest Roman of Them All,'" *CG*, July 27, 1907.

27. "All Honor to Senator Foraker"; "Booker T. Named 'Judas,' Afro-American Council Has a 'Red-Hot Finish,'" *Baltimore Sun*, June 29, 1907.

28. "Defense of the President."

29. Bruce, *Archibald Grimké*, 160–62.

30. Charles Edward Donegan, "William Henry Harrison Hart," *DANB*, 294–95. In *Hart v. the State of Maryland* (1905; 100 Md. 295, 60 Atl. 457), Hart's conviction for refusing to sit in a segregated car and compartment on an interstate trip was overturned, and Maryland's segregation law set aside.

31. "Booker T. Named 'Judas'"; "Afro-American Council, The Most Successful Meeting in the History of the Organization," *WB*, June 29, 1907. Chase admitted calling Hart's supporters "a set of pygmies" and said that one opponent reportedly likened him and his supporters to "three monkeys."

32. "The Most Successful Meeting."

33. "Afro-American Council, Officers," *WB*, June 29, 1907.

34. "Booker T. Named 'Judas.'"

35. "Afro-American Council Address," *NYA*, July 11, 1907.

36. Ibid.

37. Ibid.

38. Ibid.

39. "Attacked the President, Speakers at Afro-American Council Also Criticized Taft," *WP*, June 27, 1907; "Again Attack President, Afro-Americans Propose Taking Grievance into Close Districts," *WP*, June 28, 1907; "War on the President, Afro-Americans Publish a Political Blacklist. Make Appeal to Ballots," *WP*, June 29, 1907; "Colored Bishop Praises Foraker, Commends Senator from Ohio for His Position on the Brownsville Matter," *WES*, June 27, 1907; "Defense of the President," *WES*, June 28, 1907; "Race Prejudice Talk, Afro-American Council Discusses Injustice to Negro," *WES*, June 29, 1907.

40. Editorial, *Afro-American Ledger*, reprinted in *NYA*, July 11, 1907.

41. "Afro-American Council Resolutions," editorial, *NYA*, July 4, 1907.

42. Ibid.; "Organization and Work of Organizations," editorial, *NYA*, July 4, 1907.

43. "Mr. Fortune and the Council," *NYA*, July 18, 1907.

44. Ibid.; Thornbrough, *T. Thomas Fortune*, 302–39. Fortune worked intermittently during the next four years but was a virtual derelict until he recovered his health.

45. "Afro-American Council, The Most Successful Meeting in the History of the Organization," *WB*, July 6, 1907.

46. "At the Nation's Capital," column, *Freeman*, July 13, 1907.

47. Ibid.

48. "The Afro-American Council," editorial, *Freeman*, July 13, 1907.

49. Ibid.

50. "The Freeman Would Like to Know," *Freeman*, July 27, 1907.

51. Editorial, *Freeman*, August 31, 1907; Fox, *The Guardian of Boston*, 110.

52. "Thompson's Weekly Review," *Freeman*, September 21, 1907.

53. "The Afro-American Council," editorial, *NYA*, November 28, 1907.

Epilogue: Slouching toward Columbus

1. Fox, *The Guardian of Boston*, 110; *Guardian*, January 4 and March 21, 1908, cited in *The Guardian of Boston*, 111.

2. Fox, *The Guardian of* Boston, 111; Fleming, "Alexander Walters."

3. "Bishop Walters' Letter," *NYA*, March 26, 1908.

4. Ibid.

5. Ibid.

6. Bruce, *Archibald Grimké*, 171; "Bishop Walters and Du Bois Out for Democratic Party," *NYA*, April 2, 1908.

7. "Second Report," *WES*, April 9, 1908.

8. "The Negro Conference Splits," *WB*, April 11, 1908; Fox, *The Guardian of Boston*, 112.

9. "Union," *Horizon: A Journal of the Color Line* 3 (June 1908), 6–7.

10. Ibid.

11. Bruce, *Archibald Grimké*, 171; Fox, *The Guardian of Boston*, 162–63; editorial, *Freeman*, May 22, 1909; "Denounced President Taft," *Gazette*, June 5, 1909; Miller, "'A This Worldly Mission," 306.

12. Nancy J. Weiss, *The National Urban League, 1910–1940* (New York: Oxford Univ. Press, 1974), 59–60. According to Weiss, the NAACP attracted many Niagarites, preferring to concentrate on the "radical black leaders who rejected accommodationism and insisted upon outspoken protest and agitation to achieve immediate equality." The National Urban League, in contrast, was far closer to the views of Booker T. Washington.

13. T. Thomas Fortune, "The Quick and the Dead," *AME Church Review*, April 1916, 247–50; Thornbrough, *T. Thomas Fortune*, 353–56.

14. "The Quick and the Dead."

15. "Washington Letter," *NYA*, February 6, 1917.

16. "Sudden Death of George H. White, Esq., Saturday Morning," *Philadelphia Tribune*, January 4, 1919.

17. "T. Thomas Fortune, Noted Journalist, Succumbs," *New York Amsterdam News*, June 6, 1928.

18. Kelly Miller, "The Passing of T. Thomas Fortune," *New York Amsterdam News*, June 13, 1928.

Appendix: National Afro-American Council Constitution

1. Printed in Adams, *The National Afro-American Council*, 15–18.

Bibliography

Primary Sources

Manuscript Collections

Library of Congress, Washington, D.C.
- William McKinley. Papers.
- Daniel Murray. Pamphlet collection.
- Mary Church Terrell. Papers.
- Robert H. Terrell. Papers.
- Booker T. Washington. Papers.
- Carter G. Woodson. Papers.

Moorland-Spingarn Research Center, Howard University, Washington, D.C.
- Archibald H. Grimké. Papers.

Ohio Historical Society, Columbus, Ohio
- George A. Myers. Papers.

University Library, University of Massachusetts, Amherst
- William E. B. Du Bois. Papers (microfilmed version, Library of Congress).

Western Reserve Historical Society, Cleveland, Ohio
- John P. Green. Papers (microfilmed version, Library of Congress).

Newspapers, 1898–1928

The Appeal (Saint Paul)
Atlanta Constitution
Atlanta Journal
Baltimore Afro-American Ledger
Baltimore Sun
The Bee (Washington, D.C.)
Boston Globe
Brooklyn Daily Eagle
Chicago Broadax
Chicago Defender
Chicago Inter-Ocean
The Chicago Tribune
The Colored American (Washington, D.C.)
The Louisville (Ky.) *Courier-Journal*
Detroit Free Press

Detroit Informer
The Evening Star (Washington, D.C.)
The Freeman (Indianapolis)
The Gazette (Cleveland)
The Gazette (Raleigh, N.C.)
The Indianapolis Journal
The Indianapolis Sentinel
Indianapolis World
The New York Age
New York Amsterdam News
New York Sun
The New York Times
The News and Courier (Charleston, S.C.)
The News and Observer (Raleigh, N.C.)
Ohio State Journal (Columbus)
Philadelphia Item
Philadelphia Record
The Philadelphia Tribune
The Recorder (Indianapolis)
The Rising Son (Kansas City, Mo.)
Saint Louis Daily Globe-Democrat
Saint Louis Palladium
Saint Paul Daily Globe
The Saint Paul Pioneer Press
The Union and Advertiser (Rochester, N.Y.)
The Washington (D.C.) *Post*

Magazines and Other Publications

AME Church Review
Colored American Magazine
The Crisis
The Independent
The Horizon
Southern Workman
Voice of the Negro

Government Publications

State of Louisiana. Records of the Louisiana Supreme Court, Baton Rouge, La. (University of New Orleans Library).

U.S. Congress. *Congressional Record*, 55th–56th Cong.

———. *Preliminary Report of Commission of the Constitution League of the United States on the Affray at Brownsville, Tex.*. 59th Cong., 2d sess., Senate Document No. 107.

U.S. Department of Commerce, U.S. Bureau of the Census. *Negro Population, 1790–1915.*
GPO: Washington, D.C., 1918.

Secondary Sources

Books, Pamphlets, Dissertations

Adams, Cyrus Field. *The National Afro-American Council, Organized 1898: A History of the Organization, Its Objects, Synopses of Proceedings, Constitution and By-Laws, Plan of Organization, Annual Topics, Etc.* Washington, D.C.: Cyrus F. Adams, Secretary, 1902.

Alexander, Shawn Leigh. "'We Know Our Rights and Have the Courage to Defend Them': The Spirit of Agitation in the Age of Accommodation, 1883–1909," Ph.D. diss., Univ. of Massachusetts, 2004.

Angell, Stephen Ward. *Henry McNeal Turner and African-American Religion in the South.* Knoxville: Univ. of Tennessee Press, 1992.

Angell, Stephen Ward, and Anthony B. Pinn, ed. *Social Protest Thought in the African Methodist Episcopal Church, 1862–1939.* Knoxville: Univ. of Tennessee Press, 2000.

Aptheker, Herbert. *Selections from the Horizon.* White Plains, N.Y.: Kraus-Thomson, 1985.

Bacote, Clarence A. "The Negro in Georgia Politics, 1880–1908," Ph.D. diss., Univ. of Chicago, 1955.

Bruce, Dickson D., Jr. *Archibald H. Grimké: Portrait of a Black Independent.* Baton Rouge: Louisiana State Univ. Press, 1993.

Carter, David. "Outraged Justice: The Lynching of Postmaster Frazier Baker in Lake City, South Carolina, 1897–1899." Undergraduate honors thesis, Univ. of North Carolina at Chapel Hill, 1992.

Cecelski, David S., and Timothy B. Tyson, ed. *Democracy Betrayed: The Wilmington Race Riot of 1898 and Its Legacy.* Chapel Hill: Univ. of North Carolina Press, 1998.

Chase, Hal S. "Honey for Friends, Stings for Enemies: William Calvin Chase and *The Washington Bee*, 1882–1921." Ph.D. diss., Univ. of Pennsylvania, 1973.

Christian, Charles M. *Black Saga: The African American Experience, A Chronology.* New York: Houghton Mifflin, 1995.

Christopher, Maurine. *America's Black Congressmen.* New York: Thomas Y. Crowell, 1971.

Crow, Jeffrey J., and Robert F. Durden. *Maverick Republican in the Old North State: A Political Biography of Daniel L. Russell.* Baton Rouge: Louisiana State Univ. Press, 1977.

Culp, Daniel W., ed. *Twentieth Century Negro Literature: Or, A Cyclopedia of Thought on the Vital Topics Relating to the American Negro.* Toronto: J. L. Nichols, 1902.

Drinkard-Hawkshawe, Dorothy. "David Augustus Straker: Black Lawyer and Reconstruction Politician, 1842–1908." Ph.D. diss., Catholic Univ. of America, 1974.

Du Bois, William E. B. *The Autobiography of W. E. B. Du Bois.* New York: International Publishers, 1968.

———. *The Souls of Black Folk: Essays and Sketches.* New York: n.p., 1903.

Duster, Alfreda M., ed. *Crusade for Justice: The Autobiography of Ida B. Wells.* Chicago: Univ. of Chicago Press, 1970.

Fortier, Alcée, ed. *Louisiana: Comprising Sketches of Parishes, Towns, Events, Institutions, and Persons, Arranged in Cyclopedic Form.* Vol. 3. N.p.: Century Historical Association, 1914.

Fox, Stephen R. *The Guardian of Boston: William Monroe Trotter.* New York: Atheneum, 1970.

Franklin, John Hope, and August Meier, ed. *Black Leaders of the Twentieth Century.* Urbana: Univ. of Illinois, 1982.

Gatewood, Willard B., Jr. *Aristocrats of Color: The Black Elite, 1880–1920.* Bloomington: Indiana Univ. Press, 1990.

———. *Black Americans and the White Man's Burden, 1898–1903.* Urbana: Univ. of Illinois Press, 1975.

Gibbs, Mifflin W. *Shadow and Light.* New York: Arno, 1968.

Gilbert, Peter, ed. *The Selected Writings of John Edward Bruce, Militant Black Journalist.* New York: Arno, 1971.

Green, John P. *Facts Stranger than Fiction: Seventy-Five Years of a Busy Life with Reminiscences of Many Great Men and Women.* Cleveland: n.p., 1920.

Harlan, Louis R. *Booker T. Washington: The Wizard of Tuskegee, 1901–1915.* New York: Oxford Univ. Press, 1983.

———. *Booker T. Washington: The Making of a Black Leader, 1856–1901.* New York: Oxford Univ. Press, 1972.

Harlan, Louis R., and Raymond Smock, ed. *The Booker T. Washington Papers.* Urbana: Univ. of Illinois Press, 1972–1989.

Hine, Darlene Clark, ed. *Black Women in America: An Historical Encyclopedia.* Brooklyn: Carlson, 1993.

Johnson, Donald, comp. *National Party Platforms.* Vol. 1, 1840–1956. Urbana: Univ. of Illinois Press, 1978.

Johnson, James Weldon. *Along This Way: The Autobiography of James Weldon Johnson.* 1937. Reprint, New York: Penguin, 1990.

Jones, Beverly Washington. *Quest for Equality: The Life and Writings of Mary Eliza Church Terrell, 1863–1954.* Brooklyn, N.Y.: Carlson, 1990.

Justesen, Benjamin R. *George Henry White: An Even Chance in the Race of Life.* Baton Rouge: Louisiana State Univ. Press, 2001.

———. ed. *In His Own Words: The Writings, Speeches, and Letters of George Henry White.* Lincoln, Nebr.: iUniverse , 2004.

Kellogg, Charles Flint. *NAACP: A History of the National Association for the Advancement of Colored People.* Vol. 1, 1909–1920. Baltimore: Johns Hopkins Univ., 1973.

Kousser, J. Morgan. *The Shaping of Southern Politics: Suffrage Restriction and the Establishment of the One-Party South, 1880–1910.* New Haven: Yale Univ. Press, 1974.

Kremer, Gary R. *James Milton Turner and the Promise of America.* Columbia: Univ. of Missouri Press, 1991.

Lane, Ann J. *The Brownsville Affair: National Crisis and Black Reaction*. Port Washington, N.Y.: n.p., 1971.

Lane, Roger. *William Dorsey's Philadelphia and Ours: On the Past and Future of the Black City in America*. New York: Oxford Univ. Press, 1991.

Lewis, David Levering. *W. E. B. Du Bois: Biography of a Race, 1868–1919*. New York: Henry Holt, 1993.

Linderman, Gerald F. *The Mirror of War: American Society and the Spanish-American War*. Ann Arbor: Univ. of Michigan Press, 1974.

Logan, Rayford W. *The Betrayal of the Negro, from Rutherford B. Hayes to Woodrow Wilson* (originally *The Negro in American Life and Thought: The Nadir, 1877–1901*). Rev. ed., New York: Collier, 1965.

Logan, Rayford W., and Michael R. Winston, ed. *Dictionary of Negro Biography*. New York: W. W. Norton, 1982.

Lynch, John Roy. *Reminiscences of an Active Life*. Chicago: Univ. of Chicago Press, 1970.

McMurry, Linda O. *To Keep the Waters Troubled: The Life of Ida B. Wells*. New York: Oxford Univ. Press, 1998.

McPherson, James M. *The Abolitionist Legacy: From Reconstruction to the NAACP*. Princeton: Princeton Univ. Press, 1975.

Meier, August. *Negro Thought in America, 1880–1915: Racial Ideologies in the Age of Booker T. Washington*. Ann Arbor: Univ. of Michigan Press, 1963.

Meier, August, and Elliott Rudwick. *Along the Color Line: Explorations in the Black Experience*. Urbana: Univ. of Illinois Press, 1976.

Miller, George Mason. "'A This Worldly Mission': The Life and Career of Alexander Walters (1858–1917)." Ph.D. diss., State Univ. of New York at Stony Brook, 1984.

Moore, Jacqueline M. *Washington, Du Bois, and the Struggle for Racial Uplift*. Wilmington, Del.: Scholarly Resources , 2003.

Mossell, Mrs. N. F. [Gertrude B.] *The Work of the Afro-American Woman*, 2d. ed. Philadelphia: G. S. Ferguson, 1908.

Nelson, Paul D. *Fredrick L. McGhee: A Life on the Color Line, 1861–1912*. Saint Paul: Minnesota Historical Society Press, 2002.

Parris, Guichard, and Lester Brooks. *Blacks in the City: A History of the National Urban League*. Boston: Little, Brown, 1971.

Perman, Michael. *Struggle for Mastery: Disfranchisement in the South, 1888–1908*. Chapel Hill: Univ. of North Carolina Press, 2001.

Prather, H. Leon. *We Have Taken a City: Wilmington Racial Massacre and Coup of 1898*. Cranbury, N.J.: Associated Univ. Presses, 1984.

Pride, Armistead S., and Clint C. Wilson II. *A History of the Black Press*. Washington, D.C.: Howard Univ. Press, 1997.

Richings, G. F. *Evidences of Progress among Colored People*, 8th ed. Philadelphia: Geo. S. Ferguson, 1902.

Royster, Jacqueline Jones, ed. *Southern Horrors and Other Writings: The Anti-Lynching Campaign of Ida B. Wells, 1892–1900*. Boston: Bedford, 1997.

Saunders, John A. *One Hundred Years after Emancipation: History of the Philadelphia Negro, 1787 to 1963*. Philadelphia: F. R. S. Publishing, 1963.

Schechter, Patricia Ann. *Ida B. Wells-Barnett and American Reform, 1880–1930*. Chapel Hill: Univ. of North Carolina Press, 2001.

Scott, Emmett J., and Lyman Beecher Stowe. *Booker T. Washington, Builder of a Civilization*. New York: Doubleday, Page, 1917.

Sherman, Richard B. *The Republican Party and Black America: From McKinley to Hoover, 1896–1933*. Charlottesville: Univ. Press of Virginia, 1973.

Spencer, Samuel R., Jr. *Booker T. Washington and the Negro's Place in American Life*. Boston: Little, Brown, 1955.

Suggs, Henry L., ed. *The Black Press in the Middle West, 1865–1985*. Westport, Conn.: Greenwood Press, 1996.

Terrell, Mary Church. *A Colored Woman in a White World*, 1940. Reprint, New York: G. K. Hall, 1970.

Thornbrough, Emma Lou. *T. Thomas Fortune, Militant Journalist*. Chicago: Univ. of Chicago Press, 1972.

Walters, Alexander. *My Life and Work*. New York: Fleming H. Revell, 1917.

Wang, Xi. *The Trial of Democracy: Black Suffrage and Northern Republicans, 1860–1910*. Athens: Univ. of Georgia Press, 1997.

Washington, Booker T. *Up from Slavery*. New York: Doubleday, Page, 1901.

———. *My Larger Education: Being Chapters from My Experience*. New York: Doubleday, Page, 1909.

Washington, Ernest Davidson. *Selected Speeches of Booker T. Washington*. Garden City, N.Y.: Doubleday, Doran, 1932.

Weaver, John D. *The Brownsville Raid*. College Station: Texas A & M Univ. Press, 1992.

———. *The Senator and the Sharecropper's Son*. College Station: Texas A&M Univ. Press, 1997.

Wedin, Carolyn. *Inheritors of the Spirit: Mary White Ovington and the Founding of the NAACP*. New York: John Wiley and Sons, 1998.

Weiss, Nancy J. *The National Urban League, 1910–1940*. New York: Oxford Univ. Press, 1974.

Zangrando, Robert L. *The NAACP Crusade against Lynching, 1909–1950*. Philadelphia: Temple Univ. Press, 1980.

Articles and Essays

Adams, Cyrus Field. "The Afro-American Council, the Story of Its Organization—What It Stands For—Its Personnel." *Colored American Magazine*, March 1903.

Carroll, Patrick. "The 1905 Niagara Movement Attendants: An Interpretative Analysis of Their Lives and Ideologies." Monograph prepared for the Special Studies Department of the College of Holy Cross, 1980.

Du Bois, W. E. B. "Two Negro Conventions." *Independent*, September 7, 1899.

———. "Union." *Horizon: A Journal of the Color Line*, June 1908.

———. "Alexander Walters." *Crisis* 3 (February 1912).
Fortune, T. Thomas. "The Quick and the Dead." *AME Church Review*, Apr. 1916.
Harlan, Louis R. "The Secret Life of Booker T. Washington." *Journal of Southern History* 37 (August 1971): 393–416.
Justesen, Benjamin R. "Black Tip, White Iceberg: Black Postmasters and the Rise of White Supremacy in North Carolina, 1897–1901." *North Carolina Historical Review* 82 (April 2005).
———. "George Henry White and the End of an Era." *Washington History* 15(2) (Fall/Winter 2003–2004): 34–51.
———. "George Henry White, Josephus Daniels, and the Showdown over Disfranchisement, 1900." *North Carolina Historical Review* 77 (January 2000).
Meier, August. "Booker T. Washington and the Rise of the NAACP." *Along the Color Line: Explorations in the Black Experience*, by August Meier and Elliott Rudwick. Urbana: Univ. of Illinois Press, 1976.
———. "Booker T. Washington and the Negro Press." *Along the Color Line: Explorations in the Black Experience*, by August Meier and Elliott Rudwick. Urbana: Univ. of Illinois Press, 1976.
Mossell, [Mrs.] N. F. [Gertrude B.] "The Philadelphia Branch of the Afro-American Council." *Colored American Magazine*, August 1901, 291–95.
Scarborough, W[illiam] S. "The Negro and the Louisiana Purchase Exposition." *Voice of the Negro* 1(8) (July 1904): 313–15
Scott, Emmett J. "The Louisiana Purchase Exposition." *Voice of the Negro* 1(8) (July 1904): 300–312.
Terrell, Mary Church. "The Progress of Colored Women." *Voice of the Negro* 1(8) (July 1904).
Thornbrough, Emma Lou. "The National Afro-American League, 1887–1908." *Journal of Southern History* 27 (November 1961): 494–512.
———. "The Brownsville Episode and the Negro Vote." *Mississippi Valley Historical Review* 44 (December 1957).
Tinsley, James A. "Roosevelt, Foraker, and the Brownsville Affair." *Journal of Negro History* 41 (1956): 43–65.
Villard, Oswald G. "The Aims of the Afro-American Council, Address of Oswald Garrison Villard." *Colored American Magazine*, November 1906, 349–53.
Walters, Alexander. "The Afro-American Council and Its Work." *Colored American Magazine*, October 1906, 205–11.

Index

Benjamin R. Justesen is a freelance writer and editor. A former U.S. Foreign Service officer, he is a Ph.D. candidate in interdisciplinary studies at Union Institute and University in Cincinnati. He is the author of numerous journal articles and two previous books, a biography of George Henry White (*George Henry White: An Even Chance in the Race of Life,* nominated for the Pulitzer Prize in biography) and a collection of White's letters and writings (*In His Own Words*). He and his wife, Margaret, live in Alexandria, Virginia.